EAST ASIA AND U.S. SECURITY

Ralph N. Clough

EAST ASIA AND U.S. SECURITY

The Brookings Institution
Washington, D.C.

Library of Congress Cataloging in Publication Data:

Clough, Ralph N   1916–
   East Asia and U.S. security.
   Includes bibliographical references and index.
   1. Asia—Foreign relations—United States.
2. United States—Foreign relations—Asia.
3. United States—National security.   4. Asia—
Politics.   I. Title.
DS33.4.U6C56   327.73′05   74-274
ISBN 0-8157-1480-7
ISBN 0-8157 1479-3 pbk.

9 8 7 6 5 4 3 2 1

THE BROOKINGS INSTITUTION is an independent organization devoted to nonpartisan research, education, and publication in economics, government, foreign policy, and the social sciences generally. Its principal purposes are to aid in the development of sound public policies and to promote public understanding of issues of national importance.

The Institution was founded on December 8, 1927, to merge the activities of the Institute for Government Research, founded in 1916, the Institute of Economics, founded in 1922, and the Robert Brookings Graduate School of Economics and Government, founded in 1924.

The Board of Trustees is responsible for the general administration of the Institution, while the immediate direction of the policies, program, and staff is vested in the President, assisted by an advisory committee of the officers and staff. The by-laws of the Institution state, "It is the function of the Trustees to make possible the conduct of scientific research, and publication, under the most favorable conditions, and to safeguard the independence of the research staff in the pursuit of their studies and in the publication of the results of such studies. It is not a part of their function to determine, control, or influence the conduct of particular investigations or the conclusions reached."

The President bears final responsibility for the decision to publish a manuscript as a Brookings book or staff paper. In reaching his judgment on the competence, accuracy, and objectivity of each study, the President is advised by the director of the appropriate research program and weighs the views of a panel of expert outside readers who report to him in confidence on the quality of the work. Publication of a work signifies that it is deemed to be a competent treatment worthy of public consideration; such publication does not imply endorsement of conclusions or recommendations contained in the study.

The Institution maintains its position of neutrality on issues of public policy in order to safeguard the intellectual freedom of the staff. Hence interpretations or conclusions in Brookings publications should be understood to be solely those of the author or authors and should not be attributed to the Institution, to its trustees, officers, or other staff members, or to the organizations that support its research.

Foreword

For two decades the basic objective of U.S. policy in East Asia was to block the expansion of communist regimes. President Nixon shifted the emphasis to greater self-reliance by U.S. allies in the region; he brought about détente with China and withdrew U.S. forces from combat in Indochina. These actions partly disengaged the United States from past policies and increased the need to redefine U.S. security interests in and U.S. policy toward East Asia.

This study reassesses American interests in the light of important changes: the shift from alliance to confrontation in relations between China and the Soviet Union, Japan's emergence as a dominant economic power, and the end of U.S. combat involvement in East Asia. The author focuses on Japan, China, and the USSR—the only powers capable of posing a direct military threat to the United States and to the global balance of power—and proposes a new U.S. policy toward East Asia rooted in the vital U.S. relationship with Japan and the need for strengthening Japan's determination to remain a friendly, lightly armed, non-nuclear power.

Ralph N. Clough is a Brookings senior fellow. He is a former director of the State Department's Office of Chinese Affairs and a former member of its Policy Planning Council. He has been a Fellow of the Center for International Affairs at Harvard University and an associate of the East Asian Research Center.

The ideas reflected in this study were formulated during the lively debates of a Brookings study group on U.S. policy in East Asia. The author wishes to express his appreciation to the members of Congress, government officials, and scholars who participated in that group, and to their able chairman, Samuel Huntington. A list of the group's members is given on page 241; they do not, of course, share responsibility for the author's conclusions. He is grateful to many East Asia specialists, both government officials and private citizens, American and Asian, who gave generously of their time in discussions with him. He acknowledges particularly the help of those who reviewed parts of the study in draft: Morton Abramowitz, Michael Armacost, A. Doak Barnett, Zbigniew Brzezinski, John Dexter, Richard Erickson, Selig S. Harrison, Lawrence B. Krause, Edward Masters, Joseph Neubert, Edwin O. Reischauer, Walt Rostow, Thomas Shoesmith, and Philip H. Trezise. He is also indebted to Henry Owen, director of Foreign Policy Studies at Brookings, for his advice and encouragement. Alice M. Carroll edited the manuscript and Florence Robinson prepared the index.

The study was supported by the Ford Foundation and the Asia Foundation. The views expressed in it are those of the author and should not be ascribed to the Ford Foundation, the Asia Foundation, or the trustees, officers, or other staff members of the Brookings Institution.

KERMIT GORDON
President

October 1974
Washington, D.C.

Contents

CHAPTER ONE

The Containment Concept

"This was the week that changed the world." Thus Richard M. Nixon described his memorable visit to China in February 1972, signaling a radical change in the containment policy toward the People's Republic of China which the United States had followed for over twenty years. The President's visit was, indeed, a notable diplomatic achievement, but his oratorical hyperbole masked the fact that modification of the containment policy was more a creative adjustment to change than a cause of change. In his first foreign policy report to the Congress the President himself described the Nixon Doctrine as a needed response to the changes sweeping the world.[1]

One important change has been the decline in the military and economic preeminence of the United States. Militarily the United States is challenged by the growing power of the Soviet Union, and economically by the growing complexity and rivalry in its relations with Western Europe and Japan. But the Soviet Union also faces new problems, arising from the ideological and military confrontation with its erstwhile ally, China, and a consequent lessened ability to impose its will on its other allies.

Nations are only beginning to face up to more fundamental changes: the profound consequences of the population explosion, the accelerating deterioration of the human environment, and the rising rate of consumption of irreplaceable resources. These and other problems, whose resolution will demand a new order of international cooperation, increasingly compel the attention of national leaders. Furthermore, the big powers have, with some hesitancy, begun to recognize the declining utility of military force as a means of achieving national objectives.

1. *United States Foreign Policy for the 1970's*, H. Doc. 91-258, 91 Cong. 2 sess (1970), p. 6.

Although all of the major powers—except Japan—continue to spend heavily on armaments for deterrence or defense, they share a deep interest in avoiding nuclear war or crises that might escalate to nuclear war and a concern about the soaring costs of new weapons.

The Nixon Doctrine

The Nixon Doctrine, enunciated in 1969, was a response to the relatively short-term changes in the military and political relationships among the powers rather than to long-term world trends. It sought to induce allies of the United States to assume a larger share of the burden of providing for their own security and for the economic development of the developing nations. It proposed a partnership with Western Europe and Japan befitting their increased economic power. It also sought to cross the barriers separating the United States from its principal adversaries, the Soviet Union and China, to reach agreements that would moderate past differences and open areas for cooperation. Its objective was to create and expand pressure groups within the societies on both sides that would have a vested interest in diminishing the risk of war and promoting constructive cooperation.

The Nixon Doctrine maintained all the defense commitments that the United States assumed early in the cold war and insisted that the armed forces of the United States and its allies remain strong. It has therefore been criticized, with some justice, for overemphasizing the importance of military force and continuing the old containment policy in a new guise. But the doctrine went beyond containment in its effort to diminish the risk of war and to create a network of constructive relationships with the adversary states. The actions taken in this respect have sometimes been criticized as largely atmospherics, without real substance. And the Nixon administration has been charged with neglecting its allies in its preoccupation with dramatic advances in relations with adversaries. There is some truth in both views. Nevertheless, recent U.S. policies have on the whole been successful in managing the transition from a predominantly bipolar world to a world of greater complexity.

The need for changed U.S. policies was greatest in East Asia.[2] A

2. In this study, *East Asia* refers to the states of mainland Asia east of India and the island states of the western Pacific, including Australia and New Zealand.

costly and frustrating war had deeply divided the American people, many of whom questioned the wisdom of the containment policy in that region. Moreover, the Sino-Soviet split and the resurgence of Japan opened new possibilities for U.S. diplomacy. President Nixon, responding to domestic pressure and making astute use of diplomatic opportunities, accomplished the almost universally applauded breakthrough to China and negotiated a cease-fire agreement in Vietnam. These achievements made possible a general lowering of the U.S. military profile in East Asia.

A serious flaw in the execution of U.S. policies, particularly dangerous over the long term, was disregard for the importance of cooperation with Japan in the difficult and delicate task of creating a network of constructive relationships with the USSR and China. The massive trade between the United States and Japan, the openness of the two societies, and their common commitment to maximum freedom in the movement of goods and people should be more binding over the next ten years or more than any ties the United States might develop with the radically different societies of China or the Soviet Union. Yet, absorbed by the promise of détente and frustrated by short-term problems with the Japanese, the Nixon administration neglected the vital task of seeking the wholehearted collaboration of Japan in creating a new structure of peace in East Asia.

President Nixon's policy toward Japan was clouded with uncertainty and ambivalence. Japan's unique commitment to forgo powerful armed forces seems to have been underrated as an important factor in U.S. efforts to lower tensions with the Soviet Union and China. The President's emphasis on the need for a world power balance, with Japan becoming one of five great power centers, led many Japanese to believe that the United States expected their nation to become a strong military power. The Nixon Doctrine stressed U.S. allies' doing more for their own defense, and U.S. officials urged Japan to build up its forces.[3] Yet massive rearmament by Japan would set off an unprecedented arms race, wrecking the prospects for reducing the importance of military force.

3. See reports of the visits to Japan by Secretary of Defense Melvin Laird in *Washington Post*, July 6 and 7, 1971, and Presidential Special Assistant Peter Flanigan, in *Tokyo Shimbun*, July 27, 1973, and article by Drew Middleton in *New York Times*, Nov. 25, 1973, reporting that U.S. officials were urging the Japanese to step up their antisubmarine warfare capability.

Of course, the United States cannot control Japan's military policies. As Japan's economic power and desire for a more independent role grow, U.S. influence declines. Nevertheless, so long as the central aim of U.S. policy is to turn away from military confrontation in order to seek a more constructive, less costly, and less dangerous relationship with the adversary powers, the United States should use its still substantial influence on Japan to reinforce this purpose. It should welcome and discreetly encourage the prevailing Japanese opposition to greatly enlarged military forces, rather than regard it sourly as imposing an undesired burden on the United States.

If efforts to perpetuate and strengthen détente should fail—and the détente with Moscow is threatened by tension in the Middle East—a different U.S. policy toward Japan might become necessary. But in the long-term quest for peace, the strong desire of the bulk of the Japanese people to keep Japan a lightly armed, nonnuclear power is a valuable asset, not to be lightly cast aside. Once gone, it could not be re-created. A rearmed, nuclear Japan, even if allied to the United States, which it might not always be, would represent a regression to a more dangerous world dominated by military rivalry among the big powers.

The likelihood that Japan might soon turn to massive rearmament is slight. Opposition to such a course of action is strong in Japan. Too little emphasis on the vital importance of close collaboration by the United States and Japan in the search for expanded relations with the Soviet Union and China could gradually undermine the U.S.-Japanese alliance, however. The relationship needs reshaping to reflect Japan's growing economic power and to accommodate the shift from confrontation to negotiation in U.S. relations with the communist powers. But it is important to avoid a drifting apart over economic issues and views on how to share the burden of maintaining stability in East Asia. Should the drift become irreversible, with Japanese confidence in the U.S. defense commitment badly eroded, the probable Japanese response to sharpened conflicts of interest with China or the USSR would be to rearm rapidly.

In relation to Southeast Asia, also, the Nixon administration was slow to accept the implications of fundamental change. Here, more than anywhere else in the world, U.S. policy seems haunted by the ghosts of containment and cold war. Of course, disengaging militarily from large-scale combat while endeavoring to minimize the adverse political repercussions of that action at home and abroad presents extraordinary difficulties. The massive and coordinated military, diplomatic, and political program intended to provide an opportunity for South Vietnam to survive as a noncommunist state has been more successful than was thought possible in 1969. President Nixon and other U.S. officials, however, continued to emphasize the great importance to the United States of the survival of noncommunist governments in South Vietnam, Laos, and Cambodia. Perpetuation of this rhetoric during a period of declining ability to control events in Southeast Asia was unwise. Once the decision was made to "Vietnamize" the war, it would have been prudent to allow the character of governments in Southeast Asia to assume less importance for the United States and to gradually dissociate U.S. prestige from the trend of events there as U.S. forces were withdrawn and U.S. power to control the outcome of the struggle dwindled.

Need for a Reexamination

A fresh look at Southeast Asia reveals U.S. interests there as much less important than they were judged to be in the past from the standpoint either of U.S. security or of the major U.S. interest in Japan. No longer should the region be regarded as so important as to demand intervention with U.S forces to prevent the forcible overthrow of friendly governments. Intervention might be justified if China threatened to overrun the area with its own forces, for if the United States did nothing in the face of so blatant an act of aggression by Japan's nuclear neighbor, the vital U.S.-Japanese relationship would be severely damaged. But any such contingency is remote. No lesser disruption of local peace and stability—even the subjection of all Indochina by North Vietnam—would justify the reintroduction of U.S. combat forces into the area. Old fears that China might gain control of all Southeast Asia through its support of communist insurgency need to be reexamined in the light of the Sino-Soviet split, the rise of Japan as an economic power, and the strength of nationalism in the countries of Southeast Asia.

The Containment Policy

For twenty years the containment concept provided a coherent framework for U.S. East Asian policy. The comprehensive regional policy crystallized during the four years after the unexpected assault by Soviet-armed North Koreans across the 38th parallel on the morning of June 25, 1950. Within seventy-two hours President Harry S. Truman ordered the U.S. Air Force and Navy to give all-out support to the South Korean forces. He also took three other actions foreshadowing the lines along which U.S. policy was to develop in the region: he ordered the Seventh Fleet to prevent an attack on Taiwan—or from Taiwan against the mainland—and directed an increase in aid to Indochina and the Philippines.[4] As the war continued and the Chinese intervened, other elements of the East Asia policy were fitted into place; by the mid-fifties the main outlines of a structure to "contain" communist power had been completed. In this process the catalyzing effect of the Korean War was decisive.

At the time the blow fell in Korea, the United States conceived its defense perimeter as including only Japan, the Ryukyus, and the Philippines.[5] In Japan the United States was deeply involved, with General Douglas MacArthur carrying out step by step a program to remake the country's political and economic structure.[6] Efforts by the USSR to share in control of Japan had been rebuffed, leaving the ultimate policymaking power in the United States and the power to execute it in the supreme commander. By 1950 the U.S. government recognized that the future stability of its relationship with Japan required an early peace treaty and work on it had begun when the Korean War broke out. Thus, the importance of Japan to U.S. interests was recognized early. War in Korea gave added urgency to the work underway to make Japan the cornerstone of U.S. East Asian policy.

China policy, the subject of intense partisan debate in the United States, was at a critical turning point. American efforts to prevent civil war in China and bring the contending parties together in a coalition

---

4. See Dean Acheson, *Present at the Creation* (Norton, 1969), pp. 407–08.

5. As early as 1947 the Joint Chiefs of Staff had concluded that the United States had little strategic interest in maintaining forces in Korea and by July 1949, with the approval of General Douglas MacArthur, all U.S. combat forces had been withdrawn from the peninsula. See Harry S. Truman, *Memoirs* (Doubleday, 1956), vol. 2, pp. 325–39. Thus, Secretary of State Acheson's notable speech to the National Press Club of Jan. 21, 1950, for which he was later attacked for having excluded Korea from the U.S. defense perimeter, was strictly in accord with the views of U.S. military leaders. *Department of State Bulletin*, Jan. 23, 1950, p. 111.

6. John K. Fairbank, Edwin O. Reischauer, and Albert M. Craig, *East Asia: The Modern Transformation* (Houghton Mifflin, 1965), pp. 812–18.

government had failed. Chiang Kai-shek had withdrawn to Taiwan with the remnants of his forces. Prominent Republicans had pressed for U.S. military commitments and assistance to those forces, but President Truman had declared that "the United States has no desire to obtain special rights or privileges or to establish military bases in Formosa at this time. Nor does it have any intention of utilizing its armed forces to interfere in the present situation. The United States Government will not pursue a course which will lead to involvement in the civil conflict in China. Similarly, the United States Government will not provide military aid or advice to Chinese forces on Formosa."[7]

On the same day Secretary of State Dean Acheson pointed out that Taiwan had been turned over to China pursuant to international agreements reached at Cairo and Potsdam, that the Chinese had administered the island for four years, and that no one had raised any "lawyers' doubts" when the Chinese made Taiwan a province of China. He emphasized that the United States intended to stand by this position and would not become involved militarily in any way on Taiwan.

Acheson did add, prophetically, that "in the unlikely and unhappy event that our forces might be attacked in the Far East, the United States must be completely free to take whatever action in whatever area is necessary for its own security."[8] With the entry of U.S. forces into the Korean War, Truman invoked this freedom in order to reverse the hands-off policy toward Taiwan and thus pointed the nation's China policy in a new direction.

Except for the Philippines, the United States in 1950 had no defense commitments to states in Southeast Asia. Acheson had warned in January that the United States would not tolerate an attack on the Philippines—recently established as an independent nation and bolstered by $2 billion of U.S. economic and other aid. Should any other state in the region suffer armed attack, "initial reliance must be on the people attacked to resist it," said Acheson, "and then upon the commitments of the entire civilized world under the Charter of the United Nations." He cautioned against becoming obsessed with military considerations, warning that other problems arising from the susceptibility of many countries in the Pacific area to subversion and penetration

---

7. *Department of State Bulletin*, Jan. 16, 1950, p. 79. *Formosa* is the name given the island by an early Portuguese explorer. *Taiwan* is the name used by both Chinese regimes, by the Japanese, and in recent years by the U.S. government.

8. Ibid., p. 80.

could not be stopped by military means.[9] European states still assumed major responsibilities in Southeast Asia in 1950, the French in Indochina, the British in Malaya and Singapore, and the Dutch in Indonesia.

Americans were primarily interested in Europe in 1950, not Asia. The U.S. government was worried about Soviet intentions. Since the end of the war the Russians had concentrated on fixing their hold on Eastern Europe and probing for weak spots—in Iran, Turkey, and Greece. The Marshall Plan had been launched to redress a dangerously deteriorating economic situation in Western Europe. George Kennan's famous X article call for a "long-term, patient but firm and vigilant containment of Russian expansive tendencies"[10] had gained wide acceptance among U.S. policymakers. The Berlin blockade in the winter of 1948–49, the detonation of the first Soviet atomic bomb in August 1949, the fall of mainland China to the Chinese Communists in the same year, and the signing of the Sino-Soviet alliance in February 1950, coming in rapid succession, all added to the impression of growing Soviet strength and belligerence. By April official concerns had been spelled out in a statement of national policy that emphasized the urgent need to build the military strength of the United States and its allies if the expansionist drive of the Soviet Union were to be contained.[11] The policy was still only on paper in mid-1950, however. While administration spokesmen were busily explaining to the country why more arms were needed, the Russians, by backing the attack in Korea, provided persuasive justification.

Thus, the Korean War joined together the European and Asian policies of the United States in a "globalization of containment."[12] Soviet leaders, closely allied with the new rulers of the China mainland, wielded power across the Eurasian heartland and seemed to menace U.S. interests from two directions. The leaders of both parties and the American people rallied in support of Truman's decision to send U.S. forces into Korea under the United Nations banner to check the aggressor. And there was wide agreement with the policies of strengthening U.S. armed forces, entering into defense agreements with friendly Pacific states, and building up their strength through military and eco-

---

9. Ibid., Jan. 23, 1950, p. 116.

10. "The Sources of Soviet Conduct," *Foreign Affairs*, vol. 25 (July 1947), pp. 566–82.

11. The statement was NSC-68, issued by the National Security Council. See Acheson, *Present at the Creation*, pp. 373–81.

12. Seyom Brown, *The Faces of Power* (Columbia University Press, 1968), p. 59.

nomic aid programs. The attack in Korea, supported by the Chinese and Soviets, convinced most Americans of the reality of the Sino-Soviet threat and the evolving containment policy was accepted as a necessary counter.

Bipartisan support of the decision to fight in Korea did not, however, still partisan debate. As the costs and casualties mounted, attacks on the administration became more bitter. It was charged with "losing China," with leaving South Korea open to attack, and with following a "no win" policy in Korea. The dismissal of MacArthur polarized feelings. Above all, the vicious attacks of Wisconsin Senator Joseph McCarthy created an unparalleled atmosphere of suspicion, fear, and recrimination.

Born in such an atmosphere, the containment policy in Asia was perhaps destined to retain an emotional aura that distinguished it from its European cousin. For bureaucrat and politician alike it was easier and safer to risk overinsuring against possible communist threats than to be suspected as "soft on communism." Consequently, the dominant features of that policy were shaped as much by emotional and political reactions as by a cool-headed assessment of the threat.

Defense commitments, military bases, and U.S. forces deployed in the western Pacific formed the skeleton of the containment policy, but it was fleshed out with all the tools of modern diplomacy to restrict the power and influence of the adversaries of the United States and rapidly strengthen its allies. The purpose of the policy was not only to deter the Chinese Communists and their allies from using military force to extend their dominion, but also to confine and weaken their political influence. American leaders believed that increases in Peking's prestige and political and economic influence would facilitate its support of communist insurgents in Southeast Asia.

Although the methods by which the containment policy was carried out were many-sided and complex, its purpose was quite simply to prevent the expansion of territory in Asia under communist control. In a largely bipolar world it was assumed that seizures of power by communist parties supported by China and the USSR would add to the strength of the Sino-Soviet bloc and weaken the coalition headed by the United States.

A Clear Line of Defense

The structure of containment was based on the principle that lines between friend and foe should be clearly drawn and potential aggressors plainly warned as to the areas U.S. forces would help defend. It was widely believed, with considerable justification, that the North Koreans would not have invaded the South had they expected the United States to intervene militarily.

The security treaty with Japan, the keystone of the containment structure, was signed in September 1951 along with the peace treaty. In its train came security treaties with the Philippines and with Australia and New Zealand, which were seeking U.S. assurance against renewed Japanese aggression. These treaties did not therefore result from the Korean War, nor was the treaty system at this stage conceived of as a dike against communist expansion.

During the administration of Dwight D. Eisenhower the defense perimeter was expanded to include the two areas the United States had undertaken to defend following the attack in Korea. The defense treaties with the Republic of Korea and the Republic of China that came into force in 1953 and 1955 clearly formed part of the emerging bulwark against communist expansion. The latter treaty confirmed the reversal of the noninterference policy toward Taiwan.

Finally, Thailand came within the U.S. defense perimeter and South Vietnam, Laos, and Cambodia were made potential recipients of U.S. defense assistance. These states, all on the mainland of Southeast Asia, were among those that Acheson had said in 1950 would have to rely on themselves or "the entire civilized world" under the UN Charter for their defense. In 1954 John Foster Dulles brought Thailand within the containment line and opened the possibility of assimilation of the other three states by creating an eight-power regional defense arrangement, the Southeast Asia Treaty Organization. The United States expressly identified SEATO as aimed at containing communism by appending to the treaty an understanding that its provisions referring to armed attack applied only to "communist aggression."

As the only member capable of projecting large-scale military force into the area, the United States had the main responsibility for carrying out the provisions of the security treaty. SEATO proved to have little value as a device for mobilizing its members to take effective, united action to contain communism in Southeast Asia. Only two of the members—Thailand and the Philippines—were in Southeast Asia, and most of the others had little interest in intervening militarily in the region.[13]

13. The other members were Australia, France, New Zealand, Pakistan, the United Kingdom, and the United States.

The main beneficiary of SEATO among its members was Thailand, which gained a U.S. commitment, made explicit in the Rusk-Thanat communiqué in 1962, to act in defense of the Thais even without the unanimous agreement of SEATO members.

The SEATO pact had two features not present in other U.S. security treaties. By a separate protocol its protection extended over the non-member states of South Vietnam, Laos, and Cambodia. Cambodia soon adopted a neutralist course and withdrew from SEATO protection; and the Geneva Accord of 1962 neutralizing Laos removed that state from under the SEATO umbrella,[14] leaving only South Vietnam unambiguously in the category of a "protocol state."

The other new feature of SEATO was its provision not only for action by members in the event of armed attack against a member or protocol state, but in recognition of the danger of communist subversion or infiltration, for immediate consultation on measures to be taken for the common defense if the treaty area were threatened in any other way than by armed attack.

Thus, the extension of the containment line to mainland Southeast Asia created ambiguities, not present in the earlier bilateral U.S. commitments, about the probable U.S. response to a threat to a protocol state, as compared to a member state, and to an insurgency threat, as compared to an overt attack. Cambodia's shift to neutralism and the neutralization of Laos widened differences between states of the area and increased uncertainties.

Declaration of an American security interest in an area adjacent to one in which the U.S. commitment was clearcut seems to have set in motion a trend to assimilate such zones of uncertainty more and more closely within the containment line itself.[15] The workings of the political

14. See statement of William H. Sullivan, deputy assistant secretary of state for East Asian and Pacific affairs, on Oct. 20, 1969: "Laos agreed in its 1962 statement of neutrality, however, that it 'will not . . . recognize the protection of any alliance or military coalition including SEATO.' The United States and the other parties to the Declaration on the Neutrality of Laos which incorporated this statement agreed to respect and observe the neutrality of Laos, specifically including the Laos wish with regard to SEATO." *United States Security Agreements and Commitments Abroad,* Hearings before the Subcommittee on U.S. Security Agreements and Commitments Abroad of the Senate Committee on Foreign Relations, 91. Cong. 1 sess. (1969), pt. 2, *Kingdom of Laos,* p. 367.

15. Such zones not only included Laos, Cambodia, and South Vietnam, but also Quemoy and Matsu, where U.S. security interests were ambiguously defined by the Formosa resolution of 1955.

system, the Congress, and the bureaucracy, coupled with pressure from interested allies, tended to inflate the importance of these areas to the United States and to narrow the President's options. As perils to the areas mounted, it became increasingly difficult to decide against using U.S. forces to protect them. Finally, when U.S. reactions were put to the test, as in Quemoy in 1958, and later in South Vietnam, Laos, and Cambodia, the President decided to use U.S. forces to prevent the areas from being taken over.

The northern defense perimeter—with the notable exception of the Korean peninsula—was based on islands and therefore well suited to a policy of military containment. Combined U.S. sea and air power made any attempt to invade U.S.-protected territory extremely risky and difficult. Even Quemoy and Matsu, being islands, could be included within the containment lines when threatened, with a good chance that Peking would be deterred from pressing its attack, as demonstrated in 1958. South Korea was more exposed because of its land frontier with North Korea, lying only a short distance from Chinese and Soviet territory. But the frontier was short and the United States had shown that with superior firepower and control of the sea and air it could defend South Korea against very large Chinese and North Korean forces. Thus, it was possible for the United States to draw a sharp line across the 38th parallel in Korea and through the Taiwan Strait and deter overt military attack with its preponderant forces.

In Southeast Asia, however, neither the terrain nor political conditions were well suited to deterring attack by a policy of military containment. The political weakness, sieve-like border, and rugged terrain of the Indochina states invited probing by low-risk guerrilla warfare instead of overt attack. Because of their ambiguity, U.S. intentions proved an inadequate deterrent, and the United States committed ground, sea, and air forces to preserve South Vietnam and principally air forces to save the populous parts of Laos and Cambodia. This action, in effect, placed the containment line at the 17th parallel in South Vietnam and around the population centers in Laos and Cambodia.

Every Point on the Line Vital

Once the United States had committed its prestige to the defense of a clear line, it became difficult to differentiate between points along the line. Japan might be far more important economically and strategically to the United States than South Vietnam, but all the noncommunist areas within the containment line came to be regarded as so closely interrelated that disaster in one would powerfully affect the others. South Vietnam was less like Eisenhower's first domino in a row or his "cork in the bottle" than like a portion of a dike which, if breached, would let communist influence come swirling into nearby noncommunist areas.

The U.S. objective, as defined by Secretary of Defense Robert S. McNamara in a memorandum to President Lyndon B. Johnson on March 16, 1964, was

an independent non-Communist South Vietnam. . . . Unless we can achieve this objective in South Vietnam, almost all of Southeast Asia will probably fall under Communist dominance (all of Vietnam, Laos, and Cambodia), accommodate to Communism so as to remove effective U.S. and anti-Communist influence (Burma), or fall under the domination of forces not now explicitly Communist but likely then to become so (Indonesia taking over Malaysia). Thailand might hold for a period with our help, but would be under grave pressure. Even the Philippines would become shaky, and the threat to India to the west, Australia and New Zealand to the south, and Taiwan, Korea, and Japan to the north and east would be greatly increased.[16]

Former President Eisenhower at a White House meeting in January 1961 reportedly declared that "Laos was the key to the entire area of Southeast Asia . . . if we permitted Laos to fall, then we would have to write off all the area."[17]

Furthermore, any challenge to the line drawn by the United States was a direct test of American will and determination. No matter how insignificant the threatened area, failure to assure its security would have grave implications. Thus, Eisenhower in 1958 not only asserted the close relationship between Quemoy and Taiwan, he also declared there must be "no retreat in the face of armed aggression." Drawing parallels to the failure of the democracies to check aggression in distant Ethiopia or Manchuria, he warned that "a western Pacific Munich would not buy us peace or security. It would encourage the aggressors. It would dismay our friends and allies there."[18]

President Johnson, justifying his actions in South Vietnam, put the

16. Quoted in David Halberstam, *The Best and the Brightest* (Fawcett, 1972), p. 432.

17. Clark Clifford, "A Vietnam Reappraisal," *Foreign Affairs*, vol. 47 (July 1969), p. 604.

18. *Public Papers of Dwight D. Eisenhower, 1958*, p. 697.

case even more starkly: "If we are driven from the field in Vietnam, then no nation can ever again have the same confidence in American promise, or American protection. . . . Nor would surrender in Vietnam bring peace. We learned from Hitler at Munich that success only feeds the appetite of aggression. The battle would be renewed in one country and then another, bringing with it perhaps even larger and crueler conflict."[19]

And as late as April 1972, President Nixon could declare that "if the Communists win militarily in Vietnam, the risk of war in other parts of the world would be enormously increased. But if, on the other hand, Communist aggression fails in Vietnam, it will be discouraged elsewhere and the chance for peace will be increased."[20]

Threat of Communist Subversion

Even in 1954 when parts of mainland Southeast Asia were brought within the containment line, the U.S. government recognized that subversion, infiltration, and insurgency supported by Communist China or North Vietnam could be as serious a threat to noncommunist governments as overt invasion. Hence the provision in the SEATO treaty for consultation among the members on ways of dealing with this kind of threat.

As the United States increasingly identified its national interest with the preservation of a noncommunist government in South Vietnam, both in public statements and through military and economic aid, North Vietnamese support of rebellion in the South was equated with overt aggression. For example, Secretary of State Dean Rusk told the House Foreign Affairs Committee in August 1965 that the communists, knowing that "large-scale invasions, such as that launched in Korea 15 years ago, would bring great risks and heavy penalties . . . resorted to semiconcealed aggression through the infiltration of arms and trained military personnel across national frontiers." He stated that "the assault on the Republic of Vietnam is, beyond question, an aggression," which the United States must help that state repel. He added that the communists "already have publicly designated Thailand as the next target."[21]

Such official statements, although based on fact, blurred important distinctions. They declared, in effect, that it was as vital to the U.S.

19. Quoted in U.S. Department of State, *Why Vietnam?* (1965), p. 5.
20. *New York Times*, April 27, 1972.
21. *Why Vietnam?* pp. 9, 10.

national interest to check communist infiltration into a part of Asia where the infiltrators spoke the same language and already had a significant base among local people as to help a noncommunist government defend itself against an overt invasion by a foreign communist state.

Containment by Military Force

The Korean experience ensured that military force would be thought of as the principal means of containment. If the Russians would back the use of force by a satellite in Asia, who could be sure they would not launch a military probe wherever they saw weakness along the border between East and West? First priority therefore went to the military buildup, not just in support of the Korean War, but to strengthen defenses elsewhere, especially in Western Europe.[22]

Before the end of the Korean War, U.S. military expenditures had jumped from $13 billion a year to $50 billion. The 1,461,000 men in the armed forces in June 1950 more than doubled in two years. The 48 Air Force wings in 1950 had increased to 95 by July 1952—with another 50 expected to be added in the next four years. Naval ships increased from 671 to over 1,100.[23] The rapid demobilization of U.S. armed forces begun in 1945 was just as rapidly reversed.

When the fighting stopped in Korea the United States had a formidable military machine for use in Asia as well as in Europe. From the expanded headquarters of the Pacific commander in chief at Honolulu, lines of command stretched forward to the Seventh Fleet, to U.S. forces in Korea, and to the growing complex of bases in Japan, Okinawa, and the Philippines. Military assistance advisory groups trained and equipped the armed forces of Japan, Korea, Taiwan, Vietnam, the Philippines, and Thailand pursuant to the Eisenhower administration's policy of greater reliance on local forces. The presence in the western Pacific of important elements of U.S. forces ready to deal with military attacks ensured that military considerations would play an important part in policy decisions in that part of the world. Each of the three armed services acquired a vested interest in an elaborate establishment in East Asia and a stake in its continuance. And the capability of the United States to project military force on a large scale into the vicinity

22. Samuel Huntington, *The Common Defense* (Columbia University Press, 1961), pp. 53–64.
23. Ibid.

of China gave Washington a choice of military options not available in 1950.

In Asia, China soon came to be regarded as the front-line antagonist against which the containment policy was directed. The Chinese soldier had earned respect for his fighting ability in Korea, and during most of the 1950s the Soviet Union was not only providing the Chinese with large quantities of modern weapons, but also helping them to establish their own armaments industry. It was apparent that if the well-armed Chinese "hordes" chose to pour across the border and take over a weak neighbor, only U.S. military force could stop them.

The Chinese Communists' talk of world revolution and emphasis on violence strengthened the view in the United States that they might resort to military force. Mao Tse-tung's widely quoted aphorism that "political power grows out of the barrel of a gun," although it referred to the seizure of power by a communist party within a country, helped etch more deeply into American consciousness the image of the Peking regime as quick on the trigger. So also did the Chinese insistence on their intention to "liberate" Taiwan, by force if necessary. And when the exchange of public denunciations with the USSR began, Peking proclaimed itself more willing than Moscow to run risks that might lead to war.

Although the Chinese Communists were more restrained in their actions than in their rhetoric, they flexed their military muscles frequently enough to trouble American policymakers. Less than a year after the Korean armistice they were supplying crucial military aid to the Vietminh, making possible their victory over the French at Dienbienphu. Later the same year they heavily bombarded Quemoy, killing two American military advisers, and, in a skillful combined operation in January 1955 against one of the Ta Chen group of islands off the China coast, forced the Chinese Nationalists to evacuate the Ta Chens entirely. A brief period of relative quiet in the mid-fifties was succeeded by the Quemoy bombardment of 1958, the Indian border clash of 1962, and the first atomic explosion in 1964, all reminders of Chinese military potential. Although all of the uses of their own military forces after the Korean War were limited to territory the Chinese considered theirs, American policymakers ascribed the restraint to the deterrent effect of U.S. military force.

The U.S. priority on military force for containment has remained high throughout the past twenty years, with the emphasis changing from time to time from one form of force to another. The cry of "no more Koreas" and pressure for lower military budgets during the Eisenhower administration led to greater emphasis on building up local forces through military aid programs, reducing U.S. forces in being, and relying more on the threat of "massive retaliation" to deter possible Chinese attack.

The Kennedy administration, faced with growing insurgency in South Vietnam, and convinced that guerrilla warfare was becoming an increasing threat to U.S. interests in the Third World, overcame considerable Pentagon resistance to place greater emphasis on counterinsurgency capabilities, both in U.S. forces and local forces being trained and equipped by the United States.[24] But even counterinsurgency tended to be thought of by the U.S. military primarily in military terms. General Earle Wheeler (later Army chief of staff and chairman of the Joint Chiefs of Staff under Johnson) declared in November 1962: "Despite the fact that the conflict (in Vietnam) is conducted as guerrilla warfare, it is nonetheless a military action. . . . It is fashionable in some quarters to say that the problems in Southeast Asia are primarily political and economic rather than military. I do not agree. The essence of the problem in Vietnam is military."[25]

The conduct of the war in Vietnam, particularly after U.S. combat units were introduced in 1965, reflected the primacy of military force in the containment policy. Conventional military operations predominated over unconventional operations, and military requirements usually took precedence over the more subtle, difficult, and seemingly less certain task of building political unity and strength in South Vietnam.

Two Decades of Change

For twenty years the containment concept provided a coherent framework for U.S. East Asian policy. It had serious negative consequences, however; it caused the U.S. government to overemphasize reliance on military force, to underestimate the possibility of a break between China and the Soviet Union, and to exaggerate the Chinese threat. Nevertheless, behind the military shield it created, a great deal of constructive work went on. Japan's burst of economic energy, the

24. Roger Hilsman, *To Move a Nation* (Doubleday, 1967), chap. 28.
25. Ibid., p. 426.

thriving economic life of most of the other noncommunist East Asian states, the growing self-confidence and maturity of the independent governments of former European colonies, and the creation of institutions for regional cooperation were all stimulated by the active American presence and the consequent sense of security in the western Pacific.

At the same time that sweeping changes were occurring within the states that the containment policy was created to protect, the very threat against which the policy was erected disintegrated. The most important change in East Asia in the last decade, the Sino-Soviet dispute, split the movement known as "international communism."

The Sino-Soviet Rift

During and just after the Korean War the Sino-Soviet alliance seemed solid. The close cooperation of the two great communist powers in Korea was succeeded by the "learn from the USSR" period in China, when the Soviets provided large amounts of military and economic aid. The Chinese, heavily engaged in backing the Vietminh against the French in Indochina, appeared as the cutting edge of Soviet influence in Asia. The containing of these communist pressures was an important part of the United States' global policy. By the time that solid evidence of growing differences between Moscow and Peking became available, Washington had become so preoccupied with strengthening the instruments of containment in East Asia that top policymakers failed to realize the extent to which the Sino-Soviet split was altering the very premises on which the policy was based.

The falling out between Russia and China affected the gamut of party and state relations. By the end of the 1960s the widening gulf between Moscow and Peking had made the two-sided confrontation in East Asia triangular. This fundamental realignment in the global system of power shattered the unity of the world communist movement.

Whatever temptation the Chinese might have had to invade a neighbor—a danger that in hindsight seems to have been overestimated by the U.S. government—must have been diminished by their quarrel with the Soviets. They no longer have the benefit of the Soviet nuclear umbrella or access to Soviet weapons, a loss their own nuclear capability and industrial plant cannot compensate for. Moreover, they can no longer count on the great weight of Soviet diplomatic support or Soviet ability to threaten action elsewhere to relieve pressure on China in a crisis. Instead, they must prepare for the possibility that border clashes with Soviet troops may flare into wider war.

The Sino-Soviet split also affects the prospects for successful communist revolution. Although it does not inhibit the promotion of insurgency as it does an armed invasion by China, the split has changed the atmosphere and affected party and state relations in ways that make the life of an Asian communist revolutionary more difficult.

The Chinese Communist conquest of the China mainland in 1949 and the signing of the Sino-Soviet alliance in 1950 gave a great boost to the élan of communist revolutionaries throughout Asia. Communism seemed the wave of the future. Communists played leading parts in rebellions in Burma, Malaya, the Philippines, and Indochina. Young overseas Chinese in Southeast Asia enthusiastically acclaimed the "new China" and flocked there for their education. The intellectual atmosphere of the East was permeated with Marxist concepts, especially Lenin's theories of imperialism.

Even before the Sino-Soviet split, the optimism of revolutionaries in most parts of Asia had begun to decline, as the rebellions ran into stiff resistance. Noncommunist nationalist leaders gained the upper hand everywhere except in Indochina and were able to deny the communists control of the nationalist movements. An abortive communist rebellion in Indonesia was quickly crushed by Sukarno as early as 1948. Hope for a communist victory faded gradually in Burma, Malaya, and the Philippines. Only in Indochina, where communism and nationalism were allied, was the momentum maintained.

The serious differences between Moscow and Peking that began to appear after Khrushchev struck down the theory of the infallibility of the Soviet leadership by his denunciation of Stalin in 1956 imposed further difficulties on communist revolutionaries. By the early 1960s Russians and Chinese were trading insults publicly, and rivalry between them within the communist movement grew apace. As the contest over allies sharpened, most Asian parties either chose sides or split into factions; today they are pro-Soviet, pro-Chinese, or independent, with a variety of subcategories in each type.

Thus, a complicated and confusing set of relationships has replaced the unified communist movement of the early 1950s. The Outer Mongolian party is in the Soviet camp. The Soviets and Chinese compete vigorously for influence on North Korea and North Vietnam, both of which retain a considerable degree of independence by playing off each of the big powers against the other. The outlawed Indonesian Communist party probably retains connections with both Moscow and Peking; the substantial edge Peking had during the Sukarno era may have disappeared. The Japanese Communist party is independent and nationalistic, not hesitating to criticize both the Soviet Union and China, but in recent years its relations have been less strained with Moscow than with Peking. And in South Vietnam, Laos, and Cambodia, North Vietnam has greater influence on local communists than either of the major powers has.

The fragmentation of the communist movement has been accompanied by a transformation of the intellectual atmosphere in Asia. The influence of dogmatic Marxists of either the Moscow or the Peking persuasion is declining. The new generation of intellectuals tends to take a pragmatic, problem-solving approach to national needs and is less emotionally committed to opposition to the West. Even leaders who call themselves socialists, like Ne Win in Burma, stress the distinctiveness of their own national way to socialism, rejecting both the Chinese and Soviet models. The spectacle of communist factions quarreling among themselves has undermined the authority and appeal of communist doctrine. Though the causes of instability persist, it is not so readily exploitable as in the past.

Furthermore, the antagonism manifested in military confrontation and political infighting extends to the trade and diplomacy of China and Russia. Both are expanding their noncommunist contacts at the expense of their formerly close relationship with each other. Four-fifths of China's trade was once with the Soviet Union and other countries of the communist bloc; that portion is now with noncommunist states, and Japan has replaced the USSR as China's principal trading partner. Soviet relations with Japan likewise are steadily increasing, in trade, cultural and technological exchange, and airline agreements, and the Japanese are cooperating in the development of Siberia. The Soviet Union is also increasing its trade throughout Southeast Asia, arranging naval visits, and expanding its network of diplomatic relations. The expansion of state-to-state relationships in this region is becoming an increasingly important element in Sino-Soviet rivalry.

Since 1971 this rivalry has had a new dimension—competition for improved relations with the United States. Both communist powers pursue complex diplomatic strategies combining opposition to the United States and cooperation with it. Thus, the Sino-Soviet split has created new diplomatic options for the United States and its allies in their dealings with China and the Soviet Union.

The Resurgence of Japan

The resurgence of Japan is second only to the Sino-Soviet split in significance. The fundamental purpose of the U.S. containment policy was defense of Japan. The U.S. bases in Japan proper and Okinawa supported military actions in defense of the containment line. And those actions grew out of fear that communist gains elsewhere might undermine the vital U.S. relationship with Japan, a relationship not always spelled out by U.S. spokesmen.

Safeguarding Japan was an important reason for the American decision to send troops to defend South Korea—though deterring possible Soviet moves in the even more important European arena appears to have been uppermost in the minds of Truman and Acheson. Japan was in a vulnerable condition. Its war-devastated economy was at a low ebb,[26] it had no defense capability of its own, the socialists and communists—much more influential than they are today—were pressing hard for a disarmed, neutral Japan, and the American occupation force was small.

As the years passed, Japan's economic recovery raised doubts about the containment policy. Not only was Japan one of the most highly industrialized states in the world, but it was well on the way to becoming the predominant economic power in East Asia. It began to seem strange that American soldiers should fight in distant places to help defend the interests of a country potentially able to defend its interests itself. Americans were ambivalent, however. Many had reservations about a remilitarized Japan. But as time went on, and particularly when the costs of the Vietnam War began to pinch, the opinion grew that Japan should do more.[27]

26. It is difficult today to recall how gloomy Japan's economic outlook was at the time of the Korean War. In 1949 Edwin O. Reischauer, noting that Japan had twice the population of the United Kingdom to support on fewer natural resources, concluded: "The economic situation in Japan may be fundamentally so unsound that no policies, no matter how wise, can save her from slow economic starvation and all the concomitant political and social ills that situation would produce." *The United States and Japan* (3rd ed., Viking, 1965), p. 51.

27. See, for example, Richard M. Nixon, "Asia After Vietnam," *Foreign Affairs*, vol. 46 (October 1967), p. 120.

Even more galling than the lack of Japanese help in manning the containment line was the widespread disagreement in Japan with the containment policy. The average Japanese thought that the United States exaggerated the Chinese Communist threat and put too much emphasis on military means of dealing with it. Consequently, the general Japanese reaction to U.S. military intervention in Vietnam in 1965 was alarm rather than relief—fear of being dragged into an unwanted war with China.[28] The Japanese government expressed its "understanding" of U.S. policy and permitted the use of U.S. bases and other facilities in Japan for logistical support of U.S. operations in Vietnam, but the unpopularity of the war in Japan made it impolitic for the government to contribute large amounts of economic support to South Vietnam or even to express staunch support for the U.S. military intervention there.

The rise of Japan thus raised important questions as to the application of the containment policy elsewhere in East Asia. How could the United States protect its security interests throughout the region—or even define those interests—without giving far greater attention than in the past to the central importance of the U.S.-Japanese relationship? The need had grown inexorably for a greater measure of agreement with Japan on how to maintain peace in East Asia, and it was clear that Japan's views on how this could best be done diverged sharply from those reflected in the containment policy.

Nationalism, Modernization, and Regional Cooperation

No other East Asian state can rival Japan's postwar record of sustained economic growth and transformation in the life of its people. But other states have also changed substantially, and so also have their relations with each other, since the inception of the containment policy in 1950.

One important force in East Asia has been the thrust of nationalism—primarily against domination by Western colonial powers, but also, in some places, against Japan. More than any other Asian country, Japan has contributed to the rise of nationalism. Early, it set an example by mobilizing its population under the banner of nationalism to compete successfully with Western powers. Then by invading China and occupying Korea, it stimulated nationalism in those countries against itself.

28. Edwin O. Reischauer, *Beyond Vietnam* (Vintage Books, 1967), p. 127.

Finally, it encouraged the independence movements in the colonies of Western powers that it occupied in World War II, helping to transform them into nation-states.

The strength of nationalism has grown, unevenly but constantly, throughout the region during the past twenty years. In predominantly rural states, such as Indonesia, Burma, or Laos, most people's horizons are still limited to family, village, or religious or ethnic group. Yet even in the most tradition-bound societies change has occurred. And in the more rapidly urbanizing and modernizing states, such as South Korea or Taiwan, education and participation in modern life have fast expanded the proportion of the population capable of responding to nationalistic appeals. Armed with modern tools for fostering pride in the nation—radio, television, the press, and national school systems—political leaders and intellectuals have stimulated the growth of nationalism and have drawn on its strength to further their purposes.

The spreading and deepening sense of nationalism has been exploited in various ways. Indonesia's President Sukarno used it successfully to mobilize support for his campaign to wrest West Irian from the Dutch. The Burmese government has used it to gain popular backing for its measures putting an end to dominance of the Burmese economy by Indian and Chinese merchants. In South Korea opposition politicians appealed, unsuccessfully, to nationalistic feeling to block diplomatic relations with Japan. In the Philippines politicians have sought to improve their nationalist images by advancing the Philippine claim to Sabah and Filipino nationalists have spoken out against U.S. bases and U.S. investments.

Thus, nationalism has at times been used to fan animosities toward neighboring countries, creating friction and conflict contrary to U.S. interests, or been turned more directly against U.S. economic or security interests. But in some ways, growing nationalism accords with U.S. interests. Only in China and North Vietnam have local communist leaders been notably successful in exploiting the spirit of nationalism in their drive for power, and in most countries local communists are increasingly seen as responding to the control of either China or North Vietnam. Noncommunist leaders have been using the strength of nationalism effectively to fortify their own positions and resist communist influence.

Nationalism thus offers noncommunist leaders in Southeast Asia a means of resisting either forcible takeover by a communist party supported by Moscow or Peking or exclusive domination by the economic power of the United States or Japan. Southeast Asian states are in a substantially stronger position today than twenty years ago to maintain their national independence and balance the influence of the big powers against each other.

Closely related to the growth of nationalism is the spread of a strong desire for economic development and other attributes of modernization. The elite in the developing countries of Asia are aware of the problems economic growth has created both for developing and for highly industrialized societies. Yet, except in Burma, where economic growth has received a lower priority than elsewhere, East Asian leaders from China to Indonesia are anxious for their countries to acquire the benefits of modern technology in order to catch up with the highly industrialized nations. Leaders strong on nationalism but weak on economic development are, like Sukarno, apt to fall sooner or later, while those strong on both counts can gain wide support. Windy rhetoric is no substitute for solid achievement in which the populace can take pride.

Progress in modernization is partly dependent on internal factors, but it also occurs as the number and intensity of relations of all kinds with developed countries increase. Through economic and military aid, trade, private investment, and tourism, modernizing influences flow from the developed states to the less developed countries. Among the many other instruments, education is particularly important, as tens of thousands of young Asians study abroad or in foreign-influenced schools at home to prepare for careers in their own nations. The modern sectors attract most of the brightest and most ambitious youths, many of whom go to Japan or to Western states to study. Those East Asian states with the closest and most numerous ties with developed countries have shown the most rapid progress in modernization, while those, like Burma, that have closed themselves off have stagnated.

The United States, Japan, Australia, Canada, and Western Europe have advantages over China or North Vietnam, or even the Soviet Union, in satisfying the hunger for modernization. The industrialized Western world has larger markets for Asian products, more capital to invest, and more advanced technology to offer. The great variety of public and private institutions in Japan and the West offers more flexibility than the stiff, state-operated mechanisms of the communist countries.

Of course, China is modernizing too, along very different lines from the United States or Japan and starting from a low base. While its early appeal to many Asians as a model for development has faded, Chinese techniques may often strike Asians as more suitable to their stage of development than those of the highly industrialized countries. If China can avoid repeating the frenzy of the Great Leap Forward or the Cultural Revolution, it may refurbish its image as a model for modernization, with particular appeal to dissatisfied or disadvantaged groups in other countries. The picture of a disciplined, industrious, purposeful society, without extremes of rich and poor, is attractive to many, despite China's generally low level of economic development. Though China may thus gain an advantage over Japan and the West in certain circumstances and places, it seems unlikely, for the remainder of this decade at least, that it will be able to rival the modernizing appeal of those nations in the forefront of technological progress.

A third major trend in East Asia in recent years has been the beginnings of regional cooperation. It does not make an important difference today in the ability of governments to manage their internal problems, resist external pressures, and maintain their independence. Yet regional cooperation is potentially important. East Asian states, especially the former colonies, have traditionally trafficked more with Europe and the United States than with their neighbors. Barriers between them remain more important than the bonds uniting them. But in the past few years Asian leaders have begun to look at each other in new ways. There is a new spirit abroad.

The new-born desire to work toward Asian solutions to common problems has given rise to new institutions—the Asian Development Bank, the Association of Southeast Asian Nations (ASEAN), the Ministerial Conference on Southeast Asian Economic Development. At least equally important are the many less formal, often bilateral ways of cooperating in economic, cultural, and even security affairs. The security forces of Indonesia and Malaysia have cooperated against the communist insurgents operating near the border between the two countries, as have Malaysian and Thai forces in the vicinity of their border.

Growing nationalism, the spreading desire for modernization, and the groping for effective forms of regional cooperation do not ensure that the developing nations of East Asia will be capable of maintaining their independence in the 1970s. Local conflict, domestic disorder, and

Chinese efforts to exploit the turmoil must be anticipated in some places. Changes over the past twenty years, however, have significantly improved the chances for national leaders to maintain the independence of their nations.

The Containment Line Today

Although the Sino-Soviet split, the resurgence of Japan, and the trends of nationalism, modernization, and regional cooperation had by the mid-1960s altered the face of East Asia enough to call for a reassessment of the containment policy, the U.S. government was slow to respond. The very coherence and consistency of the containment policy became a handicap. It had a built-in tendency toward rigidity. It produced an official rhetoric and an attitude of mind in both politicians and the foreign affairs bureaucracy that led to its mechanical application in new places and through changing times. Substantial modification of the policy would inevitably involve serious risks and uncertainties, and containment, though it might not precisely fit changing conditions, appeared to work reasonably well.

The traumatic experience of the Vietnam War finally forced a thoroughgoing reappraisal of U.S. policy. The changes in East Asia made a reassessment of the containment policy desirable; the public reaction in the United States to the Vietnam War made it imperative. The length of the war, the disputable rationale and moral justification for it, the high costs and casualties, the optimistic official forecasts proved wrong—all produced deep division among the American people. Influential voices in the Congress and among the people questioned the official assessments of U.S. interests in Southeast Asia, the threat to those interests, and the use of U.S. forces to protect them.

The Sino-Soviet split and other far-reaching changes in East Asia may appear to have so strengthened noncommunist governments, and so diluted the power of China and the Soviet Union to expand their spheres of influence by aiding in the violent overthrow of such governments, that the containment line could continue to be held without the intervention of U.S. forces. This seems to be the rationale that prompted President Nixon to say that "while we will maintain our interests in Asia and the commitments that flow from them, the changes taking place in that region enable us to change the character of our involvement."[29] Thus, during the past several years, military responsibility for holding the containment line in Southeast Asia has been shifted gradually from U.S. forces to local forces.

But there is serious question whether the containment line can be held by local forces in the Indochina states, especially in Cambodia, where the administration withdrew U.S. air power from combat only when compelled to do so by the Congress. Moreover, there are still many potential causes of political unrest and disorder which the Chinese or Soviets might exploit, even though their power to expand their influence by helping in the overthrow of governments friendly to the United States has declined. Singapore President Lee Kuan-yew's public call for U.S. military forces to remain in Thailand to prevent Chinese power from surging southward was an expression of fears widely shared among Southeast Asian leaders.

Thus, the United States still faces the basic question whether, if local forces fighting to hold the containment line seem about to go under, some form of U.S. military force should again be introduced to back them up. How important is it to the United States in the 1970s that the long-established line between communist and non-communist areas in East Asia continue to hold?

29. *U.S. Foreign Policy for the 1970's*, H. Doc. 91–258, p. 54.

CHAPTER TWO

Reassessing U.S. Interests

At the heart of the public debate on U.S. policy in Southeast Asia lies the dispute over the nature and importance of U.S. interests there. The debate often lumps together different kinds of interests and brings in the threats to them and the costs and risks of defending them. The discussion is confusing, for "the fundamental question of American interests and power is never posed or answered directly or in the abstract. It is posed implicitly in terms of a number of specific immediate issues and decisions; it is answered ambiguously, if at all, by a set of responses that emerge from the unpredictable interaction of external events and domestic politics, of general policies and particular decisions, of underlying premises and pragmatic judgments." [1]

Although it is hard to abstract the idea of national interests from the foreign policy context in which it lies imbedded, some of its elements can be defined. The national interests of any state can be regarded as comprising physical survival as a nation; preservation of the most cherished values of the people of the nation and enhancement of their material well-being; and creation of an international environment favorable to these interests. It is not difficult to get agreement on such broad principles; the difficulty lies in their application. Nations clash when one appears to be pursuing its interests at the expense of another. Within a nation citizens disagree on how to define and evaluate the national interests in particular circumstances. In a world in which force remains the ultimate arbiter of disputes between nations, they may disagree most sharply on when and where to use military force to protect national interests.

1. Robert Osgood, *America and the World: From the Truman Doctrine to Vietnam* (Johns Hopkins Press, 1970), p. 1.

Nature of U.S. Interests

The United States has, of course, a great range and variety of national interests, some of substantial importance. Very few, however, are so vital that most Americans would agree on the use of armed force to protect them. But certain clusters of interests relating to particular countries or regions are of such great importance that the use of U.S. forces to protect them must be seriously considered. These clusters of interests may be defined as *general, intrinsic, derived,* or *created* interests.

General interests, those with a global reach, include the deterrence of attack against the United States and defense of the United States if attacked, as well as the avoidance of nuclear war anywhere and the kinds of conventional conflict that might escalate to nuclear war. Other general interests are the deterrence of aggression, the creation of a more stable world order, and the maintenance of confidence among those who rely on the United States for their defense. Because of the extensive involvement of the United States in the affairs of the world, many developments can affect its general interests and it is often difficult to judge the seriousness of their effect.

The intrinsic interests of the United States are inherent in its direct relationship with a particular country or area at a particular time. The U.S. economic stake in a country, traditional ties with the people of that country, the ability of that country to help protect U.S. general interests—for example, by providing land for military bases to be used in deterring attack on the United States—are intrinsic interests. So is the maintenance of friendly relations with a state whose hostility or alliance with an adversary of the United States would significantly increase the direct military threat to the United States. Only in a few countries or regions are intrinsic U.S. interests important enough to justify without question the high cost and risk in the nuclear age of using military force to defend them. The principal concentrations of industrial power in Western Europe or Japan fall in this category, as does territory so close to the United States that its control by a major hostile power could significantly increase the direct military threat to the United States.

The derived interests of the United States are those that are not intrinsic to its relations with a particular state, but flow from its important interest in a third state. The military action undertaken by the United States in Korea, for example, was based in part on worldwide general interests, but also on derived interests—that is, the damage that would be done to important intrinsic interests of the United States in nearby Japan if U.S. forces were not used.

Created interests are those that the United States itself creates in a given country by taking actions (especially by making defense commitments or by actually deploying its armed forces) that create an expectation that the United States would use armed force there in order to protect other types of interests. In making a defense commitment, the United States creates a type of interest that did not exist before, an interest in fulfilling that commitment in order to maintain the credibility to both friend and foe of its commitments elsewhere.[2] Once created, such interests are hard to extinguish. Furthermore, they tend to breed other interests. To protect existing interests, new commitments either implicit or express tend to be made in nearby areas.

Order of U.S. Interests

Without a method for the rigorous evaluation of national interests, much depends on uncertain judgments about a wide range of possible future developments. Consequently, individual views tend to be highly subjective. Nevertheless, foreign policy decisions have to be based on some express or unspoken evaluation of the national interests involved.

The United States has intrinsic interests of the highest order in only one East Asian country: Japan. In no other western Pacific nation can U.S. interests begin to compare in importance with those in Japan. In Australia perhaps they come closest, but with a population only one-tenth that of Japan, Australia has far less actual and potential impact on the region and on the world. Both countries are technologically advanced, and U.S. relations with them are more like those with Western Europe and Canada than those with the less developed states of the region.

The other noncommunist nations of East Asia, some allies, some neutrals, are at various stages along the road to development. The

2. The new created interest relates to a particular place, but the effects of making it—or failing to fulfill it—make it a form of general interest as well.

direct concern of the United States with them is in many ways like that with developing countries elsewhere. The intrinsic U.S. interests in them are small compared to U.S. interests in Japan.

The communist countries of East Asia[3]—China, North Korea, and North Vietnam—are developing states also, but the United States has at present an adversary relationship with them. China is not only a developing state, but at the same time a budding nuclear power. The long-term U.S. concern with China is comparable to that with India: both nations contain enormous and growing numbers of people who must somehow be provided an opportunity to emerge from poverty and join the modern world if they are not to become a perpetual source of trouble, discord, and danger. The short-term U.S. concern with China is more like that with the Soviet Union: the problem is to overcome the barriers of ideology and mutual suspicion in order to reduce the danger of large-scale war and little by little to develop ways of cooperating constructively.

Japan, the Chief Focus

Japan, with its 100 million people, now has the third largest economy in the world. Its capacity to cooperate with the United States in building a world order congenial to Americans or, turned hostile, to threaten American security far exceeds that of any other power in the Asian-Pacific region.

The United States and Japan are the world's two greatest trading nations. Although commercial competitors, they have a large and expanding trade with each other. The United States is Japan's most important trading partner, while, for the United States, Japan is second only to Canada. Their economic and political systems cause both countries to favor open societies and minimum restrictions on the flow of goods and people throughout the world. This shared view of a desirable world order and Japan's rapidly growing economic power create an exceptionally important U.S. interest in maintaining close and cooperative relations with Japan.

Moreover, Japan is potentially a great military power. With its broad industrial base and advanced technology Japan could quickly outstrip China in both conventional and nuclear weapons. What Japan does with its military potential will profoundly affect the course of

---

3. Excluding the USSR, which lies partly in East Asia and is a major actor there, but whose relationship with the United States is a global one.

events in East Asia and the world. It could remain a lightly armed, nonnuclear power, promoting its interests by nonmilitary means. It could become a military partner of the United States, sharing the burden of regional defense. It could rely on military strength to pursue its own objectives, disassociated from the United States. Or it could ally its military strength to that of the USSR or China.

A nuclear-armed Japan allied to one of the major communist powers would sharply increase the military force that could be used to pose a direct military threat to the United States. Even a non-aligned Japan, relying heavily on military strength in pursuit of its objectives, would make East Asia a less stable region. The other big powers, alarmed, would devote more resources to armament, thus fueling the arms race and increasing the risk of big-power war in which the United States might be involved. Prospects for arms control agreements would be reduced and the likelihood of further prolifera-tion of nuclear weapons increased.

If the United States were confronted by Soviet or Chinese efforts to expand their power in East Asia by the use of military force, it might be in the U.S. interest for Japan to develop its potential military strength and share with the United States the burden of confronting this challenge. But if China and the Soviet Union refrain from military aggression—as seems likely in this decade—Japan probably can con-tribute more to peace and stability in East Asia by remaining a lightly armed, nonnuclear power than by becoming a full military partner of the United States. In any case, it is clear that Japan's potential military power makes Japan a far more important U.S. interest in this decade than any other state in East Asia.

The interests of the United States in Japan have not been endan-gered by any serious threat of a military attack on Japan. Moreover, Japan's postwar political and economic systems have proved stable and adaptable. But the U.S. government has feared that its interests in Japan might be seriously damaged if the Soviet Union or China should gain control over other East Asian states. Concern over the threat to Japan was an important reason for the adoption of the con-tainment policy. The changes of the past twenty years call for re-examination of this concern. How much would U.S. interests in Japan actually be injured if Asian communist states should gain dominance over certain noncommunist countries elsewhere in East Asia? In other words, how important are the derived interests of the United States in particular developing countries of East Asia based on the presumption that what happened there would have repercussions on important U.S. interests in Japan?

Australia, a Secondary Focus

Although the United States has far fewer intrinsic interests in Australia[4] than in Japan, they exceed those in any one of the developing states of the region. Americans are linked to the Australians by bonds of common language and cultural background, and the U.S. economic stake in that continent is growing rapidly. Stable government, enormous reserves of easily exploited natural resources, and the mutual benefits to Americans and Australians of economic collaboration ensure that that stake will continue to grow.

Moreover, Australia is the only state in the western Pacific, other than Japan, that could within a few years produce its own nuclear weapons if it should decide to do so. It is one of a handful of countries in the world whose cooperation the United States needs to hold the line against further proliferation of nuclear weapons.

Like Japan, Australia is an industrialized state, with many interests in common with the United States, and it is capable of making a small but significant contribution to world order. Even more than Japan, Australia—also protected by the U.S. nuclear umbrella—seems secure from threat of military attack or revolution.

In addition to its intrinsic interests in Australia, the United States derives other interests from the importance of that continent to Japan. Australia is already Japan's biggest source of raw materials.[5]

The Developing States

The United States has no intrinsic interests in any of the developing countries of the East Asian region comparable to its interests in Japan.

4. New Zealand, a tiny state, less industrialized than Australia, is lumped with Australia for the purpose of this discussion.

5. The growing triangular interdependence among the United States, Japan, and Australia is typified by a contract seven Japanese steel companies signed in 1969 with an American-owned Australian mining company to provide them with 123 million tons of ore over the next 21 years. *New York Times*, Nov. 18, 1969. In May 1971, Chrysler Corp. signed an agreement with Mitsubishi Motor Corp. for 35 percent participation in Mitsubishi; Chrysler is marketing in the United States Dodge Colts built by Mitsubishi in Japan, while Mitsubishi markets in Japan Valiants produced by Chrysler's Australian subsidiary. *New York Times*, June 13, 1971.

Trade and investment are relatively small. Control of one or a group of these states by a major power hostile to the United States would not significantly increase the direct military threat to the United States. Nor can these states contribute much to maintaining a stable world order; many of them have their hands full keeping their own houses in order. Primarily, U.S. interests relating to these countries are derived and general.

KOREA. Because of Korea's close relationship to Japan, the U.S. defense commitment to South Korea is more easily justified than those to other East Asian developing nations. The Japanese have traditionally been concerned about who controlled this nearby peninsula— this "dagger pointed at the heart of Japan." The forcible seizure of South Korea in 1950 by North Korean communists, backed by the Russians, would have dismayed the Japanese and might have caused a political evolution within Japan highly unfavorable to U.S. interests. It might also have encouraged the Soviet Union or Communist China to act more boldly against U.S. interests elsewhere, thus increasing the danger of general war. The support the action taken by the United States received, both in the United Nations and from its European allies, confirmed the importance of that action. Today the growing economic and other relations between Japan and South Korea and the Japanese government's characterization of the security of the Republic of Korea as "essential to Japan's own security"[6] tie U.S. interests in South Korea to this country's primary interest in Japan.

Korea's proximity to China, the Soviet Union, and Japan, the historical involvement of these nations in Korean affairs, and the more recent deep involvement of the United States there also, make Korea important to the success of any U.S. policy designed to build a lasting structure of peace in the region. It would be difficult for any of the four big powers to stay aloof from renewed large-scale conflict on the Korean peninsula. The United States, being a distant power, could disengage more easily than the others, but if it should do so alone, while the others remained deeply involved, the prospects for Japan's remaining a lightly armed, nonnuclear power would be sharply diminished. The Japanese would have to recalculate their interest in supporting the South Korean government and, concomitantly, their own

6. Nixon-Sato communiqué, Nov. 21, 1969. U.S. Department of State, *United States Foreign Policy 1969–1970: A Report of the Secretary of State*, Publication 8575 (March 1971), pp. 503–05.

military preparedness. Still more important, they would have to decide whether the disengagement of the United States in South Korea also reduced its defense commitment to Japan. The danger that Japan would enter the big-power arms race, causing a reversal of the trend toward lessening of tension in East Asia, would rise.

The greatest danger, however, from a unilateral U.S. disengagement would be the heightened risk of conflict in South Korea. Kim Il-sung, who denounces the presence of U.S. forces as the principal obstacle to the reunification of Korea, might be tempted to revert to the use of military force to achieve his purpose (that South Korea might try to reunify the peninsula by force seems less likely but is not inconceivable). The outbreak of large-scale conflict in Korea would be a severe shock to the Japanese, particularly if North Korea should conquer South Korea. The U.S.-Japanese alliance would be severely strained and a Japanese decision to rearm massively would be probable.

Consequently, continuing U.S. involvement in Korea is important to a policy of maintaining a stable equilibrium among the four big powers in East Asia based on close cooperation with Japan and an effort to improve relations with China and the USSR. So long as this policy is succeeding, the risk of conflict in Korea is likely to remain low, and Japan can contribute more to the common purpose by remaining a lightly armed, nonnuclear power than by assuming military responsibilities in Korea. Continued U.S. involvement in Korea does not necessarily mean that the United States must maintain military forces there indefinitely. But the deep involvement of the four big powers in Korea and the potential impact of occurrences there on the Japanese make peace in that peninsula critical to peace in the region as a whole.

Not only must the abstract value of national interests that the U.S. government is prepared to defend with its own forces be weighed, but also the potential cost of defending those interests. That cost is probably lower in Korea than in most other East Asian countries. The policies of the big powers and of the two Koreas suggest that the risk of large-scale war in Korea will remain low, especially if the United States stays involved. But if war should occur, a number of circumstances would help to limit the cost of U.S. intervention. The uncertainties introduced by the Sino-Soviet split would strongly inhibit the communist powers from participating with their own forces. The military forces of South Korea are large and efficient enough to do most of the fighting against a North Korean invasion. And, because Korea is a peninsula, U.S. air and sea power could be used to great effect, while the front line in any conventional war there would be relatively short, with terrain favoring the defense.[7]

TAIWAN. Those U.S. interests in Taiwan derived from that island's relationship to Japan resemble derived U.S. interests in South Korea, although the Japanese see Taiwan as less closely related to their own security than Korea.

Japan has certain intrinsic interests in the island growing out of its long and close relationship with the Taiwanese during the colonial period and fortified by its recent substantial trade and investment there. The Japanese government would like to retain these interests, provided their retention does not conflict too severely with the larger objective of developing and improving relations with China.

Some Japanese, concerned about the potential military threat of a hostile China to their territory and their shipping lanes, are anxious that Taiwan remain free from control by mainland China. Most Japanese, however, see little prospect of a Chinese military threat to Japan and therefore do not view Taiwan in terms of their own security.[8]

Thus, the ultimate fate of Taiwan is less important to the majority of Japanese than the way in which its fate is resolved. If Taiwan were peacefully reunited to the China mainland, even though Japanese economic interests in Taiwan suffered damage, the Japanese view of China and Japanese relations with the United States would not be seriously affected.

On the other hand, if China were to resort to military threat or the actual use of military force to gain control of Taiwan, many Japanese would be deeply disturbed. The widely held view of China as a peaceable nation would be called into question. Though the Japanese concede the island to be Chinese, they would be profoundly disturbed by the operations of Chinese naval and air power so close to Japanese territory, backed by the at least implicit threat of nuclear weapons. They would have to consider what might happen in a showdown between Japan and China over the disputed Senkaku Islands, or over the overlapping claims to oil deposits under the East China Sea.

The Chinese military threat to Taiwan would deeply divide the

7. See Chapter 9.
8. See Chapter 5.

Japanese in their views of the United States. Some, fearing Japan's unwilling participation in a U.S. defense of Taiwan, would be relieved if the United States were to abandon its commitment to Taiwan in the face of the Chinese threat. Others, however, would be disturbed by the implications for Japan's own security of U.S. abandonment of Taiwan. Though they would not expect the same U.S. reaction to a threat to Japan, they could not help but be impressed by the change in the balance of power in the region represented by the Chinese willingness to use force to resolve the long-standing Taiwan problem and the U.S. decision to back away from its commitment to a peaceful resolution of the issue.

The Japanese reaction to a Chinese military threat to Taiwan would depend on many factors, including the state of Japan's relations with the United States and China. It seems probable that Chinese resort to the threat or use of force against Taiwan would strengthen support in Japan for stronger military forces. The probability would be even greater if the United States failed to fulfill its defense commitment to Taiwan and thus raised doubts about U.S. willingness to stand up militarily to China elsewhere in Northeast Asia.

The likelihood of any Chinese threat, for the next few years at least, is slight. The Taiwan issue has been successfully set to one side and China has strong reasons for not allowing it to impede the improvement and expansion of relations with the United States and Japan. Chinese leaders have shown willingness to work patiently and gradually toward a peaceful settlement with Taiwan. Therefore, the U.S. defense commitment to Taiwan is unlikely to be tested. If it should be tested, however, geography suggests that here, as in Korea, it could be fulfilled through reliance on sea power and air power.

In Taiwan, as in Korea, the United States has interests that justify continued U.S. involvement, although the case is weaker than in Korea and probably will erode further. As time passes, the importance of relations between the United States and Taiwan, and between Japan and Taiwan, is likely to decline in relation to the growing importance of U.S. and Japanese relations with Peking.

SOUTHEAST ASIA. The lack of any highly important U.S. intrinsic interests in South Korea and Taiwan hardly needs demonstrating, but the case is not so clear in Southeast Asia. The area is impressive in its bulk; as Dean Rusk pointed out in justifying U.S. military intervention in Vietnam, it "contains rich natural resources and some 200 million people."[9] But Southeast Asia is not, like Australia, a homogeneous political unit, and U.S. intrinsic interests in its heterogeneous, often politically shaky states, some of them antagonistic toward each other, cannot be viewed in the same light as U.S. interests in Australia. It is difficult to show that they are today of high importance to the United States. The U.S. economic stake in each of these countries is relatively small. None of them is capable of becoming a direct military threat to the United States for many years to come. And U.S. bases on their soil are not essential to the defense of U.S. territory. Intrinsic interests in the countries of the region may grow in importance in time, but slowly because of the diversity of peoples and languages, the political fragmentation of the region, and the generally low level of economic and political development.

Southeast Asia is frequently argued to be vital to the United States for geopolitical reasons. For Secretary Rusk, it had "great strategic importance—it dominates the gateway between the Pacific and Indian Oceans and flanks the Indian subcontinent on one side, and Australia and New Zealand on the other." The ring of authority of such a statement confirms for champions of sea power the vital nature of U.S. interests in Southeast Asia. The threat of a major power with militaristic designs closing busy straits, or gaining important forward military bases on land areas of Southeast Asia would, however, be of more direct concern to Japan and Australia than to the United States. Whatever the strategic value of Southeast Asia may be—and there is room for wide difference of opinion, mainly owing to the uncertainty whether a lengthy, large-scale conventional war between major powers is conceivable in the nuclear age—that value for the United States derives mainly from its relation to the principal U.S. interests in Japan and lesser interests in Australia or India, rather than from its direct importance to the defense of the United States.

Consequently, in judging whether U.S. interests in Southeast Asia are important enough to be defended with force, relatively little weight can be assigned to intrinsic interests. The principal concern should be the impact of what happens there on the major U.S. interest in East Asia—Japan—and on this country's global general interests.

If Japan lost confidence in the United States as a reliable ally and, deciding to go its own way, hastened to develop powerful military

---

9. U.S. Department of State, *Why Vietnam?* (1965), p. 9.

forces armed with nuclear weapons, U.S. interests in Japan would be seriously damaged. Not only could the United States no longer count on close cooperation with Japan, but it would have to face the danger that nationalistic Japanese policies might again threaten international stability in East Asia, and even that Japan might eventually align itself with either the USSR or China against the United States. How great is the chance that communist gains in Southeast Asia might cause the Japanese to turn in disillusionment from their dependence on the U.S. nuclear umbrella and enter the nuclear arms race?

Japan's intrinsic interests in Southeast Asia are more important than those of the United States, but less important than generally assumed. Only around 10 percent of Japan's trade is with Southeast Asia.[10] And that trade is growing less rapidly than trade with the industrialized nations—the United States, Canada, Western Europe, and Australia. As a source for raw materials, Southeast Asia has been declining in relative importance, for the Japanese are seeking to ensure their future needs by entering into long-term contracts in more stable areas. For example, total Japanese imports from Southeast Asia increased from $1 billion in 1966 to $1.7 billion in 1972, or about 70 percent. Imports from Australia, however, more than tripled in the same period— jumping from $687 million in 1966 to $2.2 billion—and they are expected to continue to increase rapidly.[11]

Although 90 percent of Japan's vital oil supply comes through the Malacca Strait, that route is not vital. The largest tankers are already too big to pass through its shallow, confined channel. A detour to straits farther east or even around Australia would add to transport costs, but would hardly cripple Japan's economy. After all, the closing of the Suez Canal did not cut off Japanese trade with Western Europe.

10. Based on trade statistics for 1971 in International Monetary Fund/International Bank for Reconstruction and Development (IMF/IBRD), *Direction of Trade, March 1972*. It covers trade with the geographical area generally referred to as Southeast Asia. Figures from Japanese sources are often higher because they include trade with South Korea, Taiwan, Hong Kong, and India (see, for example, *Information Bulletin* (Japanese Ministry of Foreign Affairs), June 19, 1970, which attributes 27.8 percent of Japan's exports and 15.8 percent of its imports in 1970 to this enlarged "Southeast Asia"). Since 1960 Japanese trade with Southeast Asia has been declining as a percentage of total Japanese trade.

11. IMF/IBRD, *Direction of Trade Annual, 1966–70*, pp. 145–46, and *1968–72*, pp. 137–38. Should large supplies of oil be found off Indonesia and Malaysia, Japanese imports from Southeast Asia would increase considerably. Southeast Asia's position in Japan's total trade would be unlikely to change substantially however.

Thus, although bypassing the Malacca Strait could impose an economic burden, it would hardly compare with the costs and risks of building a military force to control that strait. The naval forces provided for in the Japanese defense buildup plan for the period 1972–76 are designed only to provide protection in the seas near Japan.[12] Instead of putting money into a navy to protect the oil flow from the Persian Gulf, as they might have done before World War II, or seeking assurances from the United States that its navy would provide the necessary protection, the Japanese are trying to diversify their energy sources, both by a worldwide search for new oil fields and by seeking new sources of enriched uranium to supply their burgeoning atomic power industry.[13]

Obviously, Japan's economic and strategic stake in Southeast Asia has changed radically since World War II. Tokyo no longer considers Southeast Asia so vital that Japan should be prepared to use—or to urge the United States to use—military force there to protect its interests. The attempt to incorporate Southeast Asia into the Greater East Asia Coprosperity Sphere by military means brought disaster and disillusion to the Japanese. Japan's astounding economic comeback since World War II has convinced most Japanese that their future prosperity will rest not on military power, but on a peaceful and stable world that will assure the widest possible access to markets and raw materials. In this kind of world, with a great diversity of suppliers and markets, no single region like Southeast Asia is vital.

Japanese tend, moreover, to be less concerned than Americans about the ideological complexion of Asian governments. Gratified that Japan is the principal noncommunist trading partner for both Communist China and the Soviet Union, they do not believe that communist seizures of power in Southeast Asian countries would necessarily put a stop to trade. Moreover, they discount the danger that Peking might gain hegemony over all the states of Southeast Asia, since they see in the Sino-Soviet split evidence that national differences tend to prevail over ideology.

Damage to U.S. interests in Japan from communist gains in Southeast Asia cannot be measured, however, wholly by Japanese estimates of the damage that such gains would do to their own interests in

12. Japanese Defense Agency, *Defense of Japan* (Tokyo, 1973).
13. See article by Selig Harrison in *Washington Post*, Feb. 7, 1971.

Southeast Asia. The key question is how such communist gains might change the Japanese government's perception of the United States as a reliable ally.

The spectrum of views among Japanese about their U.S. alliance ranges from left-wing opposition to the security treaty to right-wing support for a continuing U.S. military presence in Southeast Asia. Between these extremes a broad consensus determines the limits within which any Japanese government can formulate foreign policy.

When the United States decided in 1965 on large-scale military intervention in Vietnam, the reaction of most Japanese was not relief that the United States was moving to check the spread of communism, but fear that the United States might drag Japan into war with China. Most Japanese did not see North Vietnamese gains in South Vietnam as increasing the Chinese threat to Japan.

After the United States began to withdraw its combat troops from South Vietnam, several reactions could be discerned among this broad middle group. There was general satisfaction that the war seemed to be winding down, coupled with expressions of anxiety whenever military operations were stepped up, as in the Cambodian and Laotian incursions. Sophisticated Japanese observers expressed some worry that if the withdrawal of U.S. forces were too long drawn out and costly, isolationism might increase in the United States and make the United States less likely to intervene militarily in places such as Korea, which are more important to Japan than Southeast Asia. Within the government there was sympathy for the United States as it faced the problems of conducting an orderly withdrawal. Although Japanese officials preferred a noncommunist to a communist South Vietnam, they tended to see a skillful disengagement of U.S. forces that would maintain broad domestic support in the United States for the main lines of U.S. policy in East Asia as more important than the ultimate outcome in Indochina.[14]

Both government and people welcomed the peace settlement

14. The *Washington Post*, May 14, 1970, quoted a "ranking figure in the Japanese government": "Most of us feel you should be working to salvage what you can of a bad bargain. The truth is that you have committed yourselves to un-worthy people. . . . In North China we felt our honor was at stake, just as you do, and we too failed to understand the limitations of our military power. We know you will respect your commitments, but what we are concerned about in Vietnam is not good faith, but good judgment."

reached in January 1973. The cease-fire and total withdrawal of U.S. forces from Vietnam strengthened the position of the Japanese government, for the opposition could no longer attack it for permitting the United States to use bases and facilities in Japan to prosecute an unpopular war in Indochina. Past attitudes indicate that neither the Japanese government nor the bulk of the people would favor reintroduction of U.S. forces into the countries of Indochina if the cease-fire should break down. Failure by the United States to intervene militarily would not damage Japanese confidence in the U.S. commitment to Japan, even if North Vietnam ultimately became the dominant power throughout the Indochina states.

Future Japanese confidence in the United States will probably depend less on whether communist seizures of power occur in Southeast Asia than on the way in which they come out. Certainly, the military conquest of any part of Southeast Asia by the Soviet Union or China would shock the Japanese, and U.S. inactivity in the face of such a threat would gravely damage Japanese confidence in the United States. The Japanese would see such a grab for power as only a prelude to further aggression which the United States might also not resist. They would set out to increase their military strength rapidly and to adjust their international relationships in whatever ways seemed most likely to protect their national interest in these transformed and threatening circumstances. A nuclear-armed Japan would be a real possibility.

There is little evidence, however, that either China or Russia is likely to invade Southeast Asia with its own forces. The chief threat to Southeast Asian governments in the 1970s will probably be internal rebellion backed by outside communist states, especially by North Vietnam and China. But this is unlikely to result in a sweeping and rapid victory of communist parties in one country after another, much less in Chinese hegemony over the entire region.

The conjuncture of special circumstances that have made revolution backed by the Soviet Union and China so formidable in the Indochina states does not exist elsewhere in Southeast Asia. Most governments in the region, especially if they receive outside help, have the capacity to control or defeat communist rebellions. Moreover, any communist party that did seize power probably would have freed itself of Chinese direction in the course of gaining vital local nationalist support. Like the communist parties in North Korea and North Vietnam, they would be likely to adopt independent positions, seeking support from China and the USSR, but not accepting control by either. Some increase in Chinese influence on Southeast Asia in this decade is probably inevitable, but Chinese hegemony is improbable.[15]

As Japan's economic stake in Southeast Asia grows—even though it be a diminishing proportion of its total economic interests abroad—Japan will almost inevitably become deeply involved in the political affairs of the region. In turn, competition between Japan and China for influence in the region is likely to increase. If considerable turbulence and disorder should prevail in Southeast Asia and Sino-Japanese rivalry became intense, the Japanese could become critical of the United States for having failed to hold a containment line in Southeast Asia and declining to intervene to check the spread of Chinese influence. But even if events should take this turn, it is doubtful that U.S. inaction would damage U.S. relations with Japan so severely as to cause the Japanese to undertake an independent course based on greatly strengthened military forces.

Southeast Asia is clearly a region of secondary importance to the United States. The U.S. link with Japan, whose greatly expanded economy and military potential rank it in importance close to Western Europe as a U.S. ally, is the crucial U.S. security interest in East Asia. Other U.S. security interests throughout the region derive their importance chiefly from their relation to this primary interest. Thus, U.S. security interests in Northeast Asia—especially in Korea—are important because of the impact on Japan of what may happen there. The situation in Southeast Asia is quite different; although adverse developments there might to some extent threaten the U.S. relationship with Japan, none could justify U.S. military intervention except the remote contingency of a Chinese attempt to impose its hegemony over the region by the use of its own military forces.

15. See Chapters 10 and 11.

CHAPTER THREE

The Four-Power System

The importance of Japan's remaining a lightly armed, nonnuclear power and cooperating closely with the United States emerges clearly from an analysis of the interaction in East Asia of four major powers, the United States, Japan, China, and the Soviet Union. This four-power system, a subsystem of the world balance of power, reflects the increasing political multipolarity that is developing alongside the bipolar military system in which the United States and the USSR remain preeminent.[1]

Characteristics of the System

Balance of power is a slippery term in international relations.[2] In its most common historical usage, it describes a state system prevailing at certain periods in Europe in which each state recognized that it was in its own long-term interest to preserve the system. The understanding that states would tend to combine against any member becoming too powerful and threatening to dominate the others deterred or prevented members for long periods of time from destroying the system. Britain, at times, consciously served as "balancer," shifting its policies and alliances to maintain or restore equilibrium on the continent.

1. As described by Henry Kissinger, in Kermit Gordon, ed., *Agenda for the Nation* (Brookings Institution, 1968), p. 588.
2. Cogent discussions of the varying usages and the obfuscation that careless use produces can be found in Herbert Butterfield and Martin Wight, *Diplomatic Investigations* (Harvard University Press, 1966), and Claude L. Inis, *Power and International Relations* (Random House, 1962).

44

The relationship among the four major powers interacting in East Asia today does not fit the classical mold. It is not a closed system. Two of the actors in the subsystem are the two superpowers, whose primary interests lie outside the region, and even China and Japan have important interests and influence outside it. One of the four powers, Japan, has chosen—for the present, at least—not to compete with the other three major powers in building military force. This Japanese policy reflects the fact that military power can no longer be used in the same way as in the days of the classical balance of power to threaten, force, or prevent adjustments in the power balance. Even though the constraints on the use of national military force in the nuclear age are not fully understood, there is no doubt that powerful new inhibitions exist.[3]

The rivalry among the four has an ideological dimension not present in most earlier balance-of-power systems. Ideology not only obstructs close and friendly relations between the communist and the noncommunist states; it also tends to exacerbate differences between the two communist states. Though ideological fervor is declining, important ideological differences will persist for a long time.

It is by no means clear that the actors in the subsystem perceive themselves as conducting their relations with other members of the system so as to preserve a generally accepted equilibrium. Only the United States has publicly espoused the balance-of-power concept (in its global policy) as an effective means of maintaining the peace.[4] China has never belonged to a balance-of-power system and it is doubtful that Chinese leaders today view the four-power system in that light.[5] It is true that since 1971 China has sought improved rela-

3. Thoughtful discussions may be found in Klaus Knorr, *On the Uses of Military Power in the Nuclear Age* (Princeton University Press, 1966); Stanley Hoffmann, *Gulliver's Troubles* (McGraw-Hill, 1968), chap. 2; Michael Howard, "Military Power and International Order," *International Affairs*, vol. 40 (July 1964), pp. 397–408; and Louis J. Halle, "Does War Have a Future?" *Foreign Affairs*, vol. 52 (October 1973), pp. 20–34.

4. See President Nixon's interview in *Time*, Jan. 3, 1972, in which he stated, "We must remember the only time in the history of the world that we have had any extended periods of peace is when there has been a balance of power.... I think it will be a safer world and a better world if we have a strong, healthy United States, Europe, Soviet Union, China, Japan, each balancing the other, not playing one against the other, an even balance."

5. See Coral Bell, *The Asian Balance of Power*, Adelphi Paper 44 (London: Institute for Strategic Studies, 1968).

tions with the United States and Japan to strengthen its position relative to the USSR, and in this respect might be said to be practicing
balance-of-power politics. Yet this behavior seems to spring from relatively short-term tactical considerations, rather than from a conviction
on the part of Chinese leaders that a four-power equilibrium in East
Asia is a desirable long-term condition. The official position of both
China and the USSR is that the United States should withdraw its
military power from East Asia and dissolve its security treaties with
nations in the region. Because of their rivalry with each other, neither
presses at the present time for a rapid and total withdrawal of U.S.
power, yet neither appears to hold the view that a substantial long-
term U.S. presence in the region is essential to a power balance that
would ensure lasting peace. The Japanese also shy away from the
balance-of-power concept, because they fear it implies a heavily
armed Japan, which they now strongly oppose.

The four-power system in East Asia does have several of the characteristics of a power balance. Most important is the interest of each
of the four powers in preventing any of the others from gaining
hegemony over the region. None has shown any intent to do so by
military force, but should one attempt it, the others would act to
prevent it, either singly or in combination. In the Shanghai communiqué of February 27, 1972, the United States and China expressly
disavowed any intent to gain hegemony over the Asia-Pacific region
and declared their opposition to efforts by any other state to do so.
Japan and China made a similar declaration in the Chou-Tanaka
communiqué of September 29, 1972.

Each of the four states seeks to increase its power relative to the
others, either by increasing its own military and nonmilitary instruments of power, or (as the USSR and China once did, and the United
States and Japan still do) by combining its power with another's for
joint use in certain circumstances. The spirit of rivalry that pervades
the four-power system creates tension and imposes on the actors both
pressures to act and constraints on action.

Each of the powers greatly exceeds any of the smaller nations in
the region in its combined population, economic power, and actual or
potential military power. Gains and losses in the lively contest among
the four for influence on these weaker nations cannot, therefore, decisively affect the distribution of power within the system. Only a
change in alignment among the four could have this effect.

Since the Sino-Soviet split, the alignment of military power within the system has taken the form of a triangle, with Japan's military power serving only as an addition to U.S. military power in the defense of Japan. It has not been available for independent use outside Japanese territory. Japan has acted on its own in its political and economic relations with the USSR and China—an example of the "increasing political multipolarity" observed by Kissinger—but only within limits that did not disturb its security alliance with the United States.

The military power at the three points of the triangle is not equal. Both the United States and the Soviet Union possess the power to devastate China with strategic nuclear weapons, but China has little power to retaliate. The confrontation is not so unbalanced, however, in respect to the ability of any of the three to compel another to do its will: The nuclear superiority of the United States and of the Soviet Union can deter Chinese attack but does not assure that one of the superpowers could either defeat China with conventional weapons or achieve a foreign policy objective by threatening China with nuclear weapons. China's size and population, combined with the inhibitions that exist on the use of nuclear weapons against China by either the United States or the Soviet Union, confer on China greater defensive strength than its arms alone.

Stability of the System

The four-power system is relatively stable, in the sense that neither war between the great powers nor a radical shift in alignment among them seems likely in this decade. None of the major powers seems bent on adding to its domain by military conquest. The stance of the United States and Japan is defensive, with the United States engaged in drawing down its military force in the area. The Soviet Union, although stepping up its naval activities in the Pacific somewhat, shows little tendency toward military conquest there. China, with the small strategic missile force it will have in the late 1970s, could turn to military aggression, but for many reasons it is unlikely to do so.

The chances that war might flare up between major powers, even though none was deliberately pursuing a grand design for conquest, seem to be declining. Two possible flashpoints of conflict—the demilitarized zone in Korea and the Taiwan Strait—have been stabilized for a dozen years or more. Probing, infiltration, and minor clashes have occurred, but no major effort to change the status quo. The North Koreans alone cannot hope to conquer South Korea so long as Seoul is backed by American forces, and neither the Russians nor the Chinese show any inclination to commit their own forces to unify Korea. Nor is South Korea, acting alone, in a position to use force to unify the peninsula. The Chinese do not presently appear to contemplate force to secure Taiwan; even if they did, they would hardly directly challenge the Seventh Fleet in the Taiwan Strait while the Soviets threatened their rear.

Prospects on the Sino-Soviet frontier are difficult to judge. Wars are rarely based on coldly rational calculations and it is hard to assess the depth of emotion on both sides; moreover, miscalculations and cumulative bureaucratic bungling could let border clashes get out of hand. Still, a big war seems unlikely. The Chinese clearly recognize the Soviet military advantage and would not seek war. The Soviet Union might be tempted to set back Chinese military progress—especially Peking's nuclear program—by a sudden strike, but it could not invade, occupy, and attempt to control China, as the Russians have done in Czechoslovakia, except at enormous cost and with uncertain results. Soviet leaders probably recognize, also, that even a limited preemptive strike could create in China a desire for revenge that might endure for decades. It seems hardly likely that they would take action that would destroy their hope for reconciliation with Mao's successors and risk driving China irretrievably into the arms of the United States and Japan—quite aside from the likely damage it would do to U.S.-Soviet relations.

The only other area where forces of the big powers might clash is Southeast Asia. But the Sino-Soviet conflict makes it even less likely than in the past that Chinese forces will be used there; and the reaction in the United States against the Vietnam War reduces the chances that American troops will again fight in Southeast Asia. For the Soviet Union the region is remote and of low priority among its interests. Consequently, although turmoil and disorder are probable in some parts of Southeast Asia in this decade, the forces of major powers are unlikely to be drawn into war there.

In fact, even during the 1960s, when it appeared at times that the Vietnam War might lead to a big-power clash, all four great powers behaved in ways that limited that risk. Prudence is likely to prevail in the 1970s also. Even though each of the four powers may be unhappy over some aspects of the distribution of power in East Asia, each seems prepared to live with it, rather than seek to change it by military force in the next few years. Each will maneuver to improve its position by its policies toward other members of the Big Four and by competition in Southeast Asia, but none seems likely to possess in this decade both the power and the will to upset by force the underlying stability of the four-power system.

Neither is the shape of the system likely to be changed by radical realignments among the big powers. Some rapprochement between Moscow and Peking is, of course, possible. If successors to Mao saw important advantages in warming up to the Soviet Union, both sides might be willing to make significant concessions and relations might improve considerably. But the history of growing conflicts of national interest between the Soviet Union and China and their rivalry for leadership of the communist world suggest that the path to reconciliation would be steep and rocky. Distrust on both sides would make economic and military cooperation especially difficult. China would not want to shift the bulk of its trade back to the Soviet bloc, placing its industrialization again at the mercy of Soviet caprice, nor would the USSR be inclined to give China significant help in improving either its conventional or its nuclear forces.

Nor is a de facto alliance between China and the United States likely to come about within this decade. The warming trend symbolized by President Nixon's visit to Peking may well continue. But the Taiwan issue, the ingrained hostility and suspicion between Peking and Washington, and the radically different views of the world held by American and Chinese leaders all militate against the degree of rapprochement that would radically alter alignments within the four-power system.

Japan will no doubt try to improve its relations with the USSR and China but is highly unlikely within this decade to shift its primary economic and security relationships from the United States to either of them. Japan's economy is firmly tied into the Western trade and financial system and its continued economic growth depends on these links. Neither Russia nor China, without radical and unlikely changes in its economic policies, could provide the markets, technology, or raw materials that Japan needs and has grown accustomed to getting from the noncommunist world. The Japanese will be careful not to become too dependent on the communist powers for supplies and markets, for they know that such trade could be cut off abruptly for political reasons. Moreover, the great majority of Japanese find congenial Japan's open society and democratic politics and feel greater affinity for the similar societies of Western Europe and North America than for those of China and the Soviet Union. And Japan's phenomenal economic progress has been made possible in good part by the sense of security that the mantle of U.S. protective power has fostered.

Whether Japan remains closely associated with the United States will depend, of course, at least as much on U.S. policy as on Japanese wishes. Some Americans have argued that the United States could better safeguard its security and diminish the risk of involvement in major conflict by withdrawing from its defense commitments to Japan and South Korea, taking its military forces out of Northeast Asia, and compelling Japan to assume full responsibility for its own defense.[6] The four-power system would thus become a three-power system composed of the major powers located in the region, with the United States playing only a peripheral role.

The rationale for complete withdrawal is plausible. Unlike Japan, the United States has a choice whether to incur the costs and risks of helping to maintain order in this part of the world. The United States could stand aloof from disorder there, at some economic cost perhaps, but less than the cost of military intervention. Japan has the population and technology to create a formidable military force. With their own nuclear missiles and modern conventional sea and air power, the Japanese would be in a strong position to defend their own interests in East Asia. The United States need not involve itself in conflicts of interest among the three big powers of East Asia, at least not to the extent of being prepared to intervene militarily.

These views, however, do not take account of the long-term consequences to the United States of taking action that would almost certainly cause Japan to become a major military power, no longer closely linked to the United States. By failing to take advantage of the Japanese people's present desire to avoid large-scale rearmament, the

6. See, for example, a proposal to go far in this direction in Earl Ravenal, "The Nixon Doctrine and Our Asia Commitments," *Foreign Affairs*, vol. 49 (January 1971), pp. 201–17. Also see Robert W. Tucker, *A New Isolationism: Threat or Promise?* (Universe Books, 1972), pp. 72–76.

United States would forfeit an exceptional opportunity to help build an international order in East Asia in which the role of military force in relations among the big powers would decline. Moreover, a withdrawal, in effect, of the United States from the four-power system would shock the Japanese, especially the leading politicians and businessmen who have traditionally relied on strong ties with the United States, causing them to feel betrayed. The risk would be high that, feeling isolated and rejected by the United States, they would turn to large-scale rearmament in a nationalistic, anti-American mood. The way would be opened for the possible alignment of a nuclear-armed Japan with China or the USSR in the 1980s.

A less radical course for the United States would be to withdraw only partially from defense responsibilities in Northeast Asia, retaining its commitment to Japan, but insisting that Japan share the burden of regional defense, especially in an area so close and important to it as South Korea. This course of action would not, like a full withdrawal, remove the risk for the United States of military involvement in East Asia. Its principal advantages would be to reduce military costs and possibly to create a relationship between the two countries that would seem more balanced and reasonable to Americans and Japanese. But pressure on Japan to become the military partner of the United States in East Asia, while it would appeal to Americans who resent Japan's so-called free ride under U.S. military protection, would ultimately threaten the stability of the four-power system.

If Japan again became militarily powerful, its domestic politics and its attitude toward other countries could not fail to be profoundly altered. Once the psychological barrier of regarding military forces for defense of the home islands only had been broken, military thinking in Japan would be given a strong impetus. The military and military-related industry would gain influence in national affairs; the martial spirit would be stimulated; and the government probably would be inclined to give greater weight to the option of using military force when faced with a serious clash of interest with another nation. The heightened influence of military views and concepts also could lead to restrictions on Japanese democarcy, as many Japanese fear it would. Moreover, the surge of nationalism needed to overcome the pacific inclinations inculcated in the Japanese for over twenty-five years would be likely to take on a strong anti-American coloration, for the two emotions, while not identical, are closely linked.

All this would revive memories of World War II among the nations of the region. Fear of Japanese domination, already evident in the developing nations where Japan's economic influence is growing rapidly, would be intensified were Japan to design its military forces for overseas use. The Chinese would react strongly. Rivalry between Japan and China would intensify and the prospect of expanding political and economic relations between them and thus reducing the potential importance of military force in their relations would be seriously diminished.

Perhaps the greatest disadvantage of a decision by Japan to undertake large-scale rearmament is the probability that it would lead to Japan's acquiring nuclear weapons. Once the Japanese had decided to assume a major military role in East Asia it is unlikely that they would continue to deny themselves the weapons possessed by all other nations aspiring to big-power status in the nuclear age. If Japan's defense commitments created the possibility that its forces might have to confront those of nuclear-armed China in Korea, for example, the pressure for Japanese nuclear weapons would probably become irresistible.

Of course, Japan might develop nuclear weapons even without undertaking overseas defense commitments. Some Japanese have advocated nuclear weapons as a deterrent essential to the protection of the home islands. There is little support for this view in Japan today, but it could grow if the Japanese were impelled toward military self-reliance by U.S. attempts to change the present four-power system, either by withdrawing or by pressing a regional military role on Japan.

A nuclear-armed Japan would not only increase the likelihood of further proliferation of nuclear weapons and thus augment the risk of nuclear war by accident or by miscalculation,[7] but would also radically change the character of the four-power system. Japan could become a formidable contender in the nuclear field within the next ten to fifteen years; this would alarm the Soviets and Chinese and thus create new tensions among the Big Four. As the Russians and Chinese added weapons in order to improve their capability to deter this new nuclear threat, the United States might in its turn counter with more

7. See Raymond Aron, *Peace and War* (Doubleday, 1966), pp. 637–43, for a convincing and sophisticated exposition of the case against nuclear proliferation.

weapons to redress the strategic imbalance. Thus, all four powers would probably have to devote a larger proportion of their resources to armaments. Moreover, the appearance of a fourth nuclear power in East Asia would increase the difficulty of reaching agreements on arms control: It is difficult enough for the two superpowers to agree to limit nuclear armaments. A means of bringing China into arms control agreements remains to be devised and the addition of still another nuclear power would further complicate the task.

Thus, the outlook for a stable, low-tension four-power system will be brighter if Japan remains lightly armed and nonnuclear, than if it goes in for massive rearmament. And Japan is more likely to remain so if the United States continues to be substantially involved in the four-power system than if it withdraws from the system or takes other steps that would cause the Japanese to feel exposed and isolated.

The United States derives important advantages from its participation in the four-power system. That system works to prevent any single hostile power or combination of powers from dominating all of East Asia and organizing the region to threaten others. It provides a relatively stable framework for maintaining peace in East Asia during the early years of the nuclear age, when war between big powers has become an irrational way of protecting national interests but no reliable form of international organization has been devised to replace it when states see their national interests gravely threatened. There is reason for hope that the four big powers will increasingly recognize that they all profit from the rough balance of power that obtains among them and that it is desirable to enhance the stability of that balance and dangerous to take actions that upset it. In East Asia, as in the rest of the world,

we may now have opening before us a prospect we have not seen for a very long time. There are concrete reasons to believe that the tensions between great powers may, in the next few years, be reduced to a level unknown since before the First World War. A pattern of accommodation is beginning to emerge, by which the great powers exercise restraint in asserting and pursuing their own interests and treat with respect each other's legitimate interests, even when they are in conflict. Such restraint opens the prospect of broad cooperation in areas where interests are complementary.

But it is an uncertain prospect—fragile and tentative. It would be folly to read into this possibility the attributes of certainty—or even of probability. For this is a delicate process upon which we have embarked, vulnerable to a host of difficulties, any of which could prove fatal to the emerging structure of cooperation. Indeed, it is only the recognition of the vast benefits which all would share from cooperation that gives me genuine hope that the difficulties may be overcome.[8]

Crucial to the prospect of cooperation among the four big powers is the maintenance of a close relationship between the United States and Japan and avoidance of trends in Japan unfavorable to these actions. The farther the United States and Japan drift apart, the more difficult it is likely to become to create a stable structure of increasing big-power cooperation in East Asia. Thus the primary concern of U.S. policy in the region should be to maintain a good working relationship with Japan.

8. U. Alexis Johnson, undersecretary of state for political affairs, before the Subcommittee on National Security Policy and Scientific Development of the House Committee on Foreign Affairs. Press release 196, U.S. Department of State, Aug. 8, 1972.

CHAPTER FOUR

Samurai with Briefcases

Can Japan succeed in its "grand experiment"[1] of pursuing its objectives by economic, political, and diplomatic means, abjuring great military strength? Japan's condition today affords substantial grounds for optimism. Opposition among the Japanese people to greatly strengthened military forces, and especially to nuclear weapons, is strong. International tension in the region is declining, prospects for the expansion of Japan's trade and other relations with China and the Soviet Union are favorable, and the government of Premier Tanaka has reaffirmed the fundamental importance to Japan of its ties with the United States. The danger of a nuclear-armed Japan, alienated from the United States, seems remote.

But recent trends and future possibilities are cause for concern. Growing Japanese economic power and expanding influence in East Asia are producing a rising demand for an international role less dependent on the United States, worthy of Japan's accomplishments. The U.S.-Japanese security relationship is coming under increasing strain and many Japanese are uncertain whether the United States intends in the long run to maintain its military commitments in Northeast Asia, the region of greatest concern to Japan. In Sino-Japanese relations, rivalry seems likely to predominate over cooperation, and territorial arguments with both China and the Soviet Union could build up into serious problems, stirring up the nationalistic feelings of the Japanese people. Thus, the nagging question remains: In the long run is it possible for a nation as powerful economically as Japan to remain lightly armed, dependent on its ally for defense against

1. Kei Wakaizumi, "Japan's Role in a New World Order," *Foreign Affairs*, vol. 51 (January 1973), p. 316.

powerful neighbors? Can Japan's interests in the nuclear age be protected by its modern samurai, armed only with the briefcases of the
businessman and diplomat?

Japanese Views on Military Force

Defeat in war and the actual experience of a nuclear bombing have
created exceptionally strong antimilitary sentiments in Japan. In
Article Nine of their constitution the Japanese people "forever renounce war as a sovereign right of the nation and the threat or use of
force as a means of settling international disputes" and assert that
"land, sea, and air forces, as well as other war potential, will not be
maintained." Although the Japanese people have accepted the view
that forces for self-defense are permitted by the constitution, opposition to any use of Japanese forces outside the home islands remains
strong. There is no conscription in Japan and the government has difficulty in keeping even the modest military establishment of 260,000
men up to authorized strength. Antinuclear sentiment has led the
government to formulate "three principles" of nuclear policy: Japan
will not manufacture, possess, or permit the entry of nuclear weapons.

Japan's military budget has been climbing along with the Japanese
economy, but since 1964 it has amounted to less than 1 percent of the
gross national product (as compared with 1970 figures of 11 percent
for the USSR, 8 percent for the United States, and 3–5 percent for the
other big powers).[2] The primary mission of Japan's military forces is
to defend the home islands (including Okinawa) against small-scale
outside threats. The forces are designed also to protect ships in nearby
waters, but not merchant shipping any great distance from Japan. For
that purpose, and for defense against nuclear attack or a large-scale
conventional attack, Japan continues to rely on the security treaty
with the United States. Current defense planning emphasizes naval
and air rather than ground forces, and improved weapons rather
than increases in manpower.

The rapid growth of Japan's economy, averaging 11 percent in real

---

2. International Institute for Strategic Studies, *The Military Balance, 1972–73*
(London: International Institute, 1972), pp. 70–71. Among 59 countries listed,
Japan—devoting only 0.9 percent of GNP to defense in 1971—tied with Mexico for
lowest place.

terms from 1959 to 1970, has permitted the defense budget to grow without straining Japan's resources. Thus, the defense buildup plan for the years 1972–76 provides for expenditures nearly twice those of the previous five-year program, but they still are not expected to exceed 1 percent of Japan's GNP. By 1976 Japan can be expected to have a small but very modern conventional force for defense of the home islands and adjacent waters. Although this force could not defend Japan against a large-scale Soviet conventional attack, it would provide Japan with a defense against small military probes by either the Soviet Union or China. Japan's military budget in absolute terms will probably not be far below the German, British, or French level and Japan will then have the seventh largest military budget in the world.

The range of military options available to the government will thus be broadened.[3] It will even include the production of nuclear weapons. By the mid-1970s Japan will be capable of producing enough plutonium for 200 atomic bombs a year, and this capability will continue to grow rapidly.[4] The Japanese are investigating sources of uranium and studying methods of processing it, so that they can eventually free themselves from dependence on the United States for enriched uranium. Their skill in rocketry is also increasing; Japan has already orbited several satellites. Thus, if they can assure themselves of access to uranium and should decide to make the heavy investment required, the Japanese could in time build a larger nuclear arsenal than China's.

The steady, if unspectacular, strengthening of Japan's armed forces reflects a decline in Japan's military inhibitions. The traumatic impact of defeat in war has faded, a postwar generation has grown up, and economic success has increased Japanese self-confidence. As these changes have occurred, opposition to a small defense force has declined.[5] Frank discussions in the public media of problems of Japan's security are no longer taboo. As early as 1965 former Premier Nobu-

3. Tetsuyo Senga, defense production chief of the Keidanren (the Federation of Economic Organizations), estimated that Japan would be making 80 percent of its own defense equipment by 1976. *Washington Post*, Nov. 7, 1969.

4. George Quester, "The Non-Proliferation Treaty and the IAEA," *International Organization*, vol. 24 (Spring 1970), p. 164.

5. Around 80 percent of Japanese approved the existence of a self-defense force by 1972; however, only 15 percent believed that this force should have an offensive military capability. See Paul Langer, *Japanese National Security Policy— Domestic Determinants* (Rand Corp., 1972), p. 8.

suke Kishi publicly advocated that Japan revise Article Nine of the constitution "as a means of eradicating completely the consequences of Japan's defeat and of the American Occupation. It is necessary to enable Japan finally to move out of the post-war era and for the Japanese people to regain their self-confidence and pride as Japanese."[6]

Although opposition to nuclear weapons remains strong,[7] the "nuclear allergy" had declined enough by October 1970 to permit a national defense white paper to state delicately that although Japan continued to adhere to the "three nonnuclear principles," it could theoretically possess small nuclear weapons for self-defense without violating the constitution.[8] And the statement did not evoke the violent protest that it would have several years earlier. Moreover, Japan's long delay in ratifying the nonproliferation treaty signed in February 1970 suggests that the government wishes to keep its options open as long as possible.

6. Nobusuke Kishi, "Political Movements in Japan," *Foreign Affairs*, vol. 44 (October 1965), p. 93.

7. In response to the question, "Do you think it is necessary, or not necessary for Japan to have its own nuclear weapons for the defense of the security of its own country?" 20 percent of those polled answered "necessary," 66 percent "not necessary," 13 percent "cannot say, one way or the other," and 1 percent "don't know." When asked, "Do you think that Japan will come to have its own nuclear weapons in the near future?" 28 percent thought it would, 42 percent thought not, 29 percent could not say, one way or the other, and 1 percent didn't know. *Sankei*, Aug. 7, 1973. When "learned persons" in the academic, economic, government, and other fields and college students majoring in international politics were asked, "Do you think Japan should possess nuclear weapons in the future?" 1.2 percent of the "learned persons" thought that it should, 78 percent that it should not, and 19.6 percent that the matter should be left to future option; among the students, the corresponding answers were given by 1.9 percent, 82.5 percent, and 15 percent, respectively. When asked, "Apart from your own view, do you think Japan will come to have nuclear weapons in the future?" 20.8 percent of the "learned persons" and 42.9 percent of the students thought it would, while 75.6 percent and 56 percent, respectively, thought not. When asked, "What do you think of Japan's possessing self-defense power?" 42.9 percent of the "learned persons," and 27.6 percent of the students, felt "an independent nation should have military power for self-defense, as an inherent right"; 32.7 percent and 29.8 percent, respectively, felt "possessing the self-defense force is inevitable, since neighboring countries all maintain military power"; and 22 percent and 40.7 percent, respectively, felt "the presence of military power is a threat to peace, and therefore Japan should maintain no military power." *Yomiuri*, June 27, 1973. Langer, analyzing Japanese opposition to large-scale rearmament, concludes that the domestic environment "remains exceedingly unfavorable to any massive rearmament effort." *Japanese National Security Policy*, p. 76.

8. "Defense White Paper Published," *Information Bulletin* (Japanese Ministry of Foreign Affairs), October 1970, p. 8.

Although some of the opposition to the treaty arose from the fear that it might hamper Japan in the peaceful use of nuclear energy, there is a strong undercurrent of resistance to formally committing Japan to "second-class" status.

There is still, however, a strong and pervasive antiwar sentiment among the Japanese. Most of them display resigned acceptance rather than willing support of their armed forces. Despite a widespread desire to free Japan from American influence, relatively few Japanese favor revising Article Nine of the constitution[9] and any attempt to do so would provoke a bruising political battle. Many of them fear that a strong armed service would again become dominant in domestic politics and lead Japan into catastrophe abroad. And many are concerned that Japan's chances for better relations with China would be destroyed and that its trade with Asian states that fear Japanese imperialism would be injured. Opponents of large increases in military budgets argue the urgent need for funds for social purposes. The press is quick to publicize and denounce even the smallest sign of departure from established limitations on Japan's military policy. For example, in October 1971 the press attacked as most untimely and provocative toward other Asian nations a suggestion by Director General Naomi Nishimura of the Defense Agency that Japanese troops might be sent abroad to help out in the event of natural disasters.[10]

Thus, although the inhibitions against public debate of defense matters are breaking down, many constraints against action remain. Only a substantial decline of confidence in the U.S. defense commitment, coupled with widespread fear for Japan itself, would make it possible for Japanese leaders to mobilize enough support to undertake overseas military commitments and to create the kind of force that would be needed to meet such commitments.

The Japanese remain strongly opposed to acquiring nuclear weapons, despite the decline in the "nuclear allergy." When Yasuhiro Nakasone was director general of the Defense Agency in 1970–71, he repeatedly declared that for Japan nuclear weapons are not necessary because the nuclear stalemate between the United States, the USSR, and China prevents the use of nuclear weapons; nor are they desirable, because so much of Japan's population could be wiped out in a first strike that a

---

9. See, for example, the public opinion poll in *Yomiuri*, May 31, 1970, showing that only 16 percent of those polled favored revising Article Nine.

10. *Yomiuri, Asahi,* and *Nihon Keizai,* Oct. 13, 1971.

second-strike capability would make little sense; and they are not politically feasible because any attempt by the government to change its nonnuclear defense policy would break down the consensus on which defense policy rests.

Most Japanese defense writers concur with the view that nuclear weapons would not increase Japan's security. They are keenly aware of Japan's geographical disadvantages. For example, 32 percent of the country's population and a large part of its industry are concentrated in three small areas—within a radius of 50 kilometers from Tokyo, Nagoya, and Osaka—and thus highly vulnerable to a small number of nuclear missiles. In contrast, China's thousand largest cities contain only 11 percent of its population. Thus, even to counter China's nuclear arsenal, Japan's would have to be much larger. Japan also confronts technical obstacles of finding suitable locations for testing nuclear weapons or for building uranium-enrichment plants with adequate water and safe from possible earthquake damage. Procuring uranium to produce nuclear weapons is yet another problem. Assuming that a Japanese missile system would be based at sea, its base and communications network would have to be global if it were to be within range of the principal population centers in the USSR. These technical problems could probably be overcome, but only at great cost and over a considerable number of years. Consequently, the best informed Japanese see the disadvantages of Japan's building a nuclear capacity as far outweighing the advantages. In fact, some believe that a nuclear capability might diminish Japan's security, by making the Chinese nervous and thus increasing the risk of a Chinese nuclear attack on Japan in some future crisis. While defense analysts acknowledge that the U.S.-Japan defense treaty might not guarantee Japan against attack in all conceivable circumstances, most of them doubt that an independent Japanese nuclear deterrent would be better protection.[11]

Not only is it hard to show that Japanese nuclear weapons would improve the country's security, but many Japanese believe they would impose the same problems as a large expansion in the armed forces.

11. See articles by Kiichi Saeki, *Japan Times*, July 14, 1969, and Makoto Momoi, *Mainichi*, June 23, 1970. For fuller discussions of the various factors deterring Japan from adopting nuclear arms, see John Emmerson, *Arms, Yen, and Power: The Japanese Dilemma* (Dunellen, 1971), chaps. 13 and 14; and Kunio Muraoka, *Japanese Security and the United States*, Adelphi Paper 95 (London: International Institute for Strategic Studies, 1973).

They believe that any substantial increase in Japanese military force—
nuclear or conventional—would divert funds from urgently needed
programs to improve the quality of life in Japan, would make more difficult the improvement of relations with China, and would rekindle in
Southeast Asia and Australia fear of Japan as a great military power,
thus opening old wounds and perhaps seriously hampering the expansion of Japan's economic relations with these countries. These antimilitary views have been strengthened by the decline in international
tension in East Asia since the visits of President Nixon and Premier
Tanaka to Peking and the opening of talks between North and South
Korea.

Thus, although the government's budgeting for and explanation of
Japan's security needs has become easier, defense policy remains firmly
grounded on the principles of defending the home islands only, with
conventional weapons only. Hints that Japan might some day have
to depart from these principles—definition in the 1969 Nixon-Sato
communiqué of the security of the Republic of Korea as essential to the
security of Japan; assertion in the national defense white paper of 1970
that small nuclear weapons for defense would not be contrary to the
constitution—have been carefully hedged about with assurances that
the Japanese government has no intention of departing from the principles. Any attempt to do so would arouse a storm of protest.

In short, the Japanese oppose large military forces more strongly
than do the people of any other big power. Few nations devote so small
a proportion of their resources to defense. Most Japanese see no significant military threat to Japan and fear that a large military buildup,
far from increasing Japan's security, would be more likely to decrease
it by provoking fear of Japan in neighboring states. The remarkable
success Japan has had since World War II in promoting its interests
without possessing large armed forces has created a presumption that
its interests will be best served by sticking to this policy.

Nevertheless, changes in international circumstances that caused
the Japanese to feel increasingly isolated and under pressure from
foreign countries could erode popular opposition to greatly strengthened military forces. In their resentment and anxiety the Japanese
would be likely to turn again to an emotional nationalism, and rational
arguments against nuclear weapons for Japan would have less effect.
Should the Japanese come to perceive a greater threat from China or
the USSR, and encounter growing problems with the United States,

they might be persuaded of their need to have nuclear weapons, both as a symbol of national prestige and because the United States could not be relied on to risk nuclear war to defend Japan's vital interests.

Although Japan's relations with the big powers will in the end determine whether the Japanese come to feel a need for massive rearmament, the Japanese view of their nation's place in the world and its relations with the other big powers will be significantly shaped by the rapid expansion of Japanese economic influence in the smaller nations of East Asia. Japan has already become the predominant economic power in the region and is moving slowly, but inexorably, toward a more active political role. This will probably lead to intensified Sino-Japanese rivalry for Asian leadership.

Japan's Economic Sphere of Influence

While Japanese trade with Southeast Asia has been declining as a proportion of Japan's total trade, it has steadily become a larger proportion of Southeast Asian countries' total trade. These countries are being linked economically more and more closely to Japan. In 1958 Japan took only 9.2 percent of Southeast Asian exports; by 1972 it was taking 24.4 percent. In 1958 Japan supplied only 10.4 percent of Southeast Asia's imports; by 1972, 26.9 percent.[12] Trade has also increased with South Korea, where Japan took 27 percent of the country's exports and supplied 41 percent of its imports in 1970, Taiwan, where it took 18 percent and supplied 49 percent, and Hong Kong, where it took 4 percent and supplied 24 percent. Japan's share of the trade of East Asian countries is expected to continue to climb, reaching 30 percent of the region's exports and 42 percent of its imports by 1975.[13]

Not only is Japan steadily enlarging its share of the trade of East Asian countries, it has become their largest supplier of capital. According to the Development Assistance Committee (DAC) of the Organisation for Economic Co-operation and Development all developing

12. Derived from International Monetary Fund/International Bank for Reconstruction and Development (IMF/IBRD), *Direction of Trade Annual, 1958–62* and *Direction of Trade, March 1973, July 1973, December 1973,* and *February 1974.*

13. Projections of the Japan Economic Research Center, quoted in Yoshizane Iwasa, "Japan-U.S. Economic Cooperation," *Pacific Community,* vol. 1 (April 1970), p. 386.

countries and multilateral financing agencies received $267 million in official and private funds from Japan in 1963 compared to $4.5 billion from the United States. By 1971 the Japanese figure had reached $2.1 billion, while the flow from the United States had increased only to $7.0 billion.[14] Since 51 percent of the Japanese funds went to East Asia, while the bulk of American funds went elsewhere, the Japanese appear to have replaced the United States as the principal source of foreign credits for states in the region (excluding U.S. wartime contributions to Vietnam, Laos, and Cambodia).

At the meeting of the Southeast Asian Ministerial Conference on Economic Development in May 1970 at Jogjakarta, Foreign Minister Kiichi Aichi pledged that by 1975 the flow of public and private funds from Japan to developing countries would reach the DAC-recommended level of 1 percent of gross national product. It was already close to that level in 1971, at 0.96 percent of GNP,[15] and the pledge has been reiterated by the Tanaka government. Since Japan's GNP will probably exceed $400 billion in current dollars in 1975, this would mean a flow of over $4 billion to developing countries. With the bulk of Japanese funds continuing to go to the East Asian region, they would probably far surpass those of the United States or any other nation in this area.

Not only will Japan steadily increase its share of the trade of East Asian countries in the 1970s, but most of these countries will have a growing adverse balance of trade with Japan.[16] Economic forecasters assume that the flow of Japanese resources into these countries will have to increase substantially to permit the projected increases in Japanese exports. According to one projection, Japan will have to transfer no less than $6 billion annually in financial resources to South and East Asia to finance the trade gap by 1980.[17]

14. Organisation for Economic Co-operation and Development, *Development Cooperation: 1972 Review,* December 1972, p. 214.

15. The bulk of this flow was in private loans and investment. Official aid amounted to only 0.23 percent of GNP, far below the DAC-recommended level of 0.7 percent.

16. The only East Asian nations that have had favorable trade balances with Japan in recent years are Indonesia, Malaysia, and the Philippines.

17. Tadashi Kawata, "The Asian Situation and Japan's Economic Relations with the Developing Asian Countries," *Developing Economies* (Tokyo), vol. 9 (June 1972), p. 148. This estimate is based on an economic forecast of the Japanese Ministry of Trade and Industry. Almost all of the $6 billion would presumably go to East Asia, for South Asia has not had a large unfavorable trade balance with Japan (during 1967–69 the trade balance of this region with Japan was favorable).

There are sound economic reasons for a steady and substantial increase in the flow of Japanese financial resources and exports into neighboring East Asian countries—provided those countries will tolerate the political implications of being so heavily dependent economically on Japan. The demand for raw materials is rising rapidly in Japan, causing the Japanese to invest heavily abroad to increase their production. Land for industrial plants is in short supply and costly. Pollution is heavy, and the government will probably impose increasingly strict pollution controls. The supply of labor is short and its cost high, especially in labor-intensive industry. And Japan has an increasing supply of industrial managers who can be sent abroad. In most years, moreover, Japan will probably have a surplus in its trade balance.[18]

As Japanese investment in East Asia grows, the region will become increasingly integrated with Japan's own economy. Already a number of electronics and textile plants established by Japanese in South Korea, Taiwan, and Hong Kong are exporting to Japan. Some export consumer goods, others export components or semiprocessed materials to be turned into finished goods. In effect, factories in cheap labor areas abroad have begun to take the place of the traditional subcontractors in Japan, who are being priced out of the market.[19]

As the Japanese have begun to invest in manufacturing in East Asian developing nations, they have begun to loosen their previously tight restrictions against imports of light manufactured goods. Imports of textiles from other Asian countries increased from $8 million in 1966 to $68 million in 1969 and $300 million in 1970. Japan has already become a net importer of both raw silk and cotton yarn. It will probably shift other types of traditional labor-intensive production to cheap-labor countries and import these goods in increasing quantities.[20] In August 1971, Japan adopted a system of tariff preferences for manufactured goods from developing countries.

18. See Lawrence B. Krause, "Evolution of Foreign Direct Investment: The United States and Japan," in Jerome Cohen, ed., *Pacific Partnership: United States-Japan Trade* (Heath for Japan Society, Inc., 1972).

19. See Yoshizane Iwasa, "Japan Ventures into Southeast Asia," *Columbia Journal of World Business*, vol. 4 (November–December 1969), pp. 49–54. Iwasa, president of the Fuji Bank, points out that by 1966 Japan's rural areas had been largely drained of new labor recruits; by 1968 the number of high school graduates available to industry had begun to decline; and from 1961 to 1968 average wages in industry more than doubled.

20. Statement of Saburo Okita, president of the Japan Economic Research Center, to the Subcommittee on Foreign Economic Policy of the Joint Economic Committee, U.S. Congress, Sept. 29, 1970 (processed).

Experience in developing efficient small-scale, labor-intensive light industry—which in the past produced 70 percent of Japan's exports of light manufactures—has facilitated the flow of Japanese capital and technology to the developing nations of East Asia. At their present stage of development, these countries are in need of this type of industrial know-how. Through joint ventures and technical aid agreements with local entrepreneurs, the small firms of Japan are constantly creating new links between Japan and its smaller neighbors.[21]

But the growth of Japanese economic influence in East Asia is not welcomed unconditionally. The aggressive thrust of Japanese businessmen and their lack of consideration for local sensitivities have already created some uneasiness. The Japanese, traditionally an insular, self-centered people, have difficulty in establishing easy and cordial relations with other Asian peoples. They do not learn foreign languages readily and tend to be clannish abroad, not adapting easily to foreign customs. Moreover, they carry over into international relations the sense of hierarchy that prevails within their own society and thus show a certain disdain for peoples considered inferior to them.

Asian governments, fearful of excessive Japanese economic influence, have taken steps to prevent Japanese firms from acquiring too large a share of local enterprises.[22] They continually press the Japanese—with little success in most cases—to reduce the large excess of Japanese exports over imports by buying more local goods. A Japanese official complained, "If we help develop the export of raw materials, we are accused of plundering resources; if we help construct labor-intensive industry, we are accused of exploiting cheap labor; if we help build heavy industry, we are accused of exporting pollution."[23]

Despite fears of Japanese economic domination, resentment of Japanese behavior, and unhappy memories of Japanese military occupation, the advantages of closer economic collaboration between Japan and the

21. Terutomo Ozawa, "Japan Exports Technology to Asian LDC's," *Columbia Journal of World Business,* vol. 6 (January–February 1971), pp. 65–71.

22. See, for example, the announcement by Colonel Narong Kittikachorn, assistant director of national security for the National Executive Council of Thailand, that an exclusively Thai company would be set up to handle all ore exports. He warned that "Japanese imperialism" was trying to gain control of the economy and natural resources of Thailand. *Bangkok Post,* July 30, 1972.

23. For a pioneering report on reactions to Japanese postwar economic activities in other Asian countries, see Lawrence Olson, *Japan in Postwar Asia* (Praeger, 1970). See also Hahm Pyong-choon, "The New Japan: The Chrysanthemum and the Transistor?" and Raul Manglapus, "Pacifism and the Challenge of Japan," *Pacific Community,* vol. 1 (April 1970), pp. 429–39 and 421–28.

developing countries are so compelling that few governments will be able to resist moving in that direction. The deeply felt desire for rapid modernization and the lure of profits for individual entrepreneurs in developing countries will exert strong pressures.

Thus, by 1980 Japan in all probability will have enormous economic influence in East Asia as the largest supplier of capital, an increasingly important market for raw materials and manufactured goods produced in the developing states, the largest supplier of capital goods as well as a wide range of sophisticated consumer products, and a provider of services through its banks and trading companies to producers in the developing countries exporting to the rest of the world.

The Japanese relationship to noncommunist East Asia is likely to resemble the U.S. relationship to Latin America, but more closely integrated economically, as the Japanese continue to shift their manufactures to the more complex products, relying increasingly for the simpler products on imports from East Asian developing states.

This process of economic integration will not necessarily be smooth and even. In some countries internal instability will discourage investment, in others nationalistic movements may assume an anti-Japanese character. Japanese enterprises may even be expropriated in some places, as some American investments have been in Latin America. A warning flag was raised in Thailand in late 1972 by student agitation to boycott Japanese goods because of Japan's allegedly unfair treatment of Thailand in trade and investment. The uproar that Tanaka's 1974 visits produced in Bangkok and Jakarta brought home to the Japanese the touchiness of their relations with Southeast Asia.

Japan's Quest for a Political Role

Japan will not be able to continue a wide expansion of its economic interests in East Asia without taking on greater political responsibilities there. The Japanese have been timid about doing so, in sharp contrast to the confidence and precision with which they pursue their economic interests in the region. They are still strongly affected by the trauma of defeat in World War II, and they are aware of the uneasiness about their intentions in China, Korea, and Southeast Asia. Consequently, most Japanese prefer a low posture in foreign affairs, and it is difficult to get a consensus on any policy abroad that might present either responsibilities or risks for Japan. The men who have risen to leadership in postwar Japan have responded to this public mood. Most of them have been bureaucrats, cautious and gradualist by nature, and disinclined to undertake bold or risky moves.

But the Japanese will come under growing pressure to abandon their detachment. As the Chinese saying goes, they have been privileged to "sit on the mountain and watch the tigers fight." As Japan's economic stake abroad grows, and U.S. willingness to assume burdens in East Asia declines, the Japanese government will begin to face those hard choices among distasteful options that are the lot of great powers. In public debate on foreign affairs, which has often had an air of unreality produced by facile oversimplification of complex issues, the Japanese will have to grapple more and more with tough problems directly involving national interests.

Japan already has begun to accept the challenge in the field of economic development. The Japanese see instability in the developing countries of East Asia as arising out of growing nationalism combined with frustration over lack of economic progress. They have great confidence in economic development as a means of improving political stability and reducing the danger of externally supported subversion. Economic action is a safer form of intervention than overt political action or military commitments. It is well suited to a Japan that has renounced the use of military force as an instrument of national policy.

The rapid increase in the flow of Japanese resources into East Asia first took the form of reparations and commercial credits. Gradually, longer term loans and private direct investment grew in volume, along with government loans and grants. Although by 1971 Japan was second only to the United States in its total flow of resources to developing countries, it ranked only fifth among the members of the DAC in the volume of its official development aid, and only thirteenth in its ratio of official development aid to GNP.[24] Moreover, it ranked last in the proportion of its official aid devoted to technical cooperation. The terms of its official loans were also considerably harder than those of the other aid-giving nations.

Thus, both fellow members of the DAC and aid-receiving countries will be pressing Japan to improve the terms of its loans and to increase the amount of its official aid. At the third United Nations Conference

24. *Japan Times Weekly,* Dec. 9, 1972.

on Trade and Development, Japan pledged that it would raise official development assistance to 0.7 percent of GNP. It is estimated that to reach this goal by 1980 official aid would have to be increased 33 percent each year, and domestic opposition to so high a rate of increase would be great. Nevertheless, the amount of official Japanese aid is likely to increase substantially over the decade and, as it does, Japan will feel increasing need to elaborate a development strategy and define its political objectives in East Asia.

So far the economic aid program has been seen as a means of promoting Japanese trade and as a general contribution to stability and progress in East Asia. It has not been used to any great extent as a political tool to link particular countries more closely to Japan or to mold the East Asian region into a more tightly knit group of states under Japanese leadership. Its use could change, however, as Japan comes to exercise greater influence in the region.

For Japanese leaders are beginning to acknowledge that Japan's economic weight in the region will impose political responsibility. As former Foreign Minister Kiichi Aichi put it, "influence is but another name for responsibility."[25] And Nakasone, the director general of the Defense Agency under Sato and minister of trade and industry in the Tanaka cabinet, put the need for a Japanese political role bluntly: "There will also be established such economic relations between these nations [of East Asia] that they will find it impossible to maintain themselves if they are alienated from our country. If this is so, Japan will have to formulate a larger-scale political plan, with the peace, development, and prosperity of various Pacific nations in mind."[26]

Aichi is more sensitive than Nakasone to the lack of consensus in Japan on how to go about the task of taking on political responsibilities and the need for willing cooperation from Japan's Asian neighbors in doing it. His views are probably typical of the mainstream of the Liberal Democratic party:

Economic assistance, however, is only part of the task. What is also needed is a larger objective. . . . No objective is more important than the construction in East Asia of a viable community of nations, embodying "unity in diversity." . . . Japan's role should be one of service to each country in the region that is willing to accept it, and to the region as a whole. Needless to say, this is a role we can perform only with the agreement of our partners. A long series

25. Kiichi Aichi, "Japan's Legacy and Destiny of Change," *Foreign Affairs,* vol. 48 (October 1969), p. 39.
26. *Jiyu Shimpo,* organ of the Liberal Democratic party, Feb. 17, 1970.

of talks, both bilateral and multilateral, must precede and accompany this undertaking so there will be no doubts about the intentions of all concerned. This is a task that will take a very long time, and will involve great numbers of people, Japanese and others. It will certainly cost money and energy, and will no doubt produce much criticism and little praise. Careful planning will be required; plans and priorities will have to be geared to each country's particular conditions and, of course, to our capabilities. It will be a vast and demanding enterprise, but it is in our own interest to take a vigorous part in it.[27]

Japan has been slow to formulate a new Asian role, but a growing number of Japanese feel that it can no longer comfortably stay in the shadow of the United States, keeping its head down and concentrating its efforts on economic growth—that its economic expansion has made it too important a force in East Asia to avoid taking a large part in helping to determine the political future of that region. They sense increasingly a contradiction between economic aggressiveness and political diffidence.

The rapidity of Japan's economic growth is astounding—in the hundred years from the Meiji restoration to 1965 Japan's GNP grew to $100 billion, in the next five years it doubled, and before 1980 it will again double. It is not surprising, therefore, that the Japanese, while skilled in economic planning, find it difficult to cope with the international political consequences of economic growth. The economic machine whirs along, while politicians grope for answers.

There is no consensus among the Japanese on what their role should be.[28] No grand design, or even generally agreed set of principles to guide Japan's foreign policy in East Asia, has yet emerged, except for a widely accepted conviction that Japan should exert its influence without the use of military force. Whether this conviction holds firm as the Japanese shape a new role for their nation in East Asia will depend on the evolution of Japan's relations with China and the USSR, and on the condition of the U.S.-Japanese alliance.

27. Aichi, "Japan's Legacy," p. 34.
28. Most of the Japanese who write and talk about foreign policy believe that it will take a long time to achieve a national consensus on Japan's foreign policy role—particularly the size and shape of the defense establishment that will be needed. Masayoshi Ohira, foreign minister under both Hayato Ikeda and Kakuei Tanaka, believes "a considerable amount of time will be needed by Japan in determining the scale and content in concrete terms of its defense capability and I pray from the bottom of my heart that Japan-U.S. relations and the situation in Asia will permit Japan the time needed to arrive at these decisions." "A New Foreign Policy for Japan," *Pacific Community,* vol. 3 (April 1972), p. 413.

CHAPTER FIVE

Japan, Russia, and China

It is very much in the U.S. interest that Japan succeed in its "grand experiment" as the first big power without large military forces to prosper and expand its influence widely in the world. If the Japanese continue to forgo massive rearmament, not only will Asia have a better chance to escape the harmful effects of an intensified arms race, but the world is more likely to see the further decline of military force as an instrument of foreign policy and as a measure of status in the world.

Whether the antimilitary attitudes that have taken root in Japan grow stronger or begin to wither will depend to a large extent on the nation's relationship with the United States. But they will also be affected by the evolution of Japan's relations with the Soviet Union and China. Japan's rapidly growing economic power will open new opportunities for expanded relations with these two powers, but it will also engender rivalry in East Asia, especially between Japan and China. Moreover, the Sino-Soviet confrontation, although it creates incentives for both Moscow and Peking to cultivate Japan, places Japan in a delicate position. Whenever Japan appears to draw too close to one of the big communist powers, it provokes the ire of the other and risks impeding the expansion of relations with it.

Soviet-Japanese Relations

For a century Japan and Russia have been rivals for power in East Asia. They fought each other in two major wars and their armed forces have clashed at other times in Siberia, Mongolia, and Manchuria. They have never been allies or maintained close and friendly relations. They remain suspicious and wary of each other. The Soviet Union since

World War II has usually wound up among the least-liked foreign nations in Japanese public opinion polls.

The Japanese are unlikely soon to forget the Soviet attack on their forces in August 1945, in violation of the Japan-Soviet neutrality pact, or the disappearance of thousands of Japanese prisoners who were carried off to the Soviet Union. Soviet efforts to influence Japanese domestic politics through the Japanese Communist and Socialist parties have aroused deep suspicion and resentment among the conservative leaders who have governed Japan since the end of the American occupation.

The Japanese believe that the greatest potential military threat to Japan is from the Soviet Union, which far surpasses China in air and sea power, as well as in modern equipment for ground forces and in nuclear weapons. Although most Japanese do not perceive the threat as serious today, Japanese defense planners are acutely aware that the northern tip of Hokkaido is only thirty-six miles from the southern end of Soviet Sakhalin. The potential Soviet threat thus dominates much of Japan's defense planning and constitutes the principal justification for the U.S.-Japan security treaty.

In recent years the Japanese dislike of the Soviets has been fed by the Soviet refusal to return the "northern territories"[1] taken after the last war, by frequent seizures of Japanese fishermen and boats alleged to be fishing in Soviet waters, and by Soviet naval bombing exercises in the seas near Japan. Even the Japanese Communist party, which has taken an independent position in the Sino-Soviet dispute, keeps Moscow at arm's length and calls publicly for the return of Japan's northern territories.

These territories consist of three large islands, Kunashiri, Etorofu, and Shikotan, and a group of small islands, the Habomais. Japan contends that they are not part of the Kurile chain, to which it renounced title in the San Francisco peace treaty, but an integral part of Japan. The Soviet Union refused to sign the San Francisco treaty and the dispute over the islands has blocked the negotiation of a separate peace treaty with Japan. The Soviets have indicated they would return Shikotan and the Habomais when a peace treaty was signed, but adamantly insist that the status of Kunashiri and Etorofu was finally settled when they became Soviet territory as a result of World War II.

1. For a good, brief account of the history of the northern territories issue, see John Emmerson, *Arms, Yen and Power: The Japanese Dilemma* (Dunellen, 1971), pp. 230–39.

Since 1972, when the United States returned control of Okinawa to Japan, attention has focused on these last remaining bits of territory considered unjustly seized from Japan. Japanese resentment will be exacerbated if the Soviet Union continues seizing Japanese fishermen accused of violating Soviet territorial waters around the disputed islands. The islands are intrinsically so unimportant that to an outsider it would seem foolish for either nation to allow the dispute to interfere with important national objectives. Nevertheless, the Soviet Union apparently believes that to yield on this issue would weaken its position on other revanchist claims that might be put forward by nations that had lost territory to Russia—especially by China. And to a more nationalistic Japan, with more chauvinistic leadership than it has today, the dispute could become a highly charged emotional issue.

Concern that Japan is remilitarizing and may turn to nuclear weapons has become increasingly prominent in Soviet comments on Japan since the Sato-Nixon communiqué of November 1969. Moscow has criticized growing nationalism in Japan, the increase in the military budget, the discussion among Japanese of possible nuclear weapons for Japan, the delay in ratifying the nonproliferation treaty, and the military partnership with the United States, which the Soviets profess to see as expanding Japan's role in carrying out "American imperialist policies" in Asia. The Soviets have warned that the Japanese are repeating the errors of the past and have called on them to turn away from the alliance with the United States, develop closer relations with the USSR, and cooperate with the USSR in creating a system of collective security in Asia.[2]

The increased emphasis on the theme of the remilitarization of Japan probably reflects genuine concern in the Soviet government that Japan's increasing economic power and assertiveness, combined with the smaller U.S. military presence in East Asia that the Nixon Doctrine called for, may lead to regional military commitments by Japan and increased risk that it will develop nuclear weapons. But Soviet attacks on Japanese militarism are mild in tone compared to the ringing Soviet denunciations of the "Chinese threat." Moscow clearly sees Japan as a

2. See A. Biryukov, "Operation 'Treaty Revision,'" and "USSR-Japan: Common Interests," *Pravda*, Jan. 7, 1970, and July 30, 1970; A. Grechko, "Great Victory in the Far East," *Pravda*, Sept. 2, 1970; and D. Petrov, "Japan: 25 Years After the Capitulation," *World Economic and International Relations* (USSR), September 1970, pp. 31–41.

potential, not an immediate, threat to Soviet security. Its attacks on the U.S.-Japan alliance have become almost pro forma, suggesting a certain ambivalence toward that relationship. The Russians would doubtless like to see a cooling of relations between the United States and Japan that caused Japan to draw closer to the USSR, but they would be alarmed if Tokyo turned away from Washington in order to form a closer relationship with Peking.

Despite its adamant stand on the territorial issue and its condemnation of remilitarization, the Soviet Union has in some ways sought improved relations with Japan, probably as a result of its worsening dispute with China. For several years Moscow has conducted what the Japanese refer to as "smiling diplomacy" with Japan. The Japanese government, conscious of Japan's military weakness in the face of Soviet might and recognizing the need to live at peace with the USSR, has responded to Soviet initiatives toward improving relations and has taken initiatives itself. These have resulted in visits of high-ranking officials to each capital, cultural exchanges, and an aviation agreement by which Japan became the first nation to be allowed to fly commercial aircraft across the Soviet Union with its own crews.

The Soviet campaign to cultivate Japan shifted into higher gear after the announcement of President Nixon's plan to visit China. In a surprise move, Soviet Foreign Minister Andrei Gromyko made a week-long visit to Japan in January 1972—his first visit in nearly six years—and departed with Tokyo's agreement to begin negotiations on a peace treaty in 1972. Although the Soviet position on the northern islands issue did not change, Gromyko apparently softened his tone sufficiently on this and other issues to persuade Tokyo to drop return of the islands as a precondition for entering into negotiations.

But the first formal negotiations on the peace treaty quickly deadlocked over the territorial issue. Neither side appeared willing to consider a compromise and the Japanese Foreign Ministry in late 1972 saw little hope of any early resolution of the problem.[3] Moreover, the tone of Soviet comment on Japan hardened following Tanaka's successful normalization of Japanese relations with China, with renewed attacks on increases in Japanese military spending.[4] Tanaka's visit to Moscow in October 1973 produced no perceptible progress. Thus, the atmo-

3. *New York Times* and *Yomiuri*, Oct. 11, 1973.
4. *New York Times*, Jan. 14, 1973.

sphere between the two nations remains cool, despite spasmodic efforts to improve relations.

Official visits and other largely symbolic measures to improve relations are not nearly so significant as the growing trade between the two nations, which amounted to $1.1 billion in 1972—still less than 3 percent of Japan's total foreign trade, but a somewhat larger proportion of Soviet foreign trade, and an amount equal to Japan's 1972 trade with China. For some years now, large-scale Japanese cooperation in the exploitation of Siberian resources has been expected to bring substantial growth in the two nations' trade. Soviet interest in speeding the economic development of sparsely populated Siberia may have been stimulated by the sharpening Sino-Soviet dispute. But the negotiations on Japanese cooperation, proposed in 1962, have moved slowly. The first agreement, on timber, was signed in 1968; the second, on the construction of Wrangel port, in 1970; and the third, on pulp wood and chips, in 1971. Two years later, negotiations on large-scale projects for the production of oil, natural gas, copper, and coking coal had not led to agreement.[5]

Negotiations on these large projects has been difficult because of the remote location of the mineral deposits, the heavy investment required to develop them, and disagreement between the Japanese and the Russians on the size and terms of the Japanese contribution to the development. The Japanese are also somewhat inhibited by political considerations—an unwillingness to become too dependent on trade with the USSR or to risk injuring relations with China by becoming too deeply involved in developing a region that the Chinese claim the Russians acquired from China by means of "unequal treaties." The Chinese have expressed particular concern over Japanese negotiations with the Soviet Union for loans and technical cooperation in installing a pipeline to bring central Siberian oil to the Pacific, which would considerably improve the Soviet ability to support large military forces in that region.

Nevertheless, the economic advantages to Japan and the USSR of cooperating in the development of Siberia are great. The voracious demands of the Japanese economy exert increasing pressure for new sources of raw materials, and Japan's favorable payments balances in some recent years have reduced previous constraints on large foreign

5. See Violet Connolly, "Soviet-Japanese Cooperation in Siberia," *Pacific Community*, vol. 2 (October 1970), pp. 55–65; *Washington Post*, Feb. 28, 1971; *Japan Times*, Dec. 18, 1971; *Yomiuri*, Sept. 7, 1973; and *Nihon Kogyo*, Sept. 22, 1973.

loans. The Soviet Union, on its part, is placing increasing emphasis on expanding foreign trade[6] and is urging on the Japanese the advantages of larger trade between the two countries. Soviet experts point out that between one-half and two-thirds of its investment is being allocated to Siberia and the Far East and that it is often cheaper and easier to procure equipment for plants there from Japan than from the USSR.[7]

It is probable that some of the economic development in Siberia will involve combined U.S., Japanese, and Soviet investment. In 1972, American companies were discussing possible participation in tripartite oil and gas projects,[8] and the subject was on the agenda of the talks between President Nixon and Premier Tanaka in July 1973.[9] The Japanese would welcome U.S. participation because it would make available advanced technology, reduce the share of the capital that Japan would have to provide, reduce the risk that the USSR might try to exert political pressures on Japan through these projects, and enable Japan to avoid being the sole target for Chinese resentment.

The economic advantages to both Japan and the USSR are so compelling that agreements on additional and larger Siberian projects in the next few years seem likely, if no serious political differences arise. The Japanese will bargain hard and will weigh the economic advantage of getting raw materials from the Soviet Union against their concern not to become too dependent on the Russians. Unless the Chinese should radically change past trade policies by accepting long-term loans from Japan or sharply increasing the export of minerals, it seems probable that within a few years Japanese trade with the USSR will substantially exceed that with China, both because of the larger, more highly developed Soviet economy, and because of Soviet emphasis on expanding foreign trade.[10]

During the remainder of the decade, then, Soviet-Japanese economic relations can be expected to expand, but the stiffness and distrust in the

6. *New York Times,* Feb. 16, 1971.

7. See speech by Dmitri Petrov, Soviet expert on Japanese affairs, *Mainichi,* May 14, 1970; and article on Soviet-Japanese trade by V. Akimov, acting chief trade representative in Japan, *Nihon Kogyo,* Nov. 13, 1970.

8. See *Washington Post,* March 10, 1974.

9. *New York Times,* Aug. 2, 1973.

10. The Japan Economic Research Center estimates that 4.5 percent of Japan's exports in 1980 will go to the USSR as compared to 2.5 percent to China, while 6 percent of Japan's imports will come from the USSR and only 2.1 percent from China. *Japan Report* (New York: Japanese Consulate General), July 16, 1972, p. 9.

countries' overall relationship will persist. The Soviets could improve their position considerably by compromising on the northern islands issue, but they seem determined to hold firm and this issue will probably remain an irritant in the relations between the two. Japan's conservative political and business leaders will probably continue to be aggravated by Soviet efforts to cultivate the Japanese opposition parties, especially the Socialist and Communist parties; by Soviet navy and air force activity in the Pacific; by propaganda attacks on Japanese arms programs and Japan's relations with China and the United States; and by Soviet rejection of arms control proposals initiated or supported by Japan. The common interest of the two countries in expanding economic relations may permit a gradual improvement in their relationship, but no radical change in past attitudes is likely unless Japan's relations with China and the United States should deteriorate sharply.

Sino-Japanese Relations

Japanese attitudes toward China are complex and ambivalent. The lure of the China market, racial and cultural affinity, the desire for friendly relations with a neighboring nuclear power, and a residual sense of guilt among the old over Japan's invasion of China influence the Japanese. Most of them respect Chinese culture as the main source of their own culture, but many hold a low opinion of the ability of Chinese to govern themselves and cope with the modern world. The chaos in China during much of the past century and the slow pace of China's modernization contrast sharply with the rapid, disciplined change in Japan, beginning with the Meiji restoration. This and the Japanese military superiority over China demonstrated in two wars have created a somewhat condescending attitude among Japanese toward Chinese and considerable confidence in their ability to understand and deal with Chinese.

Few Japanese today perceive China as a significant military threat to Japan or even to Japanese interests in Southeast Asia. China's acquisition of nuclear weapons has forced the Japanese to give more thought to the possible long-term threat from that quarter, but an overwhelming majority of Japanese today would rely on diplomacy rather than their own nuclear arms to forestall that threat and hold to the alliance with the United States as a safeguard against Chinese nuclear blackmail.

The Chinese, secure in their numbers, their vast territory, their centuries of predominance in Asia, their nuclear weapons, and their Maoist doctrine of historical inevitability, seem confident of their own long-run superiority. As in the days of the Celestial Empire, they expect Japanese missions to come to them seeking trade and other relations. Until the opening of the quasi-official negotiations leading to Premier Tanaka's visit to Peking in September 1972, Japanese emissaries arriving in Peking to negotiate agreements on trade—even those from Japan's governing party—were forced to perform a symbolic kowtow by denouncing their own government in a joint communiqué. The Chinese have not forgotten, however, how the Japanese military lorded it over China and they are keenly aware of Japan's rapidly growing industrial power and military potential.

There is thus a kind of brittleness and abrasiveness in the deeply ingrained attitudes of Japanese and Chinese toward one another. The Chinese feeling of superiority—the attitude of an aristocrat—seems more natural, as if bred in the bone by centuries of cultural preeminence. The Japanese attitude—that of a self-made man, proud of having reached the top through his own efforts—is somewhat patronizing toward the old aristocrat fallen on hard times, yet not entirely confident. Thus, despite racial and cultural affinities, China and Japan are unlikely to find it easy to get along comfortably with one another. Each feels that it should be the nation to which other Asian states look up.

The rapid changes in recent years affecting the relationships among the four big powers—the rise of hostility between the Soviet Union and China, the growth of Japanese economic power, the changing U.S. role in East Asia, and the rapprochement between Washington and Peking —have caused Japan and China to begin rethinking their relationship with each other. As a result, the Chinese government softened its position toward Japan, making it possible for Premier Tanaka to outflank the opposition within his own party to concessions to China and reach agreement with the Chinese in Peking in September 1972 on the normalization of relations between the two countries. Tanaka's visit was followed by an exchange of diplomatic missions, the initiation of negotiations on aviation and other official agreements, a series of visits to Japanese factories by Chinese technical missions, and the negotiation of contracts with Japanese firms for the export of industrial plants to China. The two countries have attained a new level of cordiality, but it is too early to assume that level can be held in the years ahead.

Japan and China may steadily expand their relations, submerge their differences, and arrive by the end of the decade at a close and cordial partnership. But it is also possible that relations will not develop smoothly, differences between them will grow, and by 1980 they will be in sharp contention for leadership in East Asia. While neither extreme seems probable, their relationship will tend more toward rivalry than toward cooperation. The currents that would impel them toward co-operation—mainly growing out of economic needs—seem less power-ful than those relationships with other nations that would limit their incentives to cooperate with each other or would provoke them to rivalry.

Trade

The principal force that might move the Chinese and Japanese toward partnership is the complementary nature of their economies. Certainly, both have much to gain from expanded trade. Japan needs China's raw materials; China needs Japan's capital and modern tech-nology. For some years Japan has been China's most important trading partner, in 1972 accounting for 19 percent of China's foreign trade. For Japan the China trade is less important, amounting to less than 3 per-cent of Japan's foreign trade.[11]

The rapid expansion of Sino-Japanese trade would be feasible only if there should be a radical change in Chinese economic policy, includ-ing a willingness to accept long-term loans from Japan to pay for Japanese capital goods and technical assistance and a willingness to repay loans by exporting to Japan on a large scale such basic raw materials as oil, coking coal, and iron ore or by basically reorienting the Chinese economy to stress the export of light manufactured goods, as Taiwan and South Korea have done. There are few indications that the Chinese are likely to abandon their fundamental economic policy of maximum self-reliance by incurring heavy indebtedness to Japan, expos-ing their economy to close scrutiny by Japanese technicians, and greatly increasing their dependence on trade with Japan. Even if the Chinese were to decide to seek large long-term foreign loans in order to speed

11. Four other East Asian countries bought more Japanese goods than China did in 1972. Japanese exports to China were $610 million, to Taiwan $1.1 billion, to South Korea $981 million, to Hong Kong $911 million, and to Australia $730 million. International Monetary Fund/International Bank for Reconstruction and Development (IMF/IBRD), *Direction of Trade Annual, 1968–72*, pp. 137–39.

industrialization, they would probably wish to obtain funds from a number of lenders, rather than become so dependent on a single country as they were on the USSR in the 1950s. Neither government nor business leaders in Japan expect dramatic increases in trade with China in this decade. According to their projections, Japan's foreign trade will continue to grow most rapidly with the industrialized areas of North America and Western Europe and with important suppliers of raw materials, such as Australia.

Japan and the Western World

China's attraction for Japan is based primarily on tradition and sentiment, while Japan's links with the noncommunist world grow out of strong motivations of self-interest. Most Japanese, when they consider the future, look to the West, not the East. Japan's prospects for continued economic growth depend on an expanding world trade and maximum access to markets, raw materials, and advanced technology. In industrial development, the nature of its political and economic system, its standard of living, the educational attainments of its people, the interchange of ideas, and the travel of its citizens, Japan has much more in common with North America and Western Europe than with China. Japan's greatest single stake is in its relations with the United States, which accounts for almost one-third of both its exports and imports, is its most important source of advanced technology, and has great influence on trends in the world trade and monetary system.

Japan's involvement in the politico-economic structure of the noncommunist world will not necessarily prevent it from drawing somewhat closer to China than in the past. On a variety of world issues, however, the basic interests of the two will differ, especially when China seeks to lead Third World opposition to the policies of the industrialized nations. Sharp conflicts of interest are already evident, for example, in the two countries' positions on the law of the sea, on nuclear arms control, and at international meetings, such as the 1972 UN Conference on Trade and Development and the Stockholm conference on the environment in the same year.

Only if the trend toward economic interdependence in the noncommunist world were checked or reversed by depression or a wave of protectionism, dividing the world into exclusivist economic blocs, might the Japanese be impelled to seek their economic future in close cooperation with China. If the Japanese felt unfairly discriminated against by the advanced industrial nations, their racial and cultural affinity with China would be strongly reinforced by their resentment against the West. Even in those circumstances, however, it would not be easy for Japan and China to bridge the differences in their political systems and national aspirations in order to share the leadership of an Asian bloc of nations.

Taiwan

Peking has long feared that conservative Japanese politicians with close ties to Chiang Kai-shek would so increase Japan's influence over and protection of Taiwan that the island would be permanently severed from the Chinese mainland and again made a Japanese possession, in essence if not in name. These fears were strengthened by the rapid growth of Japanese trade with Taiwan and investment there and by Premier Sato's 1969 declaration that security in the Taiwan area was a most important factor for the security of Japan. The Chinese probably believed that the expression of Japanese interest in Taiwan and Korea, taken together with the Nixon policy of asking U.S. allies to take on greater defense responsibilities, presaged the assumption by Japan of a regional defense role. In the spring of 1970 Chou En-lai laid down four principles for Japanese trade with China, aimed at inhibiting Japanese firms' deep involvement in dealings with South Korea or Taiwan. Chinese attacks on the alleged revival of Japanese militarism and de-nunciations of the presumed Japanese intention to create two Chinas grew in volume and stridency.

From late 1971, however, the attacks on Japanese militarism and on the security treaty with the United States diminished. President Nixon's approaching visit to China, agreed to in July, may have reduced fears that Washington was grooming Tokyo to take over its defense responsi-bilities in Asia. And hope for an agreement with Sato's successor on the normalization of relations between Japan and China may have been at least partly responsible for the gentler tone toward Japan. In any case, when Premier Tanaka visited Peking in late 1972, the two nations reached an understanding on Taiwan that supplemented that of Feb-ruary 1972 between the United States and China. It included recogni-tion of the People's Republic of China as the sole legitimate government of China; establishment of Japanese diplomatic relations with Peking and the breaking of relations with Taipei; a declaration of Japan's adherence to the provision of the Potsdam proclamation concerning the return of Taiwan to China; and acceptance by Japan of the view that the 1952 peace treaty with the Republic of China no longer had any effect.

In return for these concessions to the Chinese government's views on Taiwan, Japan is apparently free to continue trade and other relations with Taiwan. There are no indications that the Japanese were asked to give or gave any assurances to the Chinese of future limitations on their economic relations with Taiwan. Trade with Taiwan is large enough to be fairly important to the Japanese, in 1973 amounting to $2.5 billion and exceeding Japan's trade with mainland China by $500 million. In addition, Japanese government and private loans and investment in Taiwan totaled close to $400 million. Japanese trading companies handle a large portion of Taiwan's exports, and there are hundreds of technical cooperation agreements between Japanese and Taiwanese firms. Following the expulsion of the Republic of China from the United Nations in October 1971, Japanese companies became nervous about investing in Taiwan, and new investment slowed to a trickle. By 1973, however, the substantial flow of capital had resumed. More than 400,000 Japanese visited Taiwan in 1973, as compared to fewer than 20,000 who went to mainland China.

Soon after Japan severed diplomatic relations with the Republic of China and each nation had closed its embassy in the other country, Tokyo and Taipei made an unofficial arrangement to permit most relations between Japan and Taiwan to continue relatively undisturbed. The Japanese established a private Interchange Association, with offices in Taipei and Kaohsiung, while the Chinese created an East Asia Relations Association, with offices in Tokyo, Osaka, and Fukuoka. These nonofficial organizations are staffed mainly by diplomats of the two countries on temporary leave of absence from the foreign service. They are responsible for "promoting the development of the two nations' economic, trade, technological, cultural, and other mutual relations" and for "protecting the lives, property, and interests" of nationals of one nation residing in or visiting the other.[12] Peking appears to have made no objection to this unique arrangement, which allows relations between Japan and Taiwan to flourish—within limits determined by Peking's attitude and the priority that Tokyo gives to relations with mainland China over relations with Taiwan, when it is forced to make

12. *New York Times*, Dec. 27, 1972.

a choice. Foreign Minister Ohira, on his return from the trip to Peking with Tanaka, declared: "There are strong and deep ties between Japan and Taiwan. Consequently, even if diplomatic relations are severed, administrative relations must be respected and treasured. So long as they do not touch on the very roots of the maintenance of Japan-China relations, we intend to devote utmost efforts for the maintenance of administrative relations between Japan and Taiwan."[13]

Thus, Taiwan appears to have been laid aside for the time being as an issue between Japan and China, just as it has been between the United States and China. There was no reference in the Sino-Japanese communiqué to the U.S.-Japanese security treaty or to the question whether military bases in Japan might be used by the United States to carry out its defense commitment to the Republic of China. It must have been assumed that there would be no attack on Taiwan and that the question of its defense therefore would not arise. So long as China is willing to tolerate the separate existence of Taiwan and its various relationships with Japan, there is no reason why it should become a serious issue between the two countries. But if future Chinese leaders should be less tolerant and begin to exert pressure to force the reunion of Taiwan with the mainland, or if a movement should develop on Taiwan itself to declare independence of the mainland, Taiwan could again become a serious issue between Tokyo and Peking.

Leadership in East Asia

It is Japan's rapidly expanding economic influence in East Asia and the emerging view among Japanese leaders that a political framework for that influence is needed that is most likely to move Japan and China toward increased rivalry rather than close cooperation.

China is not in a position to compete with Japan economically. It has nothing like the broad range of export products that Japan has, nor does it have an export-oriented economy. Only a few of its exports are competitive with Japanese products on the international market. Aside from raw materials, which Japan does not export anyway, China exports mainly inexpensive consumer goods that compete more with the exports of South Korea, Taiwan, and Hong Kong than with Japan's exports. China lacks not only the range of products, but the capital, the shipping, and the services that established and experienced Japanese trading com-

13. *Asahi*, Oct. 1, 1972.

panies provide. Since 1968 Japanese exports have outstripped Chinese exports even in China's closest and most important market, Hong Kong.[14] Unless the Chinese turn from self-reliance to emphasis on a rapidly expanding foreign trade, their ability to compete with Japan's broad and sophisticated range of export products will continue to decline.

Its low level of exports will also limit China's ability to compete with Japan in providing resources to the developing countries of East Asia. Since 1954 China has pledged $2.7 billion to developing nations throughout the world, less than half of which has been delivered, while Japan provided resources, public and private, of approximately the same amount, $2.7 billion, in the single year 1972. Of course, if official aid alone is considered, the record is much less lopsided. In 1972 China extended $499 million in aid and Japan $610 million. Moreover, Chinese loan terms are much more generous—interest-free, ten to twenty years, with a five- to ten-year grace period—compared to Japan's average terms of 3.5 percent interest, and repayment over twenty-two years with a seven-year grace period. On the other hand, approximately 25 percent of Japan's official bilateral aid was in grants, while only about 5 percent of Chinese aid took this form.[15]

Thus, the generosity of their loan terms will give the Chinese a political edge over the Japanese. By concentrating on a few large, high-visibility projects, comparable to the Tan-Zam railway project in East Africa, the Chinese could reap high political rewards for a relatively small investment. Nevertheless, they lack the resources to compete on a large scale with the Japanese throughout East Asia. Moreover, the variety of ways in which it can provide private or governmental capital to developing countries gives Japan more flexibility in promoting economic growth in these countries than China is likely to possess. If Japan's unwillingness to make long-term loans on terms as generous as China should become a serious disadvantage, Japan could at relatively small cost make its terms competitive.

The Chinese denunciations of "Japanese militarism" that reached a climax in 1971 and subsequently diminished frequently laid blame for

14. Exports from Japan to Hong Kong increased from $343 million in 1967 to $893 million in 1972, while exports from China in the same years were $393 million and $681 million. U.S. Consulate General, Hong Kong.

15. Figures on Chinese aid are from U.S. Department of State, Bureau of Intelligence and Research, *Communist States and Developing Countries: Aid and Trade in 1972* (1973). Figures on Japanese aid are from *Japan Report*, Sept. 16, 1972, and *Nihon Keizai*, June 3, 1973.

the revival of militarism on Japan's rapidly expanding economic influence in East Asia. From the Marxist-Leninist-Maoist point of view, economic expansion carries the threat of military aggression. Typical of Peking's pronouncements was the *People's Daily* editorial of September 18, 1971:

Today Japan's economic strength is seven or eight times that of pre-war days and Japan has become an "economic power" in the capitalist world, second only to the United States. The contradictions between the malignant swelling of Japan's economy and her shortage of natural resources and limited market are even sharper than in pre-war times. This determines that Japanese monopoly capital must seek a way out through expansion abroad. The Japanese reactionaries have for many years practiced cunning neocolonialism with all their efforts. Behind the smokescreen of "economic cooperation," they export capital in a big way, dump their commodities everywhere, and plunder natural resources unscrupulously. Such colonial expansion inevitably encounters resistance from the people of the plundered countries and leads to clashes of interest with other imperialist countries. Japanese monopoly capital is sure to protect its colonial interests by armed force and scramble for spheres of influence. An "economic power" is bound to become a "military power" and economic expansion definitely leads to military expansion. This is an inexorable law of the development of Japanese militarism.

Chou En-lai expressed similar views to the leader of the Australian Labor party, Gough Whitlam, in July 1971: both Nakasone, head of the Japanese Defense Agency, and Premier Sato wanted nuclear weapons; Japanese economic expansion must be followed by military expansion; the Japanese claimed a "lifeline" that now seemed to stretch from Northeast China to the Malacca Strait, Chou said (reportedly, "with agitation"), and "it is not possible to have such plans without including nuclear weapons."[16]

In a later interview with James Reston, Chou elaborated his views.[17] He said flatly that an economy as highly developed as that of Japan "was bound to demand outward expansion," and that "economic expansion is bound to bring about military expansion." He pointed out that Japanese industry was fully capable of producing nuclear-armed missiles and rejected Reston's suggestion that the U.S.-Japan security treaty reduced the likelihood that Japan would add nuclear weapons to its armaments. On the contrary, the United States by extending the security treaty was promoting the growth of militarism in Japan, with

16. *Washington Post*, July 7, 1971.
17. *New York Times*, Aug. 10, 1971.

the expectation that Japan would become a stronger military partner of the United States in accordance with the principles of the Nixon Doctrine. Chou stopped short, however, of saying that a nuclear-armed Japan was inevitable. He asserted that the trend toward militarism in Japan could be checked by opposition from the Chinese and Japanese peoples, adding that "when you oppose a danger, you should oppose it when it is only budding."

The Chinese began in late 1971 to moderate this alarmist view of Japanese behavior. Probably the most important reason for their doing so was the decision to receive President Nixon and to begin radically reshaping Chinese relations with the United States. This decision, somehow related to the power struggle in China that resulted in the flight and death of Defense Minister Lin Piao, reflected a continuing high level of concern over the Soviet threat to China and a decline in concern over the U.S. threat. If U.S. intentions toward China now appeared less menacing than before, then the earlier Chinese assumptions that the United States was promoting the growth of militarism in Japan could also be revised.

Moreover, this change in the U.S.-China relationship improved prospects for the normalization of Sino-Japanese relations and made it desirable to move quickly on this front also to improve China's position relative to the USSR. Thus, the apparent decline in Chinese concern about Japanese militarism can be attributed in part to tactics. Many of the attacks on Japan were aimed at Sato personally. They were well calculated to undermine Sato's position at a time when pressures in Japan for normalization of relations with China had been greatly increased by the announcement of President Nixon's forthcoming visit and by the admission of China to the United Nations in October 1971. As the time drew nearer in early 1972 for the successor to Sato to be named, it made good tactical sense for the Chinese to ease their highly exaggerated attacks on Japanese militarism, which few Japanese could accept and which could have obstructed serious negotiations between Peking and Tokyo once the new premier took office.[18]

On his visit in Peking, Premier Tanaka emphasized the defensive nature of Japan's military forces and told the Chinese he did not want them to call Japan "militaristic." The Chinese acknowledged that it was

18. For a detailed discussion of Chinese tactics toward Japan during this period see Abraham M. Halpern, "Peking and the Problem of Japan, 1968–72" (Washington: Center for Naval Analyses, July 1972; processed).

natural for a nation to have defensive power, but added: "We are guarded, because Japan in the past had strong armed forces. Pre-war militarism inflicted great losses to the Chinese continent. There are more than a dozen million people who had their relatives or family members killed. There are some people who are not happy about your visit to China."[19]

Thus, despite the moderating of Chinese views on Japan's armed forces, an underlying distrust of Japan remains. The past history of Sino-Japanese relations combines with Chinese Communist ideology to nurture fear of Japanese economic expansion in East Asia. The Chinese have muted their concern that this must sooner or later lead to the expansion of Japanese armed forces because of their greater concern over the clear and present danger they see from the Soviet Union,[20] but it could burst into the open again as China and Japan compete for influence in the region.

Peking is likely to encourage opposition to Japanese influence in direct appeals to the people of Korea and Southeast Asia. For example, Chinese-sponsored radio stations that back local communist insurgents have denounced Japanese activities. The Voice of Malayan Revolution accused "Japanese militarism" of plotting to seize the Malacca Strait and charged "Japanese monopoly capital" with plundering Malaysian resources, damaging local industry by dumping Japanese consumer goods, attempting to gain control of the local economy through capital investment, and carrying on "cultural aggression" by sending in Japanese experts. It warned that the "sanguinary crimes committed by Japanese fascism during the second world war are still fresh in the minds of the Malayan people, who will definitely settle accounts with it."[21] The Voice of the People of Thailand accused the Japanese of infiltrating and spying on the nations of Southeast Asia through the "Japanese Youth Volunteer Corps" and other Japanese specialists and of selling arms and ammunition to Thailand and other Southeast Asian countries "to suppress the revolutionary struggle of the local people."[22]

19. *Asahi*, Oct. 1, 1972.
20. Chou En-lai is reported to have told a leading Liberal Democratic member of the Diet, Takeo Kimura, that China recognized the need both for Japanese armed forces and for the U.S.-Japan security treaty, because of the looming Soviet threat. See *Yomiuri* and *Washington Post*, Jan. 19, 1973.
21. Quoted in U.S. Government, Foreign Broadcast Information Service, *Daily Report: People's Republic of China*, Oct. 28, 1971, pp. A19–A20.
22. Quoted in ibid., March 29, 1972, pp. A5–A6.

Such attacks suggest that the Sino-Japanese rivalry in the years to come will be asymmetrical, the Japanese emphasizing economic relations with Southeast Asian countries, and the Chinese, lacking the economic power of Japan, emphasizing political and propaganda tactics and people-to-people relationships. The contest will be less unequal than it might seem. Japan's great and growing economic superiority over China will be counterbalanced, for a few years at least, by its uncertainty about its proper political role in East Asia and its inability to take vigorous and imaginative political action. Japanese political leaders are likely to be hampered by a narrowing base of support within the country, as well as by continuing unbridgeable differences between left and right on Japanese foreign policy. Unless Chinese leaders should again be distracted by domestic convulsions, they will probably have considerable advantages over Japanese leaders in developing and carrying out effective programs of political and diplomatic action in the region.

Southeast Asian governments will have ambivalent attitudes toward efforts by Japan and China to expand their influence. They will want the economic advantages of close relations with Japan but will seek to avoid excessive Japanese influence. They may see closer relations with China as one means of offsetting Japanese influence, but they may also fear Peking's tendency to support their domestic opposition.

The nature of the competition for influence between Japan and China will probably vary considerably from country to country. In the countries politically most stable the competition is likely to focus primarily on the government, with Tokyo and Peking each seeking to increase its influence on the government or on factions within the government through diplomacy. Where internal conditions are less stable and the government less firmly in control, Tokyo and Peking may give their support through a variety of conventional and unconventional means to different groups contending for power within the society. The Japanese are likely to support those who stand for order, stability, and evolutionary change, while the Chinese—concentrating their efforts on becoming the champions of the discontented or dispossessed—will tend to cultivate those who favor radical or revolutionary change. If conditions favoring armed rebellion should develop, the Chinese might support the insurgents, while Japan backed the forces of law and order. In any event, the Chinese will be the natural allies of those who oppose the growing Japanese economic influence.

How seriously conflicts of interest between Japan and China, arising out of their respective relations with developing nations of East Asia, will affect their bilateral relationship is hard to predict. In many ways the importance of good relations between the two should outweigh the effects of these conflicts of interest. Yet, in the light of the probable weaknesses and instabilities in various parts of Southeast Asia during this decade and the pride, ambition, and drive of the Chinese and Japanese, it would be unduly optimistic to assume that clashes of interest between Japan and China over this region will not grow.

Of course, Sino-Japanese relations are likely to be affected more importantly by the relations of each country with the other two countries in the four-power system than by disputes and rivalry relating to developing countries. The recent trends in Chinese policy toward Japan suggest that the Soviet threat is a strong stimulant to good relations with Japan, which will tend to prevent rivalry over developing nations from becoming intense.

Japan and the Sino-Soviet Confrontation

Japan reaps many benefits from the Sino-Soviet confrontation. Just as their fears of the USSR have caused the Chinese to mute their criticism of Japan and seek closer relations, so has the prospect of closer relations between Tokyo and Peking stimulated Moscow to increase its efforts to strike deals with Japan on the development of Siberian resources. Thus, Japan is in a favorable bargaining position and can encourage the two communist powers to vie with each other for closer ties with Japan, if it plays its cards adroitly.

Furthermore, neither power presses Japan to end its security treaty with the United States. Each would prefer that Japan remain linked to the United States for the time being rather than become linked to the other. From the Japanese viewpoint this is radically better than their early 1950s position, when the Sino-Soviet treaty aimed at Japan and the United States was in full effect, and the two communist powers were able to cooperate with each other against Japan, rather than having to compete with each other for influence on Japan as they do today.

While Japan benefits from the present confrontation, it would not gain from an intensification of the Sino-Soviet conflict and an increased risk of war in Northeast Asia. Large-scale military conflict between China and the Soviet Union would create serious dangers for Japan, because under that kind of stress each of the adversaries would probably be prepared to use severe pressure and threats, if necessary, to ensure that Japan did nothing to aid its enemy. A conflict on this scale would put an end to Japanese trade with both nations and destroy Japanese hopes for the kind of world in which its peace diplomacy could protect its interests. Consequently, Japan will use such influence as it may have—probably not very much—to prevent relations between China and the USSR from growing worse than they already are.

This will demand a delicate balance in Japanese diplomacy and will inhibit the pace at which Tokyo's relations with Peking and Moscow expand. It may also at times complicate Tokyo's efforts to accomplish a particular foreign policy objective. For example, China has publicly backed Japan's claim to the northern islands held by the Soviet Union. This Chinese move is probably more embarrassing than helpful to Tokyo, for it must reinforce Soviet fears that to yield to Japan on this issue would encourage China to press its own territorial demands. Likewise, Soviet support for the Japanese claim to the Senkaku Islands[23] would tend to stiffen Chinese opposition to the Japanese claim, for the Soviet action would raise the specter of Soviet-Japanese collaboration in the East China Sea, which might next be expanded to embrace Taiwan.

Should relations between Moscow and Peking improve, as they might in the period following Mao's death, the incentive for the USSR and China to moderate their clashes of interest with Japan and to seek closer relations with it would be somewhat weakened. Yet, a far-reaching Sino-Soviet rapprochement seems unlikely within this decade. If that is so, Japan will continue to derive advantages from carefully pursuing in a balanced way closer relations with both Moscow and Peking. Of course, this triangular equation will be powerfully affected by the state of relations within the U.S.-USSR-China triangle and by the state of relations between the United States and Japan. Generally speaking, the stronger the relationship between the United States and Japan, the stronger Japan's position will be for negotiating with the USSR and China.

23. The Senkakus (Tiao Yu T'ai to the Chinese) are a group of tiny, uninhabited islands on the outer edge of the continental shelf that lies under the East China Sea. They are about 100 miles east of the northern tip of Taiwan and about the same distance north of the southernmost group of islands in the Ryukyu chain. Peking, Taipei, and Tokyo have all claimed them. They have become important because of surveys indicating there may be large undersea oil deposits near them.

Conclusions

The commitment of the Japanese people to keep Japan a lightly armed, nonnuclear power seems remarkably solid. Conflicts of interest with the Soviet Union and China—or with the United States—have not been severe enough to affect significantly this basic attitude. Moreover, the sharpening of conflicts of interest with the two communist powers tends to be held in check by the Sino-Soviet confrontation, which impels Moscow and Peking to cultivate good relations with Japan, as well as by the desire of the Chinese and the Soviets for access to Japanese capital, goods, and technology, and by the Japanese desire to develop new markets and sources of supply.

But conflicts of interest, especially with China, are likely to become more difficult to moderate as Japan's economic influence expands further and Japan undertakes to strengthen political as well as economic links with the developing nations of East Asia. Even if the Chinese or the Soviets did not flaunt their military power in dealing with conflicts of interest with Japan, the fact that both are heavily armed nuclear powers would become more difficult to ignore. Japanese inhibitions against acquiring large military forces could be eroded, not necessarily because the Japanese perceived an increased direct military threat to Japan, but because more Japanese became convinced that a great nation could not gain the respect it deserved or make its voice heard effectively without military forces comparable to those of other great powers.

Future Japanese attitudes toward military force will be affected, of course, not only by the intensity of conflicts of interest with the Soviet Union and China—over which the United States has little control— but also by the state of relations between the United States and Japan, over which the United States has a great deal of influence. The greater the Japanese' confidence that they have the respect and support of the United States and can rely on the U.S. defense commitment, the less will be their inclination to turn to massive rearmament, even in the face of serious differences with their nuclear-armed neighbors. If they feel increasingly isolated and dependent on their own resources, both for security and for diplomatic bargaining leverage, they cannot be expected to refrain from developing powerful military forces.

CHAPTER SIX

Maintaining the Alliance with Japan

The U.S.-Japanese alliance has served both nations well for twenty years. It made possible Japan's rise from defeat to affluence; it secured for the United States the close diplomatic cooperation of the leading industrial state in Asia; and it provided a basis for the massive and flourishing trade between the two countries. There were, of course, strains, for a vociferous minority in Japan opposed the alliance, and some aspects of it irritated both Americans and Japanese. But it worked surprisingly well for two nations that had just fought a bitter and bloody war.

Drastic changes in Japan's position in the world and in U.S. policies in East Asia, particularly toward China, will change the character of the alliance. Japan's rapid economic expansion has revived the Japanese people's self-confidence, and with it their desire for national prestige and a role commensurate with their country's economic weight. When Japan began running a large surplus and the United States a large deficit in their trading accounts, disputes over economic issues became a central and probably continuing feature of U.S.-Japanese relations. As Japan's economic and political influence grows in East Asia, Japanese interests will more frequently diverge from U.S. interests. In short, the patron-protégé attitudes that have prevailed since World War II no longer fit U.S.-Japanese relations.

The alliance has also been affected by the changes in U.S. security policies in East Asia. President Nixon's breakthrough in relations with Peking, the cease-fire in Indochina, the reduction in U.S. military forces throughout East Asia, and the U.S. view that its Asian allies must rely less on the United States and do more for their own defense have greatly altered international politics in the region. Rigid confrontation

and containment have been succeeded by a more fluid diplomacy, causing Japanese to wonder about the long-term intentions of the United
States and the function of the U.S.-Japanese security treaty in the new
environment.

Both the U.S. and the Japanese governments have periodically reaffirmed the crucial importance of maintaining a close relationship.
They clearly perceive the great advantages of this course of action. But
the possibility remains that the new uncertainties introduced into international politics, combined with domestic political trends in the two
countries and increasing friction over a variety of issues, will gradually
erode the basis of trust on which the alliance has rested.

Should that happen, Japan would not necessarily turn immediately
to building powerful military forces. Japan's reaction would depend on
its sense of threat from China and the Soviet Union and on the evolution
of its domestic politics. If the threat from its communist neighbors
seemed low and the influence of left-wing parties in Japan increased
considerably, Japan could, for a time, embrace a posture approaching
the unarmed neutrality long advocated by the Japanese Socialist party.

But it is difficult to believe that a state as large and important as
Japan could long continue in a state of unarmed or lightly armed neutrality. Even Sweden and Switzerland spend heavily on arms to safeguard their neutrality. Once the U.S.-Japan security treaty had lost its
force, a relatively small increase in threats or pressures from China or
the Soviet Union could stimulate the Japanese to look to their defenses.
Feeling isolated and inferior to the nuclear powers in their diplomatic
clout, their confidence in American willingness to help defend them
gone, the Japanese could readily respond to nationalistic arguments that
they should be armed with nuclear weapons like other great powers.
Thus, the end result of a decline in trust between Japan and the United
States and a rise in friction between Japan and China or the USSR
would probably be large-scale rearmament, including nuclear weapons.

The United States and Japan have already begun to drift apart.
Some change in their relationship is, of course, inevitable and healthy,
but differences should not be allowed to proliferate until the drift
becomes impossible to check. Remodeling the U.S.-Japanese relation
to fit the new conditions will not be easy, for it runs against historical
precedent and national instinct for a nation as large and potentially
powerful as Japan to rely so heavily on another state for its defense.

Moreover, certain basic trends and attitudes in both societies run counter to a close U.S.-Japanese relationship.

Tendencies in the Japanese and American Societies

The dominant elements of Japanese society—the conservative Liberal Democratic party (LDP), business circles, and the bureaucracy—have been a buttress for the U.S.-Japanese alliance. Although none of these groups is likely in this decade to abandon the view that Japan's principal foreign relationship should be with the United States, active support for a close and cooperative relationship may decline because of a weakening in the LDP's position, combined with a spreading disillusionment among businessmen and within the bureaucracy as a result of growing economic problems between Japan and the United States.

The LDP has been responsible for Japan's economic success, and a fundamental tenet of its policy has been close cooperation with the United States. But, paradoxically, the success of conservative policies promoting rapid economic growth has set in motion sweeping social changes that may weaken the conservative grip, or at least bring to power leaders of a different stamp.

The effect of social change on politics will be accentuated by the change of generations that will occur in this decade. The generational gap is probably greater in Japan than in most industrialized states, because Japanese society has changed more rapidly. By 1975 the majority of Japanese will have been born after 1945, and the majority of voters after 1935. They will have little or no memory of the war and will have received their education after the war. The present Japanese leaders in politics, business, and the government bureaucracy, who went through the traumatic experience of defeat in war, will be passing from the scene. Their successors, who learned their trade in postwar Japan, will be more likely than they to turn to new political methods to deal with the unfamiliar problems produced by rapid social change.

The new leaders will have to deal with an accumulation of problems neglected in Japan's headlong rush to affluence: housing, transportation, pollution, social welfare, education. Social unrest will probably grow as more Japanese, especially the young, are cast loose in the big cities away from the traditional mooring of family and community and feel increasingly alienated from society. Strains within the society will increase. The strong desire to catch up with and surpass the West will clash with a reluctance to see traditional Japanese values submerged by excessive Westernization. The urge for more possessions will conflict increasingly with the desire for more leisure and a better quality of life.

The Liberal Democratic party so far has proved more adaptable in the face of social change than its principal opposition, the Japanese Socialist party (JSP). Since 1958 it has maintained a stable and comfortable majority in the House of Representatives of the Diet, while the strength of the JSP has declined by nearly one-third.[1] The JSP seats have been taken by other opposition parties, the largest number now being held by the Japanese Communist party (JCP), whose surprising gains in the December 1972 election gave it second place among opposition parties.

For years there has been talk about a unified opposition that would have some chance of challenging the LDP hold on political power, but little progress has been made in getting the opposition parties to cooperate nationally. Some gains have been made by leftist coalitions in local elections—notably in gubernatorial elections in Tokyo and Osaka in which LDP candidates were defeated—but even at the local level the LDP retains a dominant position throughout the country. The obstacles to cooperation among the disparate opposition parties are great; ideological differences within the JSP itself, deep suspicions of the Komeito and the JCP held by some members of other parties, splits within the party-affiliated Japanese labor movement, weaknesses in party organization and financing, and feuds among leaders all stand in the way. Thus, there is little basis on which to predict either a strong revival of the principal opposition party—the JSP—or an effective opposition coalition.

Despite the weakness and disarray of the opposition, the LDP has suffered a persistent secular decline in the proportion of the popular vote it has received, dropping from 58 percent in 1958 to 47 percent in 1972, although it remained well ahead of the JSP's 22 percent and the JCP's 11 percent. The LDP draws its strength mainly from rural and small-town constituencies, which have been losing population steadily to the big cities. Consequently, although the LDP's refusal to reapportion electoral districts to correspond with population changes has helped

---

1. *Information Bulletin* (Japanese Ministry of Foreign Affairs), Jan. 1, 1973, p. 2.

to protect its Diet majority, the underrepresentation of metropolitan areas in the Diet will in time create other problems. It may already be responsible, in part, for the growing tendency of the younger people in the cities to abstain from voting.

Thus, pressure on the LDP probably will increase in the latter half of the 1970s. Unless the party can devise more effective means of increasing its strength in the large cities—without losing its rural and small-town supporters—its popular base will continue to decline. The LDP will tend to suffer from the hardening of the arteries common to political organizations long in power and not presented with a real challenge to their dominant position. Although its leaders have proclaimed their determination to shift the central focus of government policy from rapid economic growth to quality of life, it remains to be seen whether they can impose on their big business backers the shift of resources from industrial investment to social infrastructure that would halt the growing frustration of the mass of Japanese with the problems of daily life. Dynamic opposition parties, such as the JCP and the Komeito, which have gathered strength by focusing on popular local issues, may make further gains, even if the opposition as a whole finds it impossible to unite against the LDP. Under these circumstances, LDP leaders may well encounter new difficulties in maintaining control over the contending factions of the party. These political pressures, heightened by the effects of social changes on the political system, could force a future LDP leader to form a coalition government with elements of other parties.[2] Because all of the opposition parties except the Democratic Socialist party (DSP) favor immediate abrogation of the U.S.-Japan security treaty, and even the DSP would eliminate the treaty gradually and cut back U.S. bases more rapidly than the government has done, any coalition would result in political compromises tending to weaken the U.S.-Japanese alliance.

Political pressure aimed at weakening the U.S.-Japanese relationship will be augmented by a similar, pronounced bias among leading Japanese newspapers. The long-established adversary relationship between press and government means that various aspects of the government's

2. See Gerald L. Curtis, "Conservative Dominance in Japanese Politics," *Current History*, vol. 60 (April 1971), pp. 207–12; Zbigniew Brzezinski, *The Fragile Blossom* (Harper and Row, 1972); and Robert Scalapino, *American-Japanese Relations in a Changing Era* (Library Press, 1972), pp. 75–77, for recent interpretations by American scholars of developing weaknesses in the Japanese political system.

policy of maintaining close relations with the United States will come under frequent attack in the press. On such issues the press and the opposition parties are natural allies. Thus, in spite of the strong parliamentary position that the LDP has always commanded, they have been able to embarrass LDP governments and force them to give ground on issues in U.S.-Japanese relations. If the LDP position in the Diet should weaken in the future, Japanese governments will be even more vulnerable to this kind of attack.

The nature of the Japanese political system and political behavior makes Japanese governments more vulnerable to attack than other governments. Even though they have large parliamentary majorities, Japanese governments are reluctant to push measures through on votes alone, without any concession to the opposition viewpoint. Rather than being accused of governing by the "tyranny of the majority," the government will delay action or make concessions on foreign policy issues on which basic differences in view make consensus impossible. This tendency to give ground is aggravated by the lack of cohesion in the LDP. The party is a coalition of faction leaders, some of them so ambitious to supplant the premier that they will purposely advocate policies that add to pressures on him to make concessions toward the opposition's position.

Pressure to weaken or end the U.S.-Japanese alliance will also come from those Japanese, including both left-wing intellectuals and right-wing nationalists, who stress Japan's historical identification with Asia. This school of thought, which has always been important in modern Japan, highlights the racial and cultural differences between Japan and the West. It rejects the view that Japan's future prosperity and security lie in expanding its relationships with the United States and other technologically advanced nations of the West, arguing that Japan's true future lies in closer relations with other Asian countries, especially China. This view, which appeals to deeply rooted feelings among the Japanese, can be readily used to fan anti-American sentiment.

Certain trends within American society may also handicap efforts by the U.S. government to maintain close relations with Japan. The general turning inward following the Vietnam War will make the United States less likely to maintain a military posture that will inspire confidence in the U.S. defense commitment among the Japanese, and will make it more difficult for the President to muster needed congressional support for a sophisticated foreign policy.

Submerged racial antipathy—the counterpart of similar feelings among Japanese—is likely to come more often to the surface as Americans become increasingly aware of Japanese economic power and affluence and as problems between the two nations increase. Americans who have long been accustomed to European travelers and European investment in the United States, and who are themselves the world's greatest overseas investors and travelers, may be jolted by the idea of Japanese buying up American real estate and taking over American firms, or Japanese tourists swarming into popular vacation spots. The traditional fascination of Americans with China, perhaps strengthened by the lengthy enforced separation of Americans from mainland China, will tend to exaggerate the relative importance to U.S. interests of relations with China, as compared to relations with Japan.

Adjusting to a Multipolar World

The overriding problem for the United States and Japan is adjusting their relationship to the new conditions of an increasingly multipolar world. In the early 1950s when U.S. foreign policy was dominated by the concept of "containing" the Soviet Union and China, Japan's leaders decided that the nation's interests would best be served by a close relationship with the United States. As a result, Japan's relations with the USSR and China have been shaped by and adjusted to the primary U.S.-Japanese relationship. Now that the emphasis in U.S. policy is moving from containment to the expansion of political and economic relations with the communist states, and Japan itself is seeking a more independent international role, the U.S.-Japanese relationship is undergoing subtle changes. Uncertainties have arisen on both sides about how the relationship should be redefined to suit the changed circumstances.

The Japanese are uncertain what military contribution the United States expects of Japan. Although the U.S. government declares it will continue to protect Japan with its nuclear deterrent, and appears to acquiesce in the Japanese policy of not using its armed forces beyond its borders, the long-term U.S. aims are clouded by official U.S. statements welcoming Japan's plans to strengthen its armed forces as the United States reduces its own in East Asia and referring ambiguously to Japan's "readiness to assume greater responsibilities."[3] Moreover, U.S. military officials have vigorously urged the Japanese to strengthen their armed forces, occasionally implying indifference to or even veiled encouragement of nuclear weapons for Japan.[4] When President Nixon spoke of an even balance in a world of five major concentrations of power,[5] the Japanese wondered how Japan could become such a power center without nuclear weapons. What, indeed, does the United States mean by its desire to inject "equality and reciprocity" into its relationship with Japan?[6]

Although the Japanese approve of the relaxation of tension in East Asia that the U.S. détente with China has brought, they are uncertain what the new U.S. relationship with China portends for their relations with the United States. The U.S. failure to consult with them prior to the dramatic announcement in July 1971 of the impending change implies a downgrading of the alliance. The U.S. government has since sought to mitigate the effects of this "Nixon shock" by taking care to keep the Japanese informed on its high-level talks with the Chinese— for example, by Henry Kissinger's stopovers in Tokyo after his visits to

3. The Report to the Congress by Richard Nixon on February 9, 1972, raised doubts in Japanese minds: "Japan had long since acquired the industrial and technological strength to assume responsibility for its own conventional defense. However, Japan continued to rely on American nuclear power for strategic security. It was, moreover, prevented by constitutional, political, and psychological factors, and by the attitudes of its Asian neighbors, from projecting military power beyond its own borders. Thus, the Mutual Security Treaty continued to serve Japan's interests, as well as our own. *Still it was clear that changes would come in our defense relationship as Japan regained its strength and pride.* . . . Japan is developing plans to strengthen its conventional defense capabilities over the next few years. *This is a reflection of heightened Japanese self-reliance and readiness to assume greater responsibilities. This welcome trend* has been accompanied by a consolidation of our own military facilities and a reduction of our forces in both Japan and Okinawa. . . . *There has, therefore, been steady progress in recent years in the assumption by Japan of a role in world affairs more consistent with its power." United States Foreign Policy for the 1970's* (February 1972), pp. 54–55. (Italics added.)

4. See report of briefing by a member of Secretary of Defense Melvin Laird's party in Tokyo in July 1971 and subsequent State Department denial that it knew of any "responsible body of opinion in Japan or the United States that advocates possession of nuclear weapons for Japan, or foresees such a necessity or possibility." *New York Times,* July 11, 1971. The denial failed, however, to eliminate suspicions that some U.S. officials saw nuclear weapons for Japan as desirable, or at least inevitable.

5. *Time,* Jan. 3, 1972.

6. Nixon, *U.S. Foreign Policy for the 1970's,* p. 54.

Peking in February and November 1973. The suspicion remains among Japanese government officials, however, that they are not being fully informed. They fear that the United States may again make a surprise move on China without consulting in advance with its principal Asian ally.

Not only are the Japanese worried about American unpredictability, they are less confident than before that the U.S. government is being candid with them on issues other than China of crucial importance to Japan. Some of the strongest supporters of the U.S.-Japanese relationship, including Premier Sato and key officials of the Japanese Foreign Ministry, felt that they had been led out on a limb by U.S. assurances of full consultation on China, only to have the limb sawed off by President Nixon. It strained credulity to accept at face value Washington's insistence that a United Nations seat for Taiwan was of great importance to the United States, when Henry Kissinger appeared in Peking at a critical point in the UN debate on the issue. For key officials in the Japanese Foreign Ministry, who had been led to believe that frequent consultations with senior State Department officials on China policy gave them a good understanding of official U.S. thinking, it was a traumatic experience to learn that the officials themselves had had no inkling of the impending abrupt change in U.S. China policy. The resulting decline in trust makes it easier for Japanese politicians and officials to entertain suspicion of U.S. intentions and to discount U.S. assurances.

Some Japanese, noting the more relaxed view of the U.S.-Japanese security treaty taken by Peking in 1972–73, suspect that the United States and China have agreed to cooperate in keeping Japan non-nuclear. Others surmise that the ultimate aim of U.S. policy is to move the United States to a diplomatic position equidistant between Japan and China. The U.S. concept of a five-power balance in the world reinforces this view. Thus, despite official U.S. reassurances that the U.S.-Japanese alliance continues to be crucially important, deep-seated suspicions remain.

Japanese uneasiness and uncertainty will be intensified as U.S. relations with China expand, particularly if friction between the United States and Japan increases and rivalry between Japan and China in East Asia grows. The many Japanese who exaggerate the prospects for trade with China also tend to exaggerate the threat of U.S. competition. They see a great expansion of trade as a major objective of the U.S. détente with China.[7] The fact that their competition in the China trade will probably have insignificant economic effects on the United States and Japan will not prevent speculation about this competition from coloring Japanese views of the direction in which U.S. policy is moving. Similarly, as Sino-Japanese rivalry in East Asia grows, the Japanese will become more sensitive to whether the United States is favoring Japan or China. This sensitivity is already evident in press criticisms of the United States for taking an equivocal position on the dispute between Japan and China over the Senkaku Islands.

The Taiwan issue will also complicate the triangular relationship. The Shanghai communiqué of February 1972 between President Nixon and Premier Chou En-lai has created an implicit—perhaps long-term—understanding that China will not attack Taiwan militarily and the United States will not promote an independent state of Taiwan. But the understanding is fragile because it is not spelled out, it leaves uncertain the ultimate resolution of the Taiwan problem, and it is open to various interpretations.

Thus the United States and Japan might misread each other's intentions toward Taiwan. So long as Peking is willing to tolerate a Taiwan that nestles under the protective wing of the United States and has fruitful and expanding economic relations with both the United States and Japan, there is little reason for Taiwan to become an issue in U.S.-Japanese relations. But if Peking were to revert to a hard line on Taiwan, perhaps as the result of a political crisis in Taiwan itself or a change in leadership in Peking and a subsequent decline in hostility between China and the Soviet Union, it could be difficult for the United States and Japan to agree on how to respond. This inability to agree could have a serious impact on their relations, for the U.S. commitment to defend Taiwan depends to a large extent on the availability of U.S. bases in Japan.

The new, more independent role for Japan that both Americans and Japanese agree must result from Japan's increased economic strength and its reborn pride and self-reliance is another area of uncertainty for the two nations. How they will put the new role into practice, and how it can be squared with a continued healthy U.S.-Japanese relation

7. Some Japanese seriously believed that the leader of the U.S. ping-pong team that visited China in the spring of 1971, who happened to be an employee of the Chrysler Corp., was there as an agent of the U.S. automobile industry to gain for the United States a large share of the Chinese import market for automobiles.

remain to be worked out. For example, will U.S. and Japanese policies toward Korea tend to diverge as Japan pursues its interests independently of the United States, and if this occurs, what is likely to be the effect on the U.S.-Japanese relationship? If the United States were to withdraw all its forces from Korea despite strong Japanese opposition, Japanese confidence in the U.S. security commitment could be undermined. Similarly, if Japan were to develop relations with North Korea, against U.S. wishes and in a way that seemed likely to increase the U.S. burden in South Korea, U.S.-Japanese relations would be badly strained by U.S. resentment. In the longer run, as Japan takes on greater political responsibility in East Asia, the United States will have to concede more frequently to its views, rather than expect Japan to follow the U.S. lead. But the change will come hard to a nation accustomed to calling the tune in the U.S.-Japanese relationship.

Maintaining the Security Treaty

The symbol of the special relationship between the United States and Japan has been the mutual defense treaty, together with the U.S. military bases in Japan authorized by that treaty, which provide the nucleus of the military force needed to fulfill the defense commitment. From the beginning, the treaty and the bases have been the target of attack led by the political opposition—principally the Japanese Socialist party and the Japanese Communist party.

The Socialists and Communists opposed the treaty on ideological grounds, and a fairly broad segment of the population joined them in opposition for other reasons. The feeling was widespread among Japanese that the treaty was imposed on Japan by the United States and primarily served U.S. purposes. Many Japanese did not perceive any serious threat to Japanese security, and they considered U.S. bases in Japan and Okinawa an irritating hangover from the period of U.S. occupation. The bases had an unhappy association with Japan's defeat in war. They occupied valuable space in land-short Japan, aggravated problems of noise and traffic congestion, and even gave rise occasionally to serious incidents, in which U.S. servicemen killed or injured Japanese. Moreover, many Japanese feared that the use of these bases by the United States to support its military actions elsewhere in East Asia might draw Japan into war against its will. The treaty and bases were seen as provocative to China and as an obstacle to the improvement of relations between Japan and China. Thus, although the ruling Liberal Democratic party considered the treaty essential to Japan's security and to the development of beneficial economic and other relations with the United States, the opposition was able to exploit opposing views among the Japanese information media and the public and keep the government on the defensive.

Circumstances have changed drastically, however, in the past several years. The return of Okinawa to Japan in 1972, with the U.S. bases there placed under the same rules as other U.S. bases in Japan, has removed a potentially explosive issue. With the cease-fire in Vietnam, the improved relations between the United States and China, the establishment of diplomatic relations between Tokyo and Peking, and the almost benevolent view of the U.S.-Japan security treaty being taken by the Chinese,[8] the arguments that the treaty might drag Japan into war with China or that it stands in the way of improved relations with China no longer carry much weight.

But the opposition view that Japan should end the U.S.-Japan security treaty and adopt an equidistant position toward each of the big powers continues to have many supporters. Adherents of this view believe Japan should remain lightly armed and nonnuclear, but should rely for its security on nonaggression treaties with each of the big powers or on some form of collective security arrangement in East Asia, rather than on the U.S. defense commitment. Advocates of this neutralist position argue that China and the Soviet Union pose no significant threat to Japanese interests. They assert that the United States cannot be relied on to help defend Japanese interests; on the contrary, conflicts of interest between the United States and Japan are likely to grow. Moreover, they contend that continued close association with the United States would create difficulties between Japan and the communist states and would increase the risk that Japan might be drawn into conflict.

The Japanese Socialists and Communists, who are the principal advocates of this position, are less nonaligned in their attitudes than the term *neutralist* would suggest, as their political views on most sub-

8. See reports of statements made by Chou En-lai to Diet member Takeo Kimura in January 1973 to the effect that the Chinese recognize the need for the U.S.-Japan security treaty at the present time because of the Soviet threat. *Asahi,* Jan. 18, 1973; *Yomiuri* and *Washington Post,* Jan. 19, 1973; and *Sankei,* Jan. 29, 1973.

jets are considerably closer to those of the Soviet Union or China than to those of the United States. But the neutralist view appeals to a wider group, for certain prevalent attitudes toward the security treaty remain unchanged: the treaty is mainly of benefit to the United States, and U.S. bases are an annoying holdover from the occupation period, nuisances that should be reduced drastically, if not eliminated entirely. Furthermore, to many Japanese, maintaining the security treaty when tension in East Asia is declining seems inconsistent with a new, independent international role for Japan.

The Japanese government thus remains on the defensive and may find it increasingly awkward politically to mount a strong defense of the treaty and the bases. The Foreign Ministry has begun to develop a new rationale for the treaty, playing down its military aspects and emphasizing its diplomatic importance. It is being portrayed in official statements as the symbol of friendly relations between the United States and Japan, as an element of strength in Japan's negotiating position with China and the USSR, and as a stabilizing force in East Asia, the abrogation of which would reverse the trend toward easing tension.

Even though the new rationale may blunt opposition attacks, the bases will remain a vulnerable aspect of the treaty arrangements, especially in Okinawa where they are so extensive. The Democratic Socialist party's position, adopted in 1959, seems to be gaining adherents: the treaty should be done away with gradually, but pending its abrogation, U.S. forces should be totally withdrawn from Japanese territory, to be returned only in an emergency at Japanese request. The Japanese government, of course, opposes this view.

The total withdrawal of U.S. forces would impair the credibility of the U.S. defense commitment. Quick return would seem both less likely to occur and less feasible technically without a nucleus of U.S. forces present in Japan. Total withdrawal of U.S. forces would thus strengthen the hand of those Japanese who would accelerate the buildup of Japanese forces. It might also incline the U.S. government to press harder for stronger Japanese forces in order to compensate for the lessened ability of U.S. forces to respond promptly in fulfillment of the continuing U.S. commitment to help defend Japan. Thus, total withdrawal of U.S. forces from Japan before the decline of tensions in Northeast Asia had achieved a momentum that was unlikely to be reversed might endanger the stability of the four-power system.

It is not only in Japan that there is likely to be declining support for the security treaty. Among the American public and in the Congress the desire to reduce U.S. burdens overseas is likely to remain strong. While this probably will not result in heavy pressure on the U.S. government to abrogate the treaty, there is likely to be a vigorous demand for Japan to share the financial burden of maintaining U.S. forces in Japan, especially if the United States should continue to run a substantial trade deficit with Japan at a time of congressional concern about rising U.S. military budgets. Criticism of the Japanese for exploiting a "free ride" will probably grow. Japanese unwillingness to compensate the United States in some way, combined with continuing Japanese public agitation against the bases, would cause many Americans to question the value of keeping U.S. forces in Japan. In a mirror image of the Japanese attitude, they would resent the United States maintaining the treaty commitment and the forces in Japan primarily for the benefit of Japan, rather than the United States. Moreover, as the base complex is consolidated and cut back, the U.S. military itself will find the changes constricting and hard to accept; the military value of the bases will tend to decline as considerations of military effectiveness have to be compromised for political reasons. Thus, both the Japanese and U.S. governments will probably find it more difficult than in the past to satisfy critics that the treaty arrangements embody a sufficient degree of reciprocity.

The Economic Confrontation

The economic problems between the United States and Japan in recent years have been due primarily to the rapid growth of Japan's economy and foreign trade and to the slowness of the two governments in adopting effective measures to counter the adverse impact of rising Japanese exports on the U.S. balance of payments. The problem, of course, was not purely bilateral; it was related to the lack of agreement among the advanced industrial nations on reforms in the world monetary system. Nevertheless, the U.S.-Japanese trade relationship attracted particular attention because of the very large deficits the United States ran in 1971 and 1972 in its trade with Japan.

Japan's economic performance has astonished the world, for between 1959 and 1970 Japan's average annual GNP growth in real terms exceeded 11 percent,[9] and its foreign trade, which grew at an average annual rate of nearly 17 percent in the 1960s, was more than double the rate of growth of world trade. By the end of 1971 Japan had become the fourth largest trading nation in the world, its foreign trade of $44 billion exceeded only by that of the United Kingdom, with $46 billion, West Germany, with $73 billion, and the United States, with $90 billion.[10]

Obviously, much of Japan's rapid economic growth was internally generated, for Japan's domestic market is much larger than that of any country of Western Europe. Foreign trade constitutes only about 10 percent of Japan's GNP, as compared to 14 percent for West Germany and 16 percent for the United Kingdom. Nevertheless, the Japanese government and Japanese business have placed exceptional emphasis on foreign trade. They are acutely conscious of the shortage of raw materials in Japan, especially those vital to modern industry, such as oil, iron ore, coking coal, copper, or bauxite. Japan's continued economic growth and the hope of a rising standard of living for its people largely rest on its ability to import raw materials and export finished products in order to pay for them.

Thus a heavy emphasis on exporting has been built into the structure of the Japanese economy and into the psychology of the people. The government has shaped its economic policy to encourage growth in those sectors of the economy that promised to be the fastest growing in world trade, such as steel, shipbuilding, chemicals, and electronics, and Japan now has a large capacity to produce these goods and possesses some of the most modern and efficient plants in the world. The export trade has further been promoted by favorable government policies and the development of large and sophisticated trading companies with expert knowledge of market conditions in all parts of the world and capable of offering a wide variety of terms and services to buyers of Japanese products. Official emphasis on exporting not only helped to

9. Analyses of the reasons for Japan's rapid economic growth may be found in P. B. Stone, *Japan Surges Ahead* (Praeger, 1969); Herman Kahn, *The Emerging Japanese Superstate: Challenge and Response* (Prentice-Hall, 1970); Robert Guillain, *The Japanese Challenge* (Lippincott, 1970); Hakan Hedberg, *Die Japanische Herausforderung* (Hamburg: Hoffmann und Campe, 1970); Angus Maddison, *Economic Growth in Japan and the USSR* (Norton, 1969); and K. Bieda, *The Structure and Operation of the Japanese Economy* (Wiley, 1970).

10. International Monetary Fund/International Bank for Reconstruction and Development (IMF/IBRD), *Direction of Trade, January 1973*, pp. 2, 5, 16, 30.

build a producing and marketing structure well suited to expanding exports, but also habituated the bureaucracy and important elements of business to giving high priority to increasing exports.

The fact that up to 1965 Japan ran a deficit on its trading account in itself provided a strong incentive to increase exports. After 1965, however, the export momentum that had been created began to produce an annual surplus. From 1970, when a business recession in Japan reduced domestic demand, the surplus built up more rapidly, for the excess industrial capacity increased the incentive to export, while lowered business activity in Japan limited increase in the flow of imports.

The recession in Japan, unfortunately, coincided with a period of inflation, recession, and unemployment in the United States. The surge of Japanese goods into the United States without a corresponding rise in U.S. exports to Japan produced a growing deficit in the U.S. balance of trade with Japan. Rapid increases in imports of Japanese textiles, steel products, electronic products, and automobiles produced alarm in the United States. Protectionist pressures grew and they were aimed especially at Japan, the nation with which the United States had the largest bilateral trade deficit.

All of this culminated in the Nixon administration's economic measures of August 1971 and the Smithsonian agreement of December 1971 aimed at improving the balance-of-payments position of the United States and laying the groundwork for fundamental reform of the world trade and monetary system. Although the Japanese yen was revalued upward nearly 17 percent, the deficit in U.S. trade with Japan grew still larger, exceeding $4 billion in 1972, accounting for two-thirds of the global deficit in the U.S. balance of trade. In February 1973 the United States devalued the dollar by 10 percent, while the Japanese and a number of European governments floated their currencies prior to seeking international agreement on changes in the international monetary system.

The Japanese government recognized that monetary adjustments alone would not permanently correct the severe imbalance in its trade with the United States and that structural changes in the Japanese economy would be required. Consequently, during 1973, it initiated a five-year program to increase government expenditures on housing, transportation, health, antipollution measures, and social security and adopted measures to slow exports and encourage imports.[11] These actions combined with those of the United States had substantially reduced the U.S. deficit in trade with Japan by the end of the year and the strain in the economic relations between the two countries had eased.

It seemed improbable that the U.S. trade deficit with Japan could again swell to the proportions reached in 1971–72. The floating exchange rates instituted by the principal trading nations and their general agreement that any new monetary system should avoid past rigidities provided assurance that the yen would not again become greatly undervalued in relation to the dollar. Moreover, the Japanese government's removal of many restrictions on foreign imports and investment and initiation of an effort to improve the quality of life meant that the pattern of investment in an affluent Japan would follow that in other highly industrialized societies.

Until the oil crisis hit Japan, most Japanese economic forecasters assumed that these changes in economic policy would take effect slowly and that throughout the 1970s Japan would enjoy a much higher rate of growth in its economy and in its exports than other major industrial states. Indeed, Premier Tanaka in the summer of 1972 stressed that rapid economic growth must continue if ambitious plans for improving the welfare of the Japanese people were to be realized. His prediction of an average annual rate of 10 percent through 1985[12] was matched by other official and private predictions of a rate of at least 9 percent through 1980.[13] The projections, of course, assumed a continued rapid growth of Japan's foreign trade.

The rapid rise in the world price of oil, accentuating the already serious inflation in Japan, radically affected Japan's economic prospects. Japanese economic forecasters began revising downward their projections of real economic growth.

The oil crisis has dramatized the high degree of economic interdependence in the world, bringing home to Japanese and Americans alike the need to find multilateral solutions to basic economic problems.

11. "Toward a Dynamic Welfare Society," *Information Bulletin*, March 15, 1973, pp. 1–4.
12. *Jiyu Shimpo*, June 27, 1972.
13. *Information Bulletin*, May 15, 1972, p. 8; and *Japan Report* (New York: Japanese Consulate General), July 16, 1972, p. 1.

Thus, their future economic problems are unlikely to be seen in the same predominantly bilateral context as the trade imbalance of 1971–72. Both nations will be involved in a multilateral effort to create a more orderly world economic system with generally agreed rules to govern monetary adjustments and access to markets and raw materials. Although the United States and Japan have a common interest in an orderly trading system favorable to the expansion of world trade, they may differ as to how to devise such a system.

Progress is likely to be hampered by the persistence of outdated stereotypes in the minds of the people of both countries, Americans continuing to view Japan as a low-wage producer whose exports to the United States threaten American jobs, and Japanese continuing to think of Japan as a small nation, unable to accept the global responsibilities that its expanded economic strength requires. As Japan's per capita GNP approaches that of the United States, Americans are likely to become uneasy and to resent the sudden affluence of people whom they have regarded with condescension. The concern already evidenced at the flood of Japanese tourists into Hawaii and the Japanese purchases of hotels, golf courses, and other valuable properties there reflects the difficulty of adjusting to Japan's new status.

The Japanese Dilemma

Some Americans believe that the Japanese have little choice but to cleave to their close association with the United States, regardless of the difficulties that arise between the two nations. Japanese leaders, despite their uncertainty about U.S. intentions and growing friction in the two nations' relations, see no practicable alternative. Neither Japanese nuclear arms nor a neutral Japan seems as desirable a choice as continuing reliance on the U.S. nuclear umbrella. And finding a substitute for Japan's economic reliance on the United States presents even greater problems. For over a hundred years, with the exception of the 1930s and the war years, Japan has consistently shipped around 30 percent of its exports to the United States, and the strong forces underlying that pattern cannot readily be altered. Not only is Japan heavily dependent on the U.S. market, but if Japanese transactions with U.S.-owned firms elsewhere in the world, U.S. investments in Japan, the flow of advanced technology from the United States to Japan, and invisible receipts from tourism and other sources are included, at least 50 percent of Japan's foreign economic relations depend directly or indirectly on the United States. The United States, on the other hand, is much less dependent on Japan. Even though Japan is the most important U.S. trading partner except for Canada, Japan accounts for only 9 percent of U.S. exports and 14 percent of U.S. imports. Many Japanese believe that this unequal dependence places Japan in a weak bargaining position with the United States, and the lack of a practicable alternative to that dependence causes them to feel increasingly frustrated.

Dissatisfaction with excessive dependence on the United States is a strong motivation for Japanese leaders to seek a more independent role for Japan. The Japanese government has moved in this direction, but it is difficult for it to move very far or fast. The LDP leaders are coming under increasing pressure from those in their own party and in the opposition who would like to see Japanese foreign policy less closely tied to that of the United States. Because Japanese governments have in the past given such great weight to their relationship with the United States, the "independence" of a Japanese policy is often judged by how much it diverges from U.S. policy. Any policy that happens to coincide with U.S. policy—even though based on an assessment of Japan's national interest—is liable to be attacked as "blind subservience to the United States."

Thus, it would be unwise to assume that the manifest advantages to Japan of a continuing close association with the United States and the difficulty of finding a desirable alternative will necessarily guide the Japanese. Should friction increase between Tokyo and Washington, resentment, frustration, and disillusionment could overwhelm dispassionate evaluations of Japan's interests. Declining support for a close relation with the United States would make it increasingly difficult for the government to mobilize support for those actions necessary to keep the relationship in good repair. Decline in support for it in Japan would tend to reduce support for it in the United States also, and once such a descending spiral of support took hold in earnest, it would be very difficult for the two governments to halt it.

Guidelines for U.S. Policy

To help Japanese leaders maintain domestic support for an association with the United States that will permit Japan to remain a lightly

armed, nonnuclear power, the U.S. government must be sensitive to
their internal problems. This means being sympathetic to Japanese
leaders' need to demonstrate convincingly to the Japanese public that
they are pursuing an independent course based on Japanese national
interests. At the same time it will require demonstration by the U.S.
government that it regards the maintenance of trust and cooperation
between the United States and Japan as its chief interest in East Asia.

Emphasizing the Value of the Alliance

It will be difficult to shed the habit of making important decisions on
U.S. policies in East Asia affecting Japan and then telling the Japanese,
rather than consulting fully with them at an early stage and at a high
level. It will be even more difficult to defer at times to Japanese views,
rather than expecting the Japanese to defer to U.S. views. The heads of
the two governments should meet regularly, not necessarily expecting
to resolve problems, but to deepen understanding of each other's thinking on foreign policy issues. The subjects on which high-level exchanges
of view are most necessary are, of course, basic economic issues, U.S.
and Japanese relations with China and the Soviet Union, and the policies of both countries toward Korea and Taiwan.

The U.S. posture will be more credible if the United States firmly
backs Japan's efforts to establish a political position in the world community compatible with its enhanced economic power. The United
States should not rest on its declaration of support for a permanent seat
for Japan in the UN Security Council; it should work closely with the
Japanese to formulate an appropriate amendment of the UN Charter
and to mobilize support for it among UN members. Even if the effort
should fail, the fact that the United States had worked hard on behalf of
its ally would serve to cement the U.S.-Japanese connection.

The United States should endorse Japan's commitment to "peace
diplomacy" as an important contribution to a world in which weapons
could become a less important element in a nation's foreign policy, a goal
the United States is working toward through its support of arms control
agreements. The United States and Japan should cooperate closely on
arms control matters in the United Nations and in the Geneva Committee of the Disarmament Conference. The United States should also
recognize Japan's contribution to the stability of East Asia through its
economic aid program.

Clarifying U.S. Objectives

The United States must try to dispel the confusion in Japanese minds about the "even" balance of power it advocates among the United States, the Soviet Union, Europe, China, and Japan. This means emphasizing that the "new structure of peace" the United States seeks in East Asia will be based on continuing close U.S.-Japanese cooperation and does not require that Japan substantially increase its military forces. The United States should, therefore, stress the desirability of Japan's ratifying the nuclear nonproliferation treaty, and seek to counter the widespread impression that important U.S. officials believe that acquisition of nuclear arms by Japan is inevitable.

If the importance of the alliance to the United States can be underlined, Japanese fears that the expansion of U.S. relations with China will diminish those with Japan are likely to decline. Moreover, if the United States makes unequivocally clear that it expects the larger responsibilities Japan is assuming in Asia to be political and economic, not military, Japanese (as well as Chinese and Soviet) suspicions that their government is being pushed to assume military commitments outside Japan will be reduced.

The Security Treaty

The nucleus of support in Japan for the security treaty is an influential group of LDP politicians, businessmen, bureaucrats, and scholars. While public attitudes toward the treaty swing widely in response to transient events, the support of this group for the treaty has remained steadfast over the years. Their continuing support will hinge on their confidence in the U.S. commitment to aid in Japan's defense, and on their ability to justify continuation of the treaty in the face of attacks from the opposition and the media. Their trust in the defense commitment will depend on the strength of the military force the United States maintains in Northeast Asia, and their success in supporting it on U.S. cooperation in deemphasizing military aspects of the treaty and easing the friction caused by U.S. bases in Japan.

The number, type, and disposition of the forces the United States needs to keep in Northeast Asia to maintain Japanese confidence in the U.S. defense commitment will vary with changes in political conditions in that area. Since 1950 the level of U.S. forces in the area has always been adequate to maintain Japanese confidence. The cease-fire in Indo-china and the general decline in international tension throughout the region provide an acceptable rationale for a large drawing down of forces in all of East Asia. Many Japanese, however, wonder how far the United States intends to go in this direction. Even if the United States and Japan continue to improve their relations with China and the USSR, some irreducible minimum of U.S. forces will be required in Northeast Asia throughout the 1970s if the confidence of Japanese leaders in the United States is to be maintained. That minimum probably will include some U.S. air power in Korea and both naval and air power in Japan, but no U.S. combat forces in Taiwan.

Close consultation between the United States and Japan does not mean that the Japanese should have veto power over the deployment of U.S. forces, except in Japanese territory. But if the primary purpose of keeping U.S. forces in Northeast Asia is to protect the U.S. relation with Japan, then it would make no sense to decide unilaterally on the deployment of U.S. forces, disregarding Japanese views and thus damaging the very interest those forces are there to protect.

To justify the continuation of the security treaty to the Japanese people and fend off opposition attacks, the Japanese government has taken steps to deemphasize its military aspects. The United States can strengthen their hand by avoiding actions or statements that highlight U.S. use of bases in Japan to support U.S. military forces elsewhere in East Asia and that provide ammunition to those Japanese who argue that the security treaty serves U.S., rather than Japanese, interests. Japanese governments can thus portray the treaty as a symbol of the broad interests that unite the two countries and as the bond that makes possible close cooperation in many fields. Emphasizing the importance of the relationship as a whole, rather than focusing narrowly on the military aspects of the security treaty, will help both governments demonstrate the reciprocity of the relationship—the United States assuming primary military responsibility, Japan primary responsibility for economic aid in the region.

Pressure to revise the security treaty will probably grow in Japan. This pressure may be mitigated by changes in interpretation and emphasis, but it may become strong enough to threaten the U.S.-Japanese relationship. In that event it would be advisable to renegotiate the treaty to reflect the changed international situation, as perceived by the majority of Americans and Japanese.

The U.S. bases in Japan are a more visible and vulnerable target for opposition attack than the security treaty itself. Pressures will be reduced if the U.S. and Japanese governments can agree on a continuing program for reducing and consolidating bases. The pace of the reduction will probably have to be accelerated, unless tension in the region mounts again. If the United States moves too slowly in response to official Japanese requests to retrench the U.S. base system in Japan, disputes between the two governments over the rate or manner of retrenchment could quickly become public. The sharper they became, the more they would feed anti-Americanism and weaken the Japanese government's efforts to maintain support for the security treaty. If disputes over bases are not to poison overall relations, the U.S. and Japanese governments will need to keep ahead of the tide of Japanese opinion on this issue, as they did on the Okinawa reversion issue, reaching agreement in time to vent pressures before they reach an explosive state.

It seems probable that, for this decade at least, Japanese pressures for reducing U.S. bases in Japan will stop short of including the U.S. Seventh Fleet.[14] Provision of the shore facilities for this chief symbol of U.S. military power in the western Pacific and for its associated air and logistic units is likely to remain more tolerable psychologically to the Japanese than the presence of other U.S. military forces now based in Japan.

The U.S. government is likely to encounter problems also in maintaining support among the American people for even a greatly reduced U.S. military presence in Northeast Asia. Criticism of Japan for taking a "free ride" at the expense of the American taxpayer, burdened by a

14. Kunio Muraoka, a Japanese diplomat, argues that the "emergency deployment" formula is the most probable and desirable form of security relationship for the United States and Japan in the future, because it would be less provocative to the Soviet Union and China and it would remove a destabilizing factor from domestic Japanese politics. He seems to assume that U.S. forces, including Seventh Fleet bases, could be removed from Japan without being removed entirely from the western Pacific (presumably by retaining U.S. forces in Korea and the Philippines), for he also argues that "the withdrawal of all U.S. forces west of Hawaii" would probably push Japan toward "extreme nationalism," very likely leading to a Japanese nuclear force. *Japanese Security and the United States*, Adelphi Papers 95 (London: International Institute for Strategic Studies, 1973), pp. 10–11. It seems unrealistic to assume that the United States would wish to maintain U.S. forces in forward positions in the western Pacific such as Korea or the Philippines without at least some supporting base in Japan.

heavy defense budget, probably will increase. This criticism would be blunted if the Japanese government could show that the Japanese tax-payer is also bearing a sizable burden in overseas economic aid which contributes indirectly to the security of the region. Many Japanese recognize that Japanese official economic aid should be increased; one proposal suggests a tenfold increase, from the 1972 level of 0.21 percent of GNP to 2 percent, as a kind of substitute for the military responsibili-ties that Japan is barred from undertaking.[15] A leap of this magnitude probably is impractical, especially in light of the oil crisis, but a dramatic move is badly needed, both to spur economic development in East Asia and as a means of strengthening American support for the security treaty.

Coping with Economic Problems

During the remainder of this decade, all highly industrialized coun-tries will confront the problems of assuring reliable access to supplies of raw materials and food, modifying the rules governing world trade to assure its continued expansion, and reforming the monetary system. Each of these problems is exceedingly complex and difficult.

The oil crisis has demonstrated the acute need for international ar-rangements to assure both reliable, adequate supplies to the consumers and a sufficient price to the producers. Japan's heavy dependence on oil, the bulk of it supplied through U.S. companies, predisposes Japan toward seeking a multilateral solution to its problem, concerting in the first instance with the United States. But if the United States, confident in its own relatively strong energy position, should be unsympathetic to Japanese difficulties, the Japanese might have to turn at great cost to independent bilateral arrangements and U.S.-Japanese relations would be severely strained.

Oil is the most immediate problem, but the need to assure orderly supply, marketing, and price arrangements for other primary products will increase. For example, the sudden U.S. decision in June 1973 to restrict the export of soybeans caused great alarm in Japan, which depends on the United States for 90 percent of its imports of this essen-tial food. Although it later proved possible to meet basic Japanese needs, the brusqueness with which the restrictions were first applied

15. Yonosuke Nagai, "Politics and the Economy in Multipolar Diplomacy," *Chuo Koron*, July 1973. See *Summaries of Selected Japanese Magazines* (Tokyo: U.S. Embassy), July 1973, p. 34.

provoked resentment and strengthened the view in Japan that it should not rely so heavily on the United States for critical imports.

International commodity agreements and reserve stockpiles of basic foodstuffs could assure producers of reliable markets and consumers of reliable access to supplies. Both the United States and Japan have a strong interest in working out arrangements with the European Community and some of the developing countries covering basic foodstuffs and other important primary products whose wide fluctuations in price have disruptive economic effects. Without multilateral agreements of this sort, friction between the United States and Japan over access to primary commodities seems certain to grow.

New negotiations under the General Agreement on Tariffs and Trade will provide an opportunity to improve trading conditions between the United States and Japan. Japan will no longer be reluctant to offer cuts in its own tariffs as it was during the Kennedy Round. The United States will have an interest in agreements that will open European markets wider to Japanese products, now that Japan can no longer be fairly regarded as a low-wage producer. On industrial tariff issues, as well as on the issues of export controls and import safeguards, Japan's interests have moved close to those of the United States and Western Europe. Revised GATT agreements that encouraged the continued growth of world trade would not only serve the interests of the three major industrial centers, but would help to moderate economic differences between the United States and Japan.

With respect to monetary reform, Japan is unlikely to wish to return to the rigid system of the past, which led to the rapid accumulation of overly large foreign exchange reserves. Like the United States, Japan is likely to prefer a system that will permit considerable exchange-rate flexibility in order to avoid the recurrent crises that have plagued the world monetary system. The United States and Japan may not easily agree on the details of a new system, but these two great trading nations have a fundamental common interest in multilateral agreement on a workable system.

In the future the strain on the U.S.-Japanese relationship is likely to arise less from the actual economic effects of U.S. or Japanese economic policies than from the political repercussions of the mishandling of particular economic problems on one side or the other, or the failure to understand and take account of the pressures of domestic politics in each country.

Economic issues could exacerbate fundamental differences over political and security issues; the manner in which the governments handle these differences will therefore be important. Both must recognize their overriding broad common interests, working to devise ways to take account of short-term domestic political considerations. If both governments take the task seriously, they will try to prevent differences being blown up out of proportion by the public media and special interest groups. They will study each other's domestic politics to gain a better understanding of what can and cannot be accomplished in bargaining over economic issues.

Increasingly, however, economic issues will have to be resolved in a multilateral framework. The bilateral concert will be replaced by close working relations among all three of the industrial centers, which will need to concert on key economic issues. Recognition of this need, in both Japan and the United States, will be the key to avoidance of economic differences between the two countries.

It will be difficult, however, to maintain the close association between the United States and Japan during the transition from a bipolar world dominated by the containment concept to a more complicated four-power equilibrium in East Asia, maintained in part by military power but increasingly by other elements of national power as U.S. and Japanese relations with the two communist powers multiply. To prevent the erosion of the U.S.-Japanese connection in this complicated and confusing new environment, it will be essential both to recognize the overriding importance of the connection and to reshape it to fit changing circumstances. The greatest difficulties may be encountered in searching for a mutually acceptable means of sharing burdens in East Asia in which Japanese economic aid contributions will be recognized as compensation for Japan's inability to assume military responsibilities in the region. Such a sharing of burdens is most likely to be acceptable to Americans if the policy of expanding relations with the USSR and China continues to permit a decline in U.S. military burdens in the region. Were tension to rise, requiring heavier U.S. military outlays, it would be difficult to persuade the American public and Congress that they should remain content to assure the defense of Japan without substantially greater Japanese defense contributions—even though massive Japanese armaments probably would accelerate rather than reverse the trend toward higher tension and greater danger of conflict among the big powers.

CHAPTER SEVEN

Expanding Relations with China

The alternating love-hate attitude Americans have had over the years toward China has tended to be the obverse of their regard for Japan; when U.S. relations with the one were good, relations with the other were bad.[1] The United States may still be on that seesaw, for relations with Japan have deteriorated since 1970, while relations with China have improved. In this decade serious deterioration of U.S. relations with Japan would endanger U.S. security in the 1980s far more than would failure to make headway in improving relations with China.

The View from Peking

The view that Chinese leaders take of the world has been strongly influenced by China's size, history, and potential power. Historically, the Chinese have seen themselves as the center of the world, surrounded by lesser peoples. The long, continuous history of the Chinese nation, the breadth of its territory, and the size of its population combined to give the Chinese the feeling of a people apart. For centuries they lived in a self-contained world, needing little from the outside. They developed a sense of invulnerability as a people and a readiness to take the long view of world events.

The humiliation of China for a century by Western powers, and most recently by its smaller neighbor Japan, temporarily shook these basic beliefs of the Chinese and undermined their self-confidence, but it did not alter the facts. The Chinese remained the largest body politic in the

1. See Harold Isaacs, *Images of Asia* (Harper and Row, 1972), pp. xiii–xxiii and 71.

world, held together by a common culture. They might be temporarily "a pan of loose sand," as Sun Yat-sen called them, but both noncommunists and communists firmly believed that the Chinese people, once properly organized and led, could resume their place as one of the leading nations, if not the leading nation, on the globe.

Consequently, the Chinese Communists came to power with a strong sense of China's potentiality for greatness and a burning desire to expunge its past humiliations. They wanted to demonstrate to the world that China had "stood up," and they had learned that to do this China must be able to rely on its own military strength. Out of this heritage grew the Chinese leaders' deep suspicions of the other big powers, their determination to have modern weapons, their insistence that China be treated as a great power, their confidence that time is on their side.

The revolutionary doctrine preached from Peking fits and reinforces the traditional world view of the Chinese. The doctrine is drawn from China's own revolutionary experience, which Mao seeks to apply universally. According to this doctrine China is the leader of the dispossessed masses of the world and the true interpreter of Marxism-Leninism. China serves as an invulnerable rear area supporting revolutionaries in the developing countries. Although China's example and support are essential to the success of revolution throughout the world, the burden of the protracted struggle must be borne by the people of each developing country as they adapt the Chinese experience to their own special circumstances. Eventually, the oppressed populations of the industrialized states, sympathizing with China, will rise up and overthrow their governments, thus bringing about the total victory of the world communist revolution.

For the Chinese, Peking's revolutionary doctrine proves that China is not just a passive receiver of modern Western culture, but an innovator, carrying on China's traditional role of spreading its influence outward. It gives China a place in the scheme of things worthy of its size and past greatness. Chinese leaders can brush aside as temporary aberrations facts apparently inconsistent with the doctrine, because they believe history is on their side.

China's revolutionary doctrine is tempered, however, by the hard facts of international politics. Chinese leaders see world communist revolution as a long-drawn-out process that requires many temporary compromises and both advances and retreats along the road. Consequently, Peking's revolutionary rhetoric is not a reliable guide to the day-to-day conduct of Chinese foreign affairs. China's foreign policy decisions, although influenced by the ideological predispositions of Chinese leaders, seem to be based on calculations of economic, political, and strategic interests not unlike those that shape the policies of the other big powers. China's size and potential power, together with the remarkable personal qualities of the architect of its foreign policy, Premier Chou En-lai, have permitted it to conduct a vigorous foreign policy befitting its great-power aspirations, despite persisting weakness in its power base.

For China is not today a superpower nor is it likely to become one during this decade. Its ability to exert influence abroad by military or economic means or by promoting revolution is severely limited, and the continued stability of its domestic political base is by no means certain.

Chinese Military Power

China's armed forces judged against those of the superpowers are weak[2] in their ability to fight beyond national borders or to deter or defend against nuclear attack or even a large-scale conventional attack with limited objectives. China is strong, however, in defense against a conventional attack aimed at total defeat or occupation of China. It is strong, even in offensive power, compared to the lesser powers on its periphery. Its strength relative to that of the superpowers seems unlikely to change much in the next decade, except for improvements in its small nuclear deterrent force.

China's defensive strength rests mainly on the size of the country (much of it rugged terrain), the paucity of roads and railroads, and the large population. Chinese regular forces could harass an invader and make his advance costly, but they are short of the air power, armor, and mechanized equipment necessary to defeat and drive back a well-prepared assault. They also lack tactical nuclear weapons. Moreover, their industry could not long replace the heavy weapons lost in large-scale modern warfare. Consequently, the Chinese count on drawing an invader into the interior of the country and wearing him down through attacks by millions of guerrillas, combined with delaying actions by the

2. The most authoritative comparison of the armed forces of the nations is International Institute for Strategic Studies, *The Military Balance, 1972–73* (London: International Institute, 1972).

regular forces. One of the principal aims since the clashes with the Russians on the Ussuri River in 1969 seems to be the strengthening of China's ability to fight this kind of war. Provinces are to be made self-sufficient and forces are to be deployed to defend each military region as a separate redoubt, rather than to defend a strong forward line near the frontier.

There is abundant evidence in Chinese military doctrine, equipment production, and deployment of forces that their military aims are primarily defensive. While they have the means to launch a spoiling attack, as they did in Korea when they saw their border threatened, there is little evidence that they could sustain a campaign far beyond their borders or that they are improving their forces for such actions. They lack the navy, air force, and logistic capability to campaign overseas. They could carry on large-scale operations near their borders, as in Korea or Thailand, but neither their propaganda nor their military dispositions and preparations along the border suggest any long-range preparations for such offensive military operations.

During the coming decade the Chinese will improve their ability to manufacture modern weapons, but probably will not be able to reduce the gap between the equipment of their forces and those of the United States and the Soviet Union. Their most significant advance will be in nuclear weapons. Although their development of missiles has been slower than predicted by U.S. officials in the late 1960s, they have begun to deploy missiles with ranges of 600 to 2,500 miles and perhaps by the late 1970s they will have deployed a few intercontinental missiles also. Most of those already in place are in soft sites where they are vulnerable to a first strike by a superpower.[3] The Chinese are also manufacturing a version of the Soviet TU-16 medium jet bomber, which can deliver nuclear weapons at a 1,500-mile range.[4]

In any nuclear exchange in this decade, China would be devastated and its opponent only moderately damaged. But even "moderate" damage could mean millions of fatalities. The United States and the Soviet Union have in the strategic arms limitation agreement chosen to forgo the very costly antiballistic missile systems that could theoretically

3. Melvin R. Laird, *Annual Defense Department Report, FY 1973*, U.S. Department of Defense (January 1972), p. 46; Thomas H. Moorer, *United States Military Posture for FY 1974*, U.S. Department of Defense (March 1973), p. 26; and *New York Times*, March 4, 1973, and July 2, 1973.

4. *New York Times*, Sept. 18, 1970, quoting "highly reliable U.S. sources."

destroy most Chinese missiles in flight. They are relying on their preponderant nuclear power to deter any Chinese use of nuclear weapons. They probably recognize that even an extensive ABM system could not prevent heavy casualties in a nuclear exchange. Consequently, the possibility that China could hit even one or two American or Russian cities with nuclear weapons will serve as a deterrent. It will make both superpowers cautious about getting into a war with China.

The Chinese are not likely to threaten use of nuclear weapons to force their nonnuclear neighbors to agree to their demands. Any such Chinese threat would necessarily transform the attitudes of both the United States and the USSR toward China. To allow Chinese nuclear blackmail to succeed in one case would improve the chances for further successes, posing serious threats to U.S. and Soviet interests. So far the Chinese have shown no tendency to brandish nuclear weapons to intimidate neighbors. On the contrary, they have declared repeatedly that they would never be the first to use nuclear weapons. It seems improbable that they would abandon this position on the strength of a very small nuclear force and expose themselves to the greater dangers and uncertainties that would inevitably ensue.

Because of their relative weakness in both conventional and nuclear weapons, the Chinese are likely to continue their cautious and predominantly defensive strategy, unless they should perceive China's vital interests threatened by a major power, as in Korea in 1950.

Chinese Economic Influence

A striking feature of China's role in international affairs is the small size of its foreign trade. So far China has failed to bear out the hope of those who see it as a vast market. The total two-way foreign trade of its 750 million people in 1972 was only $5.7 billion, approximately the size of Singapore's and less than Hong Kong's $7.4 billion trade. In world trade China is not in the league with the Soviet Union ($32 billion), Japan ($52 billion), or the United States ($105 billion).[5]

Moreover, during the 1960s when world trade was growing at

5. A useful brief description of China's foreign trade is A. H. Usack and R. E. Batsavage, "The International Trade of the People's Republic of China," in Joint Economic Committee, *People's Republic of China: An Economic Assessment,* 92 Cong. 2 sess. (1972), pp. 335–70.

8 percent annually and Japan's trade at 16 percent, China's grew not at all. In 1970 it was not quite as high as in 1959. It had dropped sharply as a result of the combined effects of bad weather, the failure of the Great Leap Forward, and the withdrawal of Soviet technicians. Though by 1966 it had recovered to the 1959 level, it dropped again because of the Cultural Revolution. In 1971 China's foreign trade increased about 7 percent and in 1972 close to 16 percent.[6]

The main reason for the small size of China's foreign trade is not a lack of resources or the poverty of the Chinese people, but Peking's official policy of maximum self-reliance. China has not, like Japan, South Korea, Hong Kong, or Taiwan, with their fast-growing economies, pushed exports as a means of acquiring imports needed for rapid economic growth. It has not, like Indonesia or the Soviet Union, solicited foreign capital to develop and export on a large scale its natural resources. Neither has it sought long-term foreign credits since it broke with the USSR and paid back the Soviet loans received in the 1950s. And it has been slow to emulate Japan's success in getting advanced foreign techniques through licensing arrangements with foreign firms.

China's policy of autarky stems in part from xenophobia, from the memory of past humiliation by Western trading powers, and from pride in the Chinese tradition of self-sufficiency. It also results from sad experience with the USSR and a consequent determination to be as invulnerable as possible to outside economic pressures. It suits the Maoist emphasis on political and social goals[7] and the desire to make each region and province self-sufficient in order to diminish the role of the central bureaucracy and to make it easier to defend China by means of "people's war." And it avoids the exposure of large numbers of Chinese to outside ideas that a large export effort would require.

The small size of its foreign trade severely limits China's ability to exert political influence either through trade or through economic aid. It can gain some advantage from projects like the Tan-Zam railway and from its no-interest loans, but it cannot compete quantitatively with the United States, the larger European nations, the USSR, or Japan.

---

6. *Japan Times Weekly*, Sept. 15, 1973, p. 8. The 1972 figure is reported as 25 percent, but that exaggerates the increase, because of the devaluation of the dollar.

7. See Dwight Perkins, "Mao Tse-tung's Goals and China's Economic Performance," *Current Scene*, Jan. 7, 1971.

China's export trade provides almost no political leverage, except for such goodwill as might be gained from offering items at less than world prices as a form of economic aid. No country is heavily dependent on Chinese exports except Hong Kong, which could obtain what it needed elsewhere, although at a somewhat higher price. China gains a little more leverage from its import trade: the lure of its "vast market," which is always ahead of its performance, the ability to purchase goods that bulk large in the production of particular states (wheat from Australia or Canada, rubber from Malaysia or Ceylon), and the threat of denying its market to states or firms that China wishes to influence. Only in Japan has China used this last, rather crude form of political pressure,[8] and there is no reason to believe it is likely to use trade extensively for political ends in the future.

China might, of course, abandon its policy of autarky during this decade and aim to become one of the world's principal trading powers. It is much better endowed with natural resources than Japan and its people are as industrious and intelligent as the Japanese. The remarkable success of Chinese emigrants to Taiwan, Hong Kong, and throughout Southeast Asia demonstrates how effectively Chinese can compete in the world market when they have freedom to exercise their talent for commerce. There are signs that Peking intends to substantially increase its foreign trade. Its initial export of 1 million tons of oil to Japan in 1973 may be increased to as much as 5 million tons in 1974.[9] It is stepping up its purchases of whole plants on deferred-payment (five- to seven-year) terms, and has begun to dispatch technical missions abroad in growing numbers; Chinese publications refer increasingly to the importance of export trade and the induction of foreign technology.

If the Chinese should seek increasing amounts of medium-term credits and abandon their past practice of balancing imports and exports, their foreign trade could surge perhaps as much as 20–30 percent annually for several years. But the growth rate could only be sustained by a radical change in their foreign trade policies: accepting long-term loans, exporting natural resources on a large scale, or greatly increasing their export of labor-intensive light manufactures.

8. See Bernard Grossman, "International Economic Relations of the People's Republic of China," *Asian Survey*, vol. 9 (September 1970), pp. 789–802.

9. This would supply only a tiny fraction of Japan's consumption, which amounted to 200 millions tons in 1972.

A fundamental question for Chinese leaders is whether the openness to outside influence that would have to accompany such a change would be compatible with the ideological controls demanded by China's totalitarian system. China's present leaders may be unwilling to risk so radical a change. Should Mao's successors turn away from some of the basic values of Maoism, China could emerge as a great trading nation. But not within this decade. China is starting from such a low base that the absolute gap between the volume of its foreign trade and that of Japan will continue to expand for a long time, whatever policies the Chinese may adopt. During the two years, 1971 and 1972, while China's foreign trade was increasing by $1.5 billion, Japan's world trade increased by $14 billion.[10]

Domestic Stability in China

China's influence in world affairs in this decade will depend in part on its internal stability. In the past whenever sharp differences arose among China's leaders—as at the time of the Great Leap Forward or the Cultural Revolution—Chinese influence abroad declined. Not only did domestic turmoil tarnish their image abroad, but Chinese leaders became so preoccupied with the internal struggle that they had less time and energy to spend on the effort to influence the outside world.

China could suffer an upheaval in the 1970s comparable to those that occurred in each of the first two decades of the existence of the People's Republic. The authority of the Communist party, badly undermined during the Cultural Revolution, is being restored. Visitors to China in 1972 and 1973 saw an orderly and disciplined society. Yet China's future is more uncertain than at any time in the past twenty years. In 1973 Mao Tse-tung reached the age of eighty and his indispensable lieutenant, Chou En-lai, became seventy-five. No one, not even Chou, has the prestige that Mao has been able to invoke to maintain his power. Mao's attempt to designate a successor and thus provide for a smooth

10. Figures on China's trade from "China's Foreign Trade in 1971," *Current Scene*, vol. 10 (October 1972), p. 1, and U.S. Department of State; on Japan's trade from International Monetary Fund/International Bank for Reconstruction and Development (IMF/IBRD), *Direction of Trade Annual, 1966–70*, p. 145, and *Direction of Trade, December 1973*, p. 29.

transfer of power at his death failed twice. Liu Shao-chi, whom Mao had elevated to the number two position in the Chinese Communist party during the 1950s, was attacked and destroyed politically by Mao during the Cultural Revolution, with the help of Defense Minister Lin Piao. Then Lin himself, named in the 1969 party constitution as Mao's successor, apparently attempted to mount a coup against Mao in 1971 and, according to Peking, was killed in a plane crash in Mongolia while fleeing to the Soviet Union. The aging Chou En-lai thus moved into the exposed number two position.

The uncertainty about the succession is compounded by the fact that the top leadership of the party was heavily purged in the course of the Cultural Revolution, then purged again as a result of the Lin Piao affair. At the tenth party congress in August 1973, which elected a new politburo and central committee, filling the numerous vacancies created by the purges, Chou En-lai warned that intraparty conflict would continue for a long time to come. Hardly had the Congress delegates returned home before a new political campaign spread across the country, ostensibly aimed at denouncing Confucius and Lin Piao, but bearing telltale signs of unresolved differences among party leaders. Chou may gradually overcome the traumatic effects of the severe party struggles and prepare the way for an orderly succession. But whether he will survive Mao; whether the transition will be prolonged and bitter or relatively smooth; how stable the new, probably collective, leadership will be are unanswerable questions that highlight the uncertainty of China's political future.

China's Political Influence

A nation's influence in the world arises only in part from its military and economic strength. Prestige, moral authority, and skilled diplomacy can give its policies a thrust exceeding the sum of its tangible instruments of power. To a great extent a state's ability to affect the course of world affairs grows out of its talent for identifying its own interests with those of other nations or influential groups therein. Its influence also depends on its leaders' ability to perceive broad trends in international relations and to move with the tide rather than against it.

The Chinese have asserted that the main trend in the world today is revolution and that revolution to be successful must be violent.[11] Their espousal of world revolution is an important instrument of their foreign policy. Their own revolution serves as a model for developing countries, and they provide textbooks for applying that model and offer to help those who would replace established governments with Maoist systems. Supporting revolutionaries is an inexpensive and low-risk means of making Chinese influence felt; the constraints that impose caution on China's use of its armed forces abroad do not apply.[12]

But the only revolutionary whom the Chinese have been notably successful in helping to power thus far is Ho Chi-minh. He qualified for large amounts of Chinese aid by demonstrating an impressive ability to organize the population of Vietnam to fight the French. Elsewhere the Chinese have not been lavish providers of aid. They doubtless believe their own maxim that successful rebels must rely for support on the people among whom they live and must be willing to wage protracted war. Nothing in Chinese Communist writings supports the view that foreign aid could provide a shortcut to revolutionary success. If a Southeast Asian communist leader could duplicate Ho's feat of organizing and inspiring large numbers of people to make revolution, the Chinese would be inclined to provide large amounts of aid—especially to rebels in adjacent Thailand or Burma—but Ho's example is not an easy one to follow.

Thus, although the leaders of China are revolutionaries—and there

11. The following authoritative pronouncement appeared in joint editorials of the *People's Daily, Red Flag,* and the *Liberation Army Daily* on March 17, 1971: "Violent revolution is the universal experience of proletarian revolution. . . . Historical experience shows that the seizure of political power by the proletariat and the oppressed people of a country and the seizure of victory in their revolution are accomplished invariably by the power of the gun; they are accomplished under the leadership of a proletarian party, by acting in accordance with that country's specific conditions, by gradually building up the people's armed forces and fighting a people's war on the basis of arousing the broad masses to action, and by waging repeated struggles against the imperialists and reactionaries. This is true of the Russian revolution, the Chinese revolution and the revolutions of Albania, Vietnam, Korea and other countries, and there is no exception." *Peking Review,* March 19, 1971, p. 5.

12. Thomas Robinson, "Peking's Revolutionary Strategy in the Developing World," *Annals of the American Academy of Political and Social Science,* vol. 386 (November 1969), pp. 64–77, concludes that the constraints on Chinese support for revolutions abroad are considerable. His stress on economic weakness seems an error, however, because the material needs of revolutionaries are very small relative to Chinese resources.

is no reason to doubt their sincere dedication to world revolution—their opportunities to move toward their long-term goal by direct aid to revolutionaries in other countries are limited. For the most part they must pursue their national purposes through the more conventional methods of state-to-state relations.[13] Their ability to function simultaneously on two levels—the diplomatic and the subversive—gives them added leverage on foreign governments in some circumstances. Only great skill and a profound understanding of the internal political dynamics of foreign states, however, can prevent gains on one level from being offset by losses on the other. China's two-level policies can easily backfire—and frequently have done so.

Although Peking in its foreign policy has always emphasized state-to-state relations (with the possible exception of the most frenzied phase of the Cultural Revolution, when diplomatic relations were largely in abeyance and revolutionary rhetoric reached new heights), the relative emphasis on support for revolution has varied. Since 1970 the pendulum has swung away from revolution. One evidence of this shift is Peking's highly successful drive to expand its diplomatic relations around the world, which was given great impetus by the seating of the People's Republic of China in the United Nations in October 1971. From late 1970 to early 1973 Peking established diplomatic relations with thirty-six nations, making a total of eighty-six with which it had such relations.

Peking's attitude toward the governments of those Southeast Asian states where Peking-backed insurrections are under way is also shifting. For example, Burma's Ne Win, who only a few years before had been excoriated in the Chinese press as the running dog of American imperialists and Soviet revisionists, made a state visit to Peking in 1971. Malaysia established diplomatic relations with China in 1974, and various types of contact and feelers have also begun between Peking and the governments of Thailand and the Philippines. Peking has not ended its support of revolution in these states, but it has turned from treating the governments as enemies of China to cultivating them.

The most striking evidence of Peking's increased emphasis on diplomacy, however, is its change of policy toward the United States.

13. Peter Van Ness, in *Revolution and Chinese Foreign Policy* (University of California Press, 1970), concludes that the most important factor determining the Chinese attitude toward a particular government is the degree to which that government agrees with China on foreign policy, not the prospects for revolution within that state.

At one stroke this new departure strengthened China's position relative to the Soviet Union, improved its prospects for normalizing relations with Japan on satisfactory terms, assured its seating in the United Nations, gained it greater influence in world councils, and set in motion a rapid erosion of the international position of the Republic of China on Taiwan. At the same time, however, this action weakened Peking's position as the champion of world revolution and made less plausible its attacks on the Soviet Union as a backslider for collaborating with the United States. By deciding to improve relations with the United States, the Chinese chose to give up some of their influence with revolutionaries in order to gain greater influence on governments.

The obstacles to China's making its influence felt can be only partially overcome by the prestige conferred on it by its size, its nuclear weapons, and its considerable skill in the diplomatic arts. In the 1970s it will be neither a military nor an economic superpower. It will gain some leverage from its reputation as a new and attractive social order, but its political influence may be impaired again by domestic troubles, this time brought on by a struggle for succession. Opportunities for Peking to help communist revolutionaries seize power probably will be few, for evolutionary change—accompanied by sporadic outbursts of violence—seems more the world trend than the seizure of power following the classic Chinese Communist pattern. Although Peking may attempt to mobilize the medium-sized and small countries of the world under its leadership, its ability to do so will be severely limited by clashes of national interest among these countries. Peking's failure to impose its views on the states planning the abortive second Bandung conference in Algiers in 1965 demonstrates the difficulty of using the developing countries to serve Chinese purposes. China's influence in world affairs in the 1970s is likely to depend more on its ability to identify its interests with those of other big powers than to promote revolution or to command a distinctly Chinese-oriented group of powers.

China's limited influence when standing alone was highlighted during the Cultural Revolution. At the outset of this curious episode in the life of the People's Republic of China, Foreign Minister Ch'en Yi proclaimed defiantly: "If the American imperialists have decided to launch a war of aggression against us, we hope that they will come, and the sooner the better. Let them then come tomorrow! Let the Indian reactionaries, the British imperialists, and the Japanese militarists come with them! Let the modern revisionists support them in the North! We will finish nevertheless by triumphing."[14] China's self-sufficiency and great defensive capability put it in a better position than any other country to throw out such a challenge—but even for China, going it alone proved an ineffective way to advance national interests.

Only by aligning itself to some degree with other states—particularly the larger and more influential—can China effectively achieve its national purposes. Mao's writings recognize this in their call to "unite with all forces that can be united." An important article published not long after the announcement of President Nixon's intended visit to China draws analogies with the use of united front tactics in the war against Japan, and emphasizes the importance of distinguishing between the "primary enemy" and the "secondary enemy," "temporary allies" and "indirect allies."[15] It calls for "waging all kinds of struggles in a flexible way" in order to make use of the four major contradictions—between the oppressed nations and imperialism and social-imperialism (the USSR); between the proletariat and the bourgeoisie in the capitalist and revisionist (USSR) countries; between imperialist nations and social-imperialist nations and among imperialist nations; and between the socialist nations (China) and imperialism and social-imperalism.

The article goes on to point out that although "U.S. imperialism and social-imperialism" are both collaborating and competing with each other, their contradictions are irreconcilable and daily becoming more acute. In order to take advantage of these contradictions, it is necessary to unite all forces that can be united. But the united front is

neither all alliance and no struggle nor all struggle and no alliance, but combines alliance and struggle. . . . The dual policy of alliance and struggle is built on the dual character of all allies in the united front. . . . If we only think of struggle without unity, we will not be able to unite with the forces that can be united, or to consolidate and develop the united front. We will not be able to force our principal enemy into a narrow and isolated position, and our struggle against the enemy will not be successful.

Obviously, so complex a picture of political forces, both within and between nations, can be used to justify all kinds of twists and turns in policy. This article was widely disseminated in Chinese media in the summer of 1971, perhaps with the immediate purpose of explaining

14. Press conference, Sept. 29, 1965, quoted in O. Edmund Clubb, *China and Russia: The Great Game* (Columbia University Press, 1971), p. 478.

15. *Red Flag;* see U.S. Government, Foreign Broadcast Information Service (FBIS), *Daily Report: People's Republic of China,* Aug. 18, 1971, pp. B1–B7.

President Nixon's forthcoming visit, but also probably for the more general purpose of justifying the flexibility that will be required in the years ahead.

There are, of course, limits on the extent to which the Chinese might wish to align their policies with others of the Big Four. The main content of Sino-Japanese relations in this decade is more likely to be rivalry than cooperation. Rapprochement with the United States is limited by the Taiwan problem, by deep ideological differences, and by conflicting positions on many world issues. And a far-reaching rapprochement between Moscow and Peking is unlikely.

Sino-Soviet Relations

China's relations with the Soviet Union differ basically from its relations with Japan or the United States because of their dispute over ideological orthodoxy and, especially, their geographical proximity. China and the USSR confront each other directly along a 4,500-mile border. There is no sea or neutral state between them to serve as buffer. Outer Mongolia could theoretically serve as a buffer along part of the border, but the Soviet Union has assimilated the China-Outer Mongolia border into its own defenses. Moreover, for each of the governments the border is exceptionally sensitive because the disaffection of the minority nationalities along the border can be exploited by a hostile power. Thus, for the Chinese, territorial issues are a major point of dispute with the Russians, whereas with the Japanese they are a minor issue (for example, the Senkaku Islands), and with the United States no issue at all.

The border disputes between China and Russia over large areas revolve around the justness of the treaties by which Tsarist Russia annexed parts of Siberia. The two also contest over relatively small pieces of territory of little intrinsic importance to either country. If relations between them were reasonably good, these border demarcation disputes could be resolved without much difficulty. Because of their profound suspicion and mistrust of each other, however, serious military clashes can flare up over these disputed bits of territory, as occurred on Damansky Island (Chen Pao Tao) in the Ussuri River in March 1969. As to the large areas, the Chinese, in a government statement of October 8, 1969, formally declared that they "had never demanded the return" of the territory annexed by the tsars.[16] They have, however, insisted that the Soviet Union acknowledge the "unequal" nature of the treaties by which Russia obtained it—which the USSR refuses to do. China is too weak militarily for its implied claim to Soviet territory to threaten the Soviet Union today—but so long as the Chinese maintain their position, the Russians must look to the future, when the Chinese will be much stronger and their numerical advantage even greater than it is today.

Tension over the border dispute has declined since the high point of 1969. Moscow no longer floats veiled threats to wipe out China's nuclear facilities in a preemptive strike. Ambassadors have returned to their posts in Moscow and Peking. But negotiations on border problems, which began in October 1969, have made no apparent progress. Polemics continue. Mutual suspicion does not seem to have diminished, nor does either side appear to feel under pressure to make significant concessions. The Soviet Union continues the strengthening of its forces along the border begun in the mid-sixties, although at a slower pace. China continues building an extensive system of air raid shelters throughout the country and pursues its program of local self-sufficiency aimed at improving the nation's capacity to fight a "people's war" against an invader.

The other singular aspect of Peking's rivalry with Moscow is the dispute over the leadership of the world communist movement. The two have engaged in hot debate over points of doctrine and a fierce struggle for predominant influence over communist parties throughout the world. And the ideological conflict has tended to intensify conflict over national interests. Leaders on each side, accused of heresy by the other and faced with dissidence in their own camp, have stirred up nationalistic feelings to strengthen their position. Consequently, this dispute is so basic as to be almost impossible to resolve. The Chinese government has admitted "that there exist irreconcilable differences of principle between China and the Soviet Union and that the struggle of principle between them will continue for a long period of time."[17]

The contest for national advantage has left the Chinese with a long litany of grievances against the USSR: inadequate Soviet economic and military aid, abrupt withdrawal of Soviet technicians in 1960, cancellation of the Soviet agreement to provide China with the technical knowl-

16. *New York Times*, Oct. 8, 1969.
17. Ibid.

edge for manufacturing nuclear weapons, Soviet support of India against China, Soviet unwillingness to confront the United States militarily (in Cuba, Lebanon, and the offshore islands—1958), and alleged Soviet collaboration with the United States against China, especially in signing the nuclear test-ban and nonproliferation treaties. These and many other concrete points of friction have added to the burden of Chinese antagonism toward the Russians.

The Soviets have their own list of complaints against the Chinese:

Speaking bluntly, what does Peking's foreign policy amount to today? It amounts to absurd claims to Soviet territory, to malicious slander of the Soviet social and political system, of our peace-loving foreign policy. It amounts to undisguised sabotage of the efforts to limit the arms race and of the struggle for disarmament and for a relaxation of international tension. It amounts to continuous attempts to split the socialist camp and the communist movement, to foment discord among the fighters for national liberation, to range the developing countries against the Soviet Union and the other socialist states. Lastly, it amounts to unprincipled alignments on anti-Soviet grounds with any, even the most reactionary forces—the most rabid haters of the Soviet Union from among the English Tories or the revenge-seeking elements in the FRG, the Portuguese colonialists or the racists of South Africa.[18]

The combination of past grievances, border disputes, great-power rivalry, and competition for ideological leadership in the world has created great barriers to reconciliation. To these must be added personal antipathy between the leaders. It is hard to envisage significant rapprochement so long as Mao is the leader in China. Scathing Soviet personal attacks on him rule out deals with him. Mao, for his part, holds the Soviet leaders in at least equal contempt. He regards them as backsliders, who led the Soviet Union down the road of revisionism. He launched the Cultural Revolution in part to prevent China from following the Soviet example. The intensity of his hostility came out clearly in the spring of 1966 when Mao rejected a plea by the Japanese communist leader, Kenji Miyamoto, for united action by China and the Soviet Union in support of Vietnam.[19] He did this at a time when there was considerable evidence that China feared an open clash with the United States over Vietnam and when a degree of reconciliation with the Soviets could have been important to China's security.

18. President Leonid I. Brezhnev, reported in FBIS, *Daily Report: Soviet Union,* Dec. 22, 1972, p. AA23.

19. Clubb, *China and Russia,* p. 484.

Since the military clashes on the Ussuri River in 1969, Chinese leaders have become obsessed with their quarrel with the USSR. They have publicly identified the Soviet Union as China's "primary enemy" against which they will try to "unite all forces that can be united."[20] Not only has this Chinese view made possible the spectacular change in Chinese policy toward the United States and Japan, it has come to dominate all aspects of Chinese foreign policy. The North Atlantic Treaty Organization (NATO), the European Community, the U.S.-Japan security treaty, Japanese military forces—once objects of Chinese hostility—are now viewed benignly by China as checks on Soviet expansionism. Verbal clashes between China and the Soviet Union have become a prominent feature of debates in the United Nations. The Chinese regularly denounce Soviet moves toward closer relations with any nation in the arc from India to Japan as part of a Soviet scheme to encircle and contain China. No opportunity is lost to impress on the growing stream of visitors to China the military threat posed by Soviet forces along the Chinese border and the energy being devoted by the Chinese to digging air raid shelters and storing food to meet this threat.

If Mao's death brought to power leaders who favored better relations with the USSR, and if the Soviet Union should make conciliatory moves—particularly by reducing its military forces along the Chinese border—the intense hostility between Moscow and Peking could be moderated, and partial reconciliation between the two would be possible. But a return to the closeness of the early 1950s seems out of the question. The Chinese could no longer accept the role of junior partner and the Soviets would find it hard to treat the Chinese as equals. The unwillingness of the Chinese to become again economically and militarily dependent on the USSR would be matched by the unwillingness of the Russians to risk their own security for the sake of Chinese ambitions. Their long-term concern over territorial claims by an increasingly powerful China would cause the Russians to limit the supply of advanced technology to China. Moreover, they could never accept the Chinese version of historical determinism, while the pride of the

20. *Red Flag*, in FBIS, *Daily Report: People's Republic of China*, Aug. 18, 1971. A joint editorial in the *People's Daily*, *Red Flag*, and the *Liberation Army Daily* declared: "The Soviet revisionist renegade clique has further revealed its true colors of social-imperialism. With a growing appetite, it is reaching out its hands everywhere. It is even more deceitful than old-line imperialist countries and therefore more dangerous." Ibid., Oct. 2, 1972, p. B2.

Chinese and faith in their future would make it hard for them to abandon their concept of China as the leader of the world's dispossessed. Thus, although both China and the USSR could improve their positions in the four-power contest in East Asia by overcoming their differences and aligning their policies, the obstacles to their doing so are great.

U.S. Policy toward China

The United States and China are far apart in their declared positions on most major world issues. Finding common ground on arms control, the law of the sea, relations between developed and developing countries, or the desirability of armed revolution in large parts of the world is difficult. Fundamental differences on such broad issues will not, however, prevent the two countries from adopting parallel and mutually supportive policies on various occasions when tactical objectives coincide. Lasting improvement in U.S.-Chinese relations will require the more frequent adoption of parallel policies, as well as progress on strictly bilateral issues and the expansion of trade and travel. Prospects for improvement of U.S.-Chinese relations along all these lines will continue to be strongly affected by the state of Sino-Soviet relations.

The Sino-Soviet Conflict

The hostility between China and the Soviet Union created an exceptional opportunity for U.S. diplomatic initiatives, especially after the massive buildup of Soviet forces on the Chinese border and the bloody clashes on the Ussuri River had convinced Chinese leaders that the Soviets might be preparing for a large-scale attack on China. The Soviet military occupation of Czechoslovakia not long before the Ussuri incidents must have added to Chinese concern. But this was an opportunity that the United States had to handle with care. It could not afford to jeopardize its central task of making more stable the strategic balance between the United States and the USSR. The improvement of relations with China had to be managed so that it would neither interfere with progress on that task nor increase the risk of a Sino-Soviet war by giving added force to the arguments of those within the Soviet Union who might have been urging an early preemptive strike on Chinese nuclear facilities.

The United States' determination to strike a balance was spelled out early in the Nixon administration by Under Secretary of State Elliot Richardson:

In the case of Communist China, long-run improvement in our relations is in our own national interest. We do not seek to exploit for our own advantage the hostility between the Soviet Union and the People's Republic. Ideological differences between the two Communist giants are not our affair. We could not fail to be deeply concerned, however, with an escalation of this quarrel into a massive breach of international peace and security. Our national security would in the long run be prejudiced by associating ourselves with either side against the other. Each is highly sensitive about American efforts to improve relations with the other. We intend, nevertheless, to pursue a long-term course of progressively developing better relations with both. We are not going to let Communist Chinese invective deter us from seeking agreements with the Soviet Union where those are in our interest. Conversely, we are not going to let Soviet apprehensions prevent us from attempting to bring Communist China out of its angry, alienated shell.[21]

So far the policy of seeking improved relations with both Moscow and Peking has worked well, helped along by the removal of U.S. troops from combat in Vietnam and the international agreement on a cease-fire there. China has been surprisingly quick in moving to expand its relations with the United States. Meanwhile, relations between the United States and the USSR have also improved. These trends suggest that a certain pressure exists on each of the communist rivals to continue expanding relations with Washington, lest the other gain a lead.[22]

The United States had strong independent motives for wanting improved relations with both China and the USSR, whatever the relationship between the two might have been. Although the United States has benefited from the hostility between them, it had little to do with creating that hostility and there is no basis for believing that it could now play one of the rivals off against the other so as to maintain their mutual hostility to the continued advantage of the United States.

The estrangement between China and Russia was not brought about by U.S. policies, but grew out of the direct interaction between the two

21. *Department of State Bulletin,* Sept. 22, 1969, p. 260.

22. The Soviet scholar V. P. Lukin, acknowledging the advantages to the United States of the triangular relationship, implies that pursuit of the U.S.-Soviet détente by the USSR is the best counter to the danger that improvement in U.S.-Chinese relations might work to the disadvantage of the USSR. *USA,* in FBIS, *Daily Report: Soviet Union,* Feb. 20, 1973, pp. D2–D13.

countries, an interaction in which internal factors were dominant.[23] Of course, U.S. influence was a significant part of the international environment in which the two states carried on their foreign policies and each found it convenient to seize on aspects of U.S. policy as clubs to beat the other, but the effect of U.S. action or inaction was clearly secondary to the effect of the internal momentum in the conflict. Moreover, even those U.S. actions that did exacerbate Sino-Soviet hostility, such as the handling of the Cuban missile crisis or the signing of the test-ban treaty, were taken by the United States for reasons other than their effect on the Sino-Soviet dispute.

The United States could conceivably adopt a finely tuned triangular strategy toward China and the USSR designed to preserve the estrangement between them—without pushing them to the brink of war—and increase U.S. influence on both. Such a subtle concept unfortunately cannot be fitted to policymaking as it must be practiced by the U.S. government. A country like the United States would confront great obstacles in seeking to manipulate to its advantage with countries like China and the USSR a complex and sophisticated triangular diplomacy; it even encounters problems in conducting simple bilateral diplomacy with a close and friendly ally.

Misperceptions between two governments as open and well known to each other as the American and British governments can lead to crisis, as Richard Neustadt has shown.[24] The national security bureaucracy through which the United States conducts its foreign relations is a blunt instrument, which Neustadt doubts can be adapted to subtle diplomacy. Consequently, he recommends simplicity—"limiting our claims on other governments to outcomes reachable by them within a wide range of internal politics, under a variety of personalities and circumstances." If these outcomes do not depend on "precise conjunctions of particular procedures, men, and issues," then U.S. officials should be capable of perceiving other governments' concerns with enough accuracy to take effective action.

The scope for misperceptions in U.S. diplomatic relations with China vastly exceeds that in U.S. relations with the United Kingdom. Little is known about the views of the principal Chinese officials or the inner

23. See Donald Zagoria, *The Sino-Soviet Conflict 1956–61* (Princeton University Press, 1962); William Griffith, *The Sino-Soviet Rift* (M.I.T. Press, 1964); and Clubb, *China and Russia.*

24. *Alliance Politics* (Columbia University Press, 1970), pp. 148–49.

workings of the Peking government, and most of what has been learned about the course of the Sino-Soviet dispute has come out long after the event—too late to be of much use in devising current policy to influence that dispute. The struggle for succession in China will make the U.S. government's crystal ball even more turbid. Thus, the United States can have little confidence in its ability to predict how the Chinese might react to a particular U.S. move aimed at influencing China, and even less in its ability to predict how that move might affect Soviet policies toward the United States or the recondite sphere of Sino-Soviet relations. The same is true of attempts to influence Chinese policy through U.S. actions toward the USSR. A carom shot might easily go astray and bring about a result the opposite of that intended.

Consequently, the United States is most likely to be effective in carrying out its policies toward China and the USSR if it sets rather broad, direct objectives for its relations with each of them. The Sino-Soviet dispute probably will continue to be a catalyst to the improvement of U.S. relations with both China and the USSR so long as the United States maintains a rough balance, not leaning too far to either side, and avoids complex maneuvers whose success would depend heavily on uncertain judgments as to how the third state might react.

The Taiwan Issue

The United States and Japan have gone part way—but not all the way—to accepting Peking's view that Taiwan is an integral part of the People's Republic of China and that the relationship of Taiwan with the mainland is a domestic issue in which no outside power has the right to interfere.

The United States, in the Shanghai communiqué of February 27, 1972, acknowledged "that all Chinese on either side of the Taiwan Strait maintain there is but one China and that Taiwan is part of China. The United States Government does not challenge that position. It reaffirms its interest in a peaceful settlement of the Taiwan question by the Chinese themselves. With this prospect in mind, it affirms the ultimate objective of the withdrawal of all U.S. forces and military installations from Taiwan. In the meantime, it will progressively reduce its forces and military installations on Taiwan as the tension in the area diminishes."[25]

25. *New York Times,* Feb. 28, 1972.

With this declaration the United States almost ruled out the possibility of U.S. support for any movement by the people of Taiwan to establish the island as an independent state. The statement was heavily weighted toward encouraging the reunion of Taiwan with the mainland, but through a peaceful settlement by the Chinese themselves. The ultimate withdrawal of U.S. forces from Taiwan is linked in the communiqué to the "prospect" of a "peaceful settlement." The U.S. security treaty with the Republic of China remains in force and the intention of the United States to adhere to this commitment has been reaffirmed since President Nixon's visit to China.

The government of Japan in the Tanaka-Chou communiqué of September 29, 1972, declared it "fully understands and respects" Peking's position that Taiwan is an "inalienable part of the territory of the People's Republic of China."[26] The Japanese government also reaffirmed its adherence to the provision in the Potsdam communiqué concerning the return of Taiwan to China. Thus Japan, like the United States, has gone a long way toward disavowing any intent to support independence for Taiwan. And it has gone a step further by formally recognizing the People's Republic of China as the "sole legal government of China" and by breaking diplomatic relations with Taipei in order to establish them in Peking.

The international position of the Republic of China has been radically altered by the loss of its seat in the United Nations in October 1971 and by subsequent actions by the United States and Japan to improve their relations with Peking. Many nations are shifting their diplomatic relations to Peking, and before long probably only a handful of nations will have diplomatic relations with Taipei. Nevertheless, Taiwan's economic relations with the world continue to grow rapidly. In 1972 Taiwan's foreign trade surpassed that of mainland China. Taipei is adjusting to the loss of its diplomatic relations by conducting relations with its trading partners increasingly through official or quasi-official trade agencies.

It is doubtful that Peking and Taipei can arrange a peaceful reunification of Taiwan with the mainland within a few years. The loss of diplomatic relations with most nations of the world will not, in itself, put great pressure on Taiwan to accept the terms likely to be offered by Peking. So long as the island can continue to trade and prosper and

26. Ibid., Sept. 30, 1972.

is not seriously threatened militarily, the government on Taiwan will be able to persist in its separate existence if it wishes to do so.

For twenty years the political and economic systems in the two parts of China have diverged. The standard of living in Taiwan is considerably higher than that on the mainland and the gap continues to grow. Taiwan's expanding economic relations with the noncommunist world include substantial amounts of foreign investment, a monetary system closely linked to that of the noncommunist world, and a tourist trade that exceeds that of any area of East Asia except Japan and Hong Kong. Most of the two million or so mainlanders in Taiwan, the only group that has links of kinship and sentiment with the mainland, are deterred from seeking reunification by deep-seated mistrust of the communists and by personal vested interest in their situations in Taiwan. The thirteen million Taiwanese want a greater part in governing Taiwan, but few have shown any desire to see Taiwan ruled by mainland China.

It is thus improbable that the Taiwan problem can be resolved within the next few years by a freely negotiated settlement between the Chinese on the mainland and the Chinese in Taiwan. The United States, to break this stalemate, could abandon its present policy and back an independence move by the government of the island, or it could withdraw its defense commitment, in order to put pressure on the island government to reach a settlement with the mainland. The more reasonable course, however, is for the United States to continue its commitment to protect the people in Taiwan until a settlement agreeable to both sides can be reached.

Support for independence for Taiwan would damage U.S. relations with both China and Japan. The Chinese would, justifiably, regard this course as violating the spirit if not the letter of the Shanghai communiqué, and they would be likely to renew military threats to Taiwan. The Japanese would be torn over the issue; many would approve in principle self-determination for Taiwan, but more would be shocked by the danger of renewed military confrontation between the United States and China and fear that Japan might be drawn into the conflict because the most important U.S. military bases for the defense of Taiwan are located on Japanese territory. Peking could take advantage of this Japanese concern and put strong pressure on Japan not to support the U.S. position.

While a move away from the U.S. commitment to Taiwan might improve U.S. relations with mainland China, it would risk seriously undermining the U.S. relationship with Japan. Should the United States break relations with Taipei, abrogate the defense commitment, and set Taiwan adrift, the people of Taiwan could be compelled to accept control by Peking. China would not necessarily resort to the use or threat of force, but it might be tempted to resolve the Taiwan problem quickly once U.S. forces were out of the way, and the government of Taiwan, which is well armed, might refuse to capitulate without a struggle. Whatever the outcome, Japanese attitudes toward Japan's need for military force and toward the United States could be profoundly affected. As the Chinese thrust military forces into the Pacific close to territory disputed between Japan and China, and the United States in the face of military threat abandoned fifteen million people whom it had pledged for over twenty years to help defend, the shift in the power balance could not fail to make a deep impression in Japan. Moreover, the U.S. action would immediately raise grave questions about the reliability of the U.S. defense commitment to South Korea and increase the risk of conflict there.

There is no pressing need for the United States to run the risks involved in abandoning its present commitment to Taiwan. For the next few years at least, there is a strong probability that China will not wish to press the Taiwan issue because of its confrontation with the USSR and its consequent desire to continue to improve relations with the United States and Japan. Chou En-lai, in conversations with visiting overseas Chinese, reportedly has rejected the use of force to reunite Taiwan to the mainland, declaring that China will rely instead on a long-term program of educating Chinese in Taiwan to the advantages of reunification. There is little evident pressure on Chinese leaders to bring about a settlement of the Taiwan issue soon; they have many more urgent problems to concern themselves with. So long as there is no move by Chinese in Taiwan or by the United States or Japan to foreclose the prospect of Taiwan's eventual reunification with the mainland, and so long as Taiwan refrains from the kind of small-scale military raids against the mainland it occasionally attempted in the past, Peking probably will be able to tolerate Taiwan's separate existence just as it has tolerated British control over Hong Kong, which it also regards as part of China.

Taiwan might remain for a long time in limbo—neither a fully independent state nor an actual part of China. A reunion that would satisfy Peking's desire to treat the island as an integral part of its territory and satisfy the people of Taiwan that their lives would not suffer drastic and undesired changes once they had agreed to give up the protection of the Seventh Fleet is not easy to design. Certainly, an offer of the nominal autonomy that Peking allows Tibet could hardly be expected to appeal to the people of Taiwan and lead to the voluntary acceptance of Peking's control. Even Chou En-lai has acknowledged that Taiwan would have to be given special treatment.[27]

Taiwan's continued economic development, at a much faster pace than the mainland's, will steadily enhance the value to Peking of creating at least economic links with the island. There would be some reciprocal advantages for Taiwan in gaining access to China's market and resources. Taiwan's relatively advanced technology, its own defensive capability, its defense link with the United States, and Peking's desire to improve relations with the United States combine to give the government on Taiwan a degree of bargaining power in working out a relationship with the China mainland. Consequently, it is conceivable that contacts and trade may gradually develop, leading ultimately to a loose association that would not demand the imposition of China's political and economic system on Taiwan. Neither Americans nor Japanese would have any reason to oppose such a peaceful, uncoerced reassociation of Taiwan with the China mainland—improbable though it now seems.

Conditions for the peaceful reassociation of Taiwan with the China mainland will be most propitious if overall relations between the United States and China continue to improve. The two governments agreed in the Shanghai communiqué that the need to improve their relations was so important that the Taiwan issue could no longer be allowed to stand in the way. Consequently, a formula was found to set the Taiwan issue aside. If the United States continues to support the principle of eventual settlement of the issue by the Chinese themselves and carries out its pledge to withdraw its forces from Taiwan, there is no reason why the issue need obstruct the improvement of relations. The United States must, of course, make it clear to the government on Taiwan that it could not support militarily the formal independence of Taiwan from China. Withdrawal of the five thousand or so U.S. military personnel on Taiwan before the issue is settled will not significantly affect the ability of the United States to intervene decisively in the defense of

27. *Wall Street Journal,* Oct. 9, 1972.

Taiwan with air and sea power. As U.S.-Chinese relations improve, the relative importance of Taiwan as an issue will continue to decline, as will the significance of the U.S. defense commitment. A gradual fading of the commitment will be more conducive to the peaceful reassociation of Taiwan with the mainland than abrogation of the treaty. The policies toward the United States and Taiwan that the Chinese have followed since President Nixon's visit to China suggest that such a resolution would be acceptable to them.

Intensifying rivalry between Japan and China would cloud prospects for peaceful reassociation of Taiwan with the China mainland, since it would strengthen the influence on the Japanese government of Japanese who have ties with Taiwan and of those who are worried about the strategic disadvantages to Japan of Chinese control of Taiwan. It would also increase Chinese suspicion that the Japanese hope to bring Taiwan again under their control. Mounting distrust between Japan and China would thus inevitably make negotiations between Taiwan and China more problematical. The United States ought therefore to continue its defense ties with Taiwan to help hold in check Chinese and Japanese suspicion of each other's intentions.

Should the United States do as Japan has done and shift its formal diplomatic relations from Taipei to Peking, replacing the U.S. embassy in Taipei and the Republic of China's embassy in Washington with quasi-official representation? The establishment of liaison offices in Washington and Peking headed by distinguished diplomats serves most of the purposes that an embassy could serve, but the logic of the U.S. policy of seeking improved relations with China argues for the establishment of embassies. The legal and political effect that this action would have on the U.S. defense commitment to the Republic of China is a critical problem. If the United States decides to recognize the People's Republic of China as the sole legitimate government of China and to reduce the U.S. representation in Taipei to quasi-official status, some means will have to be found to assure that the defense commitment continues in force, even as it declines in significance.

If the Chinese should revert to the view that Taiwan is the fundamental issue between the United States and China, revive the threat to take Taiwan by military force, and demand that the U.S. security treaty be abrogated, should the United States accede to this demand or face the serious risk of direct conflict with nuclear-armed China? Much would depend on the Japanese view and the likely effect at that time of alternate courses on the Japanese desire to remain a lightly armed, non-nuclear power. If the Japanese government were unwilling to back U.S. participation in the defense of Taiwan, it is doubtful that the American people would or should support such action. Whether the United States and Japan became involved in conflict over Taiwan or not, the renewed willingness of China to resolve the Taiwan problem by military force would severely set back hope for permanent peace in the region.

The best way of working toward the U.S. goal of a stable, low-tension four-power system in East Asia is to preserve the understanding reached between the United States and China in the Shanghai communiqué that Taiwan should be set aside as an issue between them pending eventual peaceful settlement of the problem among the Chinese themselves. The peace of the region will be best assured if Taiwan becomes neither an American base, nor a Chinese military outpost, nor a precinct of Japan, but a genuinely autonomous territory, loosely linked to China, with which all three powers have useful relations.

Arms Control and Security

At some point China must be drawn into serious negotiations on arms control, lest its growing nuclear force eventually have a destabilizing effect on the strategic balance between the United States and the USSR. But that will not happen in this decade because the two superpowers will continue to have great superiority over China in nuclear strategic weapons. Whatever limitations may be agreed to in the strategic arms limitation talks, both will have enough strategic nuclear weapons to deter China and each other. The Chinese now see no advantage in limiting the expansion of their own nuclear force. Only after Chinese leaders believe they have a reliable second-strike capability may they become aware of an advantage for China in negotiating limitations on nuclear weapons.

Chinese demands for total abolition and destruction of nuclear weapons and their other pronouncements on arms control matters are so sweeping and propagandistic in tone as to discourage hope that they might soon participate in major arms control negotiations. The hostility between Moscow and Peking is another serious obstacle to negotiations. But certain types of arms control arrangements between China and the United States might be negotiable. These would not, like the partial test-ban agreement or the types of limitations on major weapons systems agreed in the strategic arms limitations talks, obstruct Chinese efforts to build their own nuclear deterrent. One possibility is an agreement such as the United States concluded with the Soviet Union to reduce the risk of accidental or unauthorized launch of nuclear weapons. Such an agreement might include the establishment of a "hot line" for emergency communications between Washington and Peking.[28] A useful first step might be initiation of a dialogue with China on the subject of arms control, either officially or through private channels, like the Pugwash meetings with the Soviet Union. The sooner the process of exchanging views is begun, the better the chances of offsetting the long-term threat to U.S. security posed by China's growing nuclear force.

The prospect that Sino-Soviet antagonism will persist, even if it becomes less intense under Mao's successors, should continue to favor U.S. efforts to reduce the danger of big-power involvement in military conflict in Korea, Taiwan, and Southeast Asia. These efforts might include an attempt to involve China in four-power arrangements to make Korea more stable (see Chapter 9) and to reduce the danger of big-power military conflict in Southeast Asia (see Chapters 10 and 11).

Economic Relations

The United States, together with Japan, is likely to find growing opportunities to expand economic relations with China. The evident Chinese desire to speed the introduction of modern technology, induced in part by the Soviet threat, will gradually create influential groups in China, Japan, and the United States with an interest in seeing such trade continue. The process of expanding trade could be accelerated by granting China most-favored-nation treatment and by making available funds from the Export-Import Bank to finance U.S. exports to China. Even though trade with China is unlikely to become a large proportion of U.S. or Japanese trade, a solid enough base may be established to preserve the trade in a possibly adverse climate in the future.

A serious potential conflict of interest with China may arise, however, over the oil resources beneath the Yellow Sea and East China Sea. Peking has already denounced an agreement between Japan and South Korea for oil production in one portion of the continental shelf. Japan's

28. A detailed discussion of the possibilities of involving China in arms control negotiations and recommendations for U.S. government actions is given in Ralph N. Clough and others, *The United States, China, and Arms Control* (Brookings Institution, forthcoming).

demand for oil is rising so rapidly and the advantages of a source close to Japan would be so great (particularly in light of events in the Middle East) that the discovery of large amounts of oil in this area would create an important national interest for Japan. China and Japan seem certain to clash over claims to the continental shelf, and the dispute could become serious if the prize should prove to be of high value. The United States would become involved, because of the participation of U.S. companies in producing the oil, because of the U.S. interest in maintaining close relations with Japan and in seeing Japan obtain a new source of oil, and because of the U.S. interest in keeping the severity of conflicts between Japan and China below the level of military confrontation.

The United States might try to persuade Japan and China to work out arrangements for sharing the oil resources of the continental shelf, together with the two Koreas and Taipei, but the political differences among these governments will make such arrangements extremely difficult to agree upon. Nevertheless, the United States, because of its technological lead in underwater oil drilling, is in a position to bring some influence to bear on both China and Japan. And if the negotiations involving U.S. and Japanese participation in the Soviet oil and natural gas development in Siberia should be successful, the Chinese might modify their opposition to foreign participation in developing Chinese natural resources. In that event, tripartite oil projects on parts of the continental shelf might be feasible.

An Overview

An important requirement for the U.S. policymaker in the 1970s will be to keep U.S. relations with China in proper perspective and not to exaggerate their importance in comparison to U.S. relations with the Soviet Union or Japan. For the remainder of this decade and probably well into the next, the primary strategic problem for the United States will be to maintain a stable strategic balance with the USSR, a task that will require continuing close and fruitful U.S. relations with the great industrial and trading centers of Western Europe and Japan. China, with the majority of its population engaged in agriculture, will be industrializing at a steady pace but will still be much weaker militarily than the Soviet Union and much weaker economically than Japan. While China's potential for future development calls for a continuing effort to improve U.S. relations with Peking, in this decade that effort needs to be carefully proportioned to the more urgent demands of relations with the Soviet Union and Japan.

Maintaining the proper balance will not be easy. Relations with China may seem more compelling than U.S. relations with Japan because China has nuclear weapons. If the Japanese become convinced that they must have nuclear weapons to gain the respect that Americans accord to China, however, they will not only acquire those weapons but do so in an atmosphere of growing nationalism and alienation from the United States. The risks inherent in Japan's becoming a great military and nuclear power for the next ten years, at least, far exceed the risks to U.S. security posed by China's modest offensive power.

The rapidity with which Mao and Chou have acted to open relations with the United States and Japan probably reflects their consciousness that they do not have much time. They are men in a hurry. They seem to be trying to create a momentum in the expansion of China's relations with Washington and Tokyo that a successor regime would have difficulty reversing. The greater the vested interests of the Chinese bureaucracy in continuing those relations, the more resistant will they be to change. The effort to improve relations with the United States and Japan, like the campaign to denigrate Lin Piao by his association with the Soviet Union, seems part of an effort by Mao and Chou to fix China's foreign policy course for possibly stormy times after Mao's death. It will be in the U.S. interest to make it easier for them to do this.

CHAPTER EIGHT

Moderating Rivalry with the USSR

The Soviet Union's policies toward East Asia are dictated largely by its global confrontation with the United States and by its conflict with the Chinese—particularly the presumed long-term Chinese threat to Soviet territory and the contest for influence on Asian governments and for leadership of the communist parties of the world. Everywhere there is a strong element of rivalry with both the United States and China. In some places, however, rivalry with the United States has predominated, as in Vietnam, where the Russians and the Chinese both helped North Vietnam against the United States; and in other places rivalry with China has been more important. Nowhere does the Soviet Union cooperate with or coordinate its policies with either of the other powers. At most, its policies sometimes parallel those of the United States or China, when national interests overlap.

Soviet Activity in East Asia

Although rivalry with the United States is the overriding preoccupation of Soviet foreign policy in the world, the USSR's actions in East Asia in recent years probably have been determined more by its concern about China. Its principal objectives appear to be to deter or contain any possible Chinese threat to the Soviet frontier, preserve or improve the Soviet position relative to China with governments and major communist parties in East Asia, and keep open the possibility of improving relations with Mao's successors; to improve the Soviet position in East Asia relative to the United States; and to improve Soviet relations with Japan and keep Japan from acquiring nuclear weapons.

Soviet state-to-state activities in pursuit of these aims have included military deployments, military aid programs, economic aid, trade, diplomatic intercourse, and cultural exchange. Military activities in Asia have been largely geared to the defense of the frontier with China. Since 1965, forces deployed in the border area have more than doubled. Compared with the large deployment of forces against China, Soviet air and naval activities in the Pacific directed toward the United States or Japan are small. Still less significant, militarily, is the small number of Soviet naval vessels that have regularly cruised the Indian Ocean since 1968,[1] to show the flag and demonstrate to the littoral states that the Pacific and Indian Oceans are no longer monopolized by the American and British fleets.

In two East Asian countries, military aid is a major instrument of Soviet influence. The Soviet Union's ability to supply advanced weapons to the governments of North Korea and North Vietnam may be its strongest lever in competing for influence with Peking. One other East Asian state—Indonesia—was between 1958 and 1965 a recipient of large amounts of Soviet military aid, but this investment of more than a billion dollars gave the USSR disappointingly little influence. The Indonesian Communist party, and later President Sukarno, aligned themselves closely with China against the USSR, and the present leaders of Indonesia are oriented toward the West.[2] The Soviets are now supplying only small amounts of military spare parts—for cash.

In economic aid, where the Soviet Union is competing with China rather than the United States, North Korea and North Vietnam have been the principal beneficiaries. Burma and Cambodia received small amounts of Soviet economic aid in the 1950s and early 1960s but no longer receive it. A substantial flow of economic aid that accompanied military aid to Indonesia ended with the fall of Sukarno in 1965. Not until mid-1971 did a survey team arrive to study the feasibility of completing the unfinished steel and fertilizer plants that the Russians had

---

1. In 1969 the U.S. Defense Department announced that the USSR had some 125 ships on international waters (about 10 percent of the active Soviet fleet), of which more than 60 were in the Mediterranean, about 40 in the Atlantic, 15 in the Pacific, and 10 in the Indian Ocean. *New York Times*, Aug. 21, 1969. See also Barry M. Blechman, *The Changing Soviet Navy* (Brookings Institution, 1973), especially pp. 12–15.

2. See Uri Ra'anan, *The USSR Arms the Third World* (M.I.T. Press, 1969), for a good account of how the Soviet investment in arms aid to Indonesia failed to buy influence.

begun. The total amount of economic aid provided by the USSR in recent years has declined, as the Soviets have tended to concentrate their aid in a few countries and to be more selective in the projects that they support. They will probably continue to give high priority to countries such as North Vietnam, where rivalry with China is intense.

Soviet trade with noncommunist East Asian countries is meager. In 1971 none of them exported to the USSR as much as 2 percent of its total exports, except Malaysia, which sold 3 percent of its exports to the Russians.[3] Soviet foreign trade is increasing, but at a slower rate than world trade and much more slowly than Japanese foreign trade. Even though the Soviet Union will probably continue its policy of seeking to expand its trade with the noncommunist world, problems inherent in its state-managed economy and trading system seem likely to prevent extensive and rapid expansion of trade with East Asian countries. Hence, it appears unlikely that trade with the USSR in this decade will become a larger proportion of the total trade of East Asian states; for most of them it will probably become a smaller proportion.

The Soviet Union is gradually expanding diplomatic and other ties with East Asian states, concentrating particularly on Japan. During the past several years it has established diplomatic relations with Malaysia and Singapore. It has sent trade and goodwill missions to the Philippines, the only Southeast Asian state other than South Vietnam with which it does not have diplomatic relations. Through cultural exchanges, official visits, and the increasing numbers of Soviet merchant ships and aircraft in the area, the USSR gives an impression of increasing activity—not large in absolute terms, but a large increase from a low base.

Soviet Interests in Southeast Asia

Soviet interests in Southeast Asia have traditionally been small, not comparable to those in Europe, the Middle East, South Asia, or North-

3. Data on Malaysia from International Monetary Fund/International Bank for Reconstruction and Development (IMF/IBRD), *Direction of Trade, November 1973*, pp. 59–60. Japan exported 1.6 percent of its total exports to the USSR in 1971, Burma 1.2 percent, Thailand 0.7 percent, Indonesia 0.8 percent, Singapore 0.5 percent, and the Philippines none. IMF/IBRD, *Direction of Trade, January 1973* and *May 1973*.

east Asia. But the global confrontation with the United States after
World War II demanded greater Soviet activity even in parts of the
world where Soviet interests were small. The breakup of colonial em-
pires offered new opportunities, especially in Indochina and Indonesia.
The Soviet Union moved in to become the chief supplier of arms to
Indonesia and to play an important part in easing the French out of
Indochina at the Geneva conference of 1954. Soviet aircraft flew supplies to neutralist forces at the Plaine des Jarres in Laos in 1961 and the
USSR was cochairman with the United Kingdom of the 1962 Geneva
conference on Laos. After the 1954 accords, Khrushchev seemed ready
to downgrade the importance of Indochina to the USSR, but the Soviet
Union was drawn into sharp confrontation with the United States over
U.S. bombing of North Vietnam. Moscow had to support its fellow
communist state under external attack in order to maintain its self-
respect and standing among communist parties and in order to compete
effectively with the Chinese for influence in North Vietnam. With the
winding down of the U.S. combat role in Indochina, the flow of Soviet
resources into North Vietnam dropped, although it remained high
enough to compete with Peking's aid.

Its recent behavior in Southeast Asia suggests that the Soviet Union
will continue to regard its interests in that area as small compared to
Europe, the Middle East, South Asia, or Northeast Asia. The region is
far from the centers of Soviet power; the Russians have no important
direct interests in these countries, and they would suffer from severe
logistical handicaps in projecting military power into the area. They are
expanding their activities there, but in an economical way, not investing
large resources except in Vietnam, and those investments are tapering
off. Since Sukarno's overthrow, they have not tried to compete seriously
in Indonesia, as they are competing in India, with Western and Japanese economic aid. They seemed more willing than the Chinese were
(at least until 1971, when relations between Peking and Washington
began to improve) to go along with a negotiated settlement of the conflict in Indochina.

This low Soviet posture in Southeast Asia will probably continue.
While their global competition with the United States and China will
require that they try to keep their hand in and be alert for opportunities
to exploit, the Russians will probably not, failing an exceptional opportunity, invest in Southeast Asia valuable resources better used elsewhere.

The present situation in Southeast Asia, however, favors a generous payoff for a small Soviet investment. Even though Soviet activity—in the form of official visits, the presence of ships and aircraft, trade, cultural exchanges, and so forth—is very small compared to U.S. or Japanese activity, it gets a great deal of publicity. For a while, at least, the Soviets will be able to trade on the novelty of their presence and the impression of U.S. withdrawal from the region to get a lot of attention for a little activity. But this advantage may wear thin once the Soviet presence becomes familiar and its small size more apparent.

The Soviet Union is likely to favor stability over turmoil in Southeast Asia during this decade—except in the unlikely event that a strong, pro-Soviet communist party should come into existence in one of the states of the region—for the Soviets probably recognize that the Chinese are in a better position than they are to exploit disorder. Emphasis on state-to-state relations and consequent reluctance to aid insurgent movements is a worldwide trend in Soviet policy, but in Southeast Asia it probably also reflects a realistic recognition that the Chinese have long had the inside track in most Southeast Asian communist parties, making it hard for the Soviets to break in. If Chinese-backed communist insurgents threatened to seize power in a Southeast Asian state, the Soviets would be placed in an awkward position. They would be loath to see a successful revolution bring increased influence to China, but it would be difficult for them to aid a noncommunist government threatened by communist revolution. Consequently, relative stability in which the USSR can cultivate state-to-state relations with the conventional instruments of diplomacy would seem to serve Soviet purposes better than the eruption of revolutionary violence.

The Soviet Union has been more deeply involved in Indochina than in other parts of Southeast Asia because there the confrontation with the United States and the rivalry with China were particularly intense. Following the introduction of U.S. combat forces into South Vietnam in 1965, the Soviet Union rapidly expanded its military and economic aid to North Vietnam. The Chinese also increased their aid, but Mao Tse-tung rejected Soviet proposals for "united action" in support of Hanoi. Moscow and Peking accused each other of colluding with the United States and letting Hanoi down as they maneuvered for predominant influence in North Vietnam.

But this was a contest that neither could win, for North Vietnam needed both countries too much to align itself with one. North Vietnam needed China as a "reliable rear area" safe from U.S. bombing from which to support the front, as a corridor for the transportation by land of Soviet military supplies, and as a continuing threat that Chinese forces might intervene should U.S. ground forces invade North Vietnam. It needed the Soviet Union as the sole source of advanced weapons and as insurance against falling under the domination of the Chinese, past invaders and occupiers of Vietnamese territory. Consequently, the North Vietnamese played their diplomatic cards shrewdly to maintain a balance in their relations with the two big communist powers.

By 1971 the confrontation of the Soviet Union and China with the United States over Indochina began to decline in severity. Soviet and Chinese leaders became increasingly convinced that the Nixon administration was in the process of withdrawing most, if not all, U.S. forces from South Vietnam. And their tense military confrontation with each other gave both Moscow and Peking increasing incentive to improve their relations with the United States. As the United States continued to withdraw its forces from combat, the desire for improved relations with the United States came to overshadow the confrontation in Indochina sufficiently that in the spring of 1972 neither Moscow nor Peking would allow the mining of North Vietnamese harbors and the intensified U.S. bombing of North Vietnam to interfere with steps to improve their relations with Washington. Despite Hanoi's resentment manifested in its propaganda attacks on both China and the Soviet Union, neither was willing to seek advantage over its rival by all-out support of Hanoi at the risk of jeopardizing more important objectives in its relationship with Washington.

Both Moscow and Peking may have helped the United States to bring about the agreement on a cease-fire in Indochina. As a result of that agreement, the flow of resources from the Soviet Union into Indochina is likely to continue to decline, and the importance of Indochina as an issue between the United States and the USSR will diminish further. Should the settlement break down and the United States resume bombing North Vietnam, the flow of Soviet military aid would rise, but even in this event the U.S.-Soviet confrontation over Indochina seems unlikely to attain its former level of intensity.

Thus the Soviets will continue to cultivate relations with Hanoi so as to protect their position relative to China, but probably with a much smaller investment of resources. The Soviets could not hope for predominant influence in Hanoi in any case, for it will continue to be in the North Vietnamese interest to strike an approximate balance in their relations with the two big communist powers. The Soviet Union will by various means jockey for position with China, not only in North Vietnam, but also in Laos, Cambodia, and Thailand. Confrontation with the United States will also continue to be a force in Soviet relations with those countries of Southeast Asia, but it is likely to be less intense than in the past. As the United States reduces its involvement in the nations of mainland Southeast Asia, both the opportunities and the incentives for Soviet intervention there will also tend to decline, for neither the United States nor the Soviet Union has very important interests in this region.

Concern over the possible expansion of Chinese influence in the countries of mainland Southeast Asia could, of course, compel the USSR to increase its emphasis on that part of the world, especially if U.S. influence there declines. No doubt the Soviets will continue to be active there diplomatically and with a variety of relatively low-cost programs in an effort to counter Chinese influence. But it seems improbable that the USSR would pour large amounts of military and economic aid into this area or enter into defense commitments with countries of the area for the purpose of "containing China."

Asian Collective Security

The proposal that President Brezhnev put forward at the Moscow meeting of communist and workers' parties in June 1969 for a collective security system for Asia was widely interpreted at the time as primarily aimed at China, although the Russians denied this and pointed out that China was invited to participate. The idea was broached, however, at the high point of Sino-Soviet tension, and rivalry with China for influence with Asian countries was probably an important motivation.

Since then, Soviet publications have stressed the need for a collective security system to replace the U.S. system of military bases and alliances which, the Russians charge, brought war and suffering to the Asian peoples. Creation of the new system "presupposes the end of imperialist aggression in Asia, the withdrawal of American troops and the troops of the accomplices of the United States from the territory of Asian countries."[4] Or, as Mikhail Suslov told the chairman of the Japanese Socialist party, the Brezhnev plan requires "the withdrawal of U.S. troops from Indochina, the dissolution of SEATO, and the abrogation of the ANZUS pact, the US-Japan security treaty, and the defense treaties with South Korea and Taiwan."[5]

Although Brezhnev's proposal has been presented primarily as a replacement for the U.S. system of defense treaties, it also seems intended as a counter to such regional associations as the Asian and Pacific Council (ASPAC) and the Association of Southeast Asian Nations (ASEAN), which the Soviets regard as devices for the indirect expansion of U.S. influence. After the fall 1970 meeting of the signatories to the security treaty between Australia, New Zealand, and the United States (the ANZUS treaty), a Soviet commentator pointed out that the group's communiqué "underlines the necessity of close collaboration of the members of ANZUS with Japan, who on her side is not only a partner of the United States in the 'security treaty', but is also the most influential member of the so-called ASPAC, which unites the direct and indirect associates of American adventures in Asia."[6] Another commentator expressed doubts about the declared economic and cultural interests of ASEAN: "The United States, from the day of creation of ASEAN, declared its full support—including financial support—if the new organization would take on certain military-political responsibilities in Asia. . . . The official representatives of the countries belonging to ASEAN openly recognize the identity of the objectives and tasks of this organization and those of the closed military-political group of ASPAC, where the leading role belongs to Japan and Australia."[7]

The sweeping conditions attached to realization of the Soviet collective security proposal, and the failure of Soviet diplomats to push it hard, suggest that it was made more for its propaganda effect than as a serious proposal which the Soviets expected to lead to concrete results. It is the kind of proposal that thrives on its own vagueness, because interested Asians can speculate on its meaning in accordance with their

4. K. T. Mazurov, head of Soviet delegation to celebration of 25th anniversary of liberation of Korea, quoted in *Pravda,* Aug. 16, 1970.

5. *Mainichi,* July 20, 1970.

6. *Pravda,* Sept. 9, 1970.

7. M. Andreev, "ASEAN—Economic Bloc with Political Objectives," *World Economics and International Relations* (USSR), February 1969, p. 90.

own predilections. It has not, however, attracted significant support from Asian governments.

The Soviets' policy toward regional organization in East Asia has been mainly to attack organizations to which the United States belongs or of which the United States has expressed approval; so far the Soviets have not made a serious effort to organize any group of countries in the region under their own leadership, nor have they attempted to compete with the United States in expressing approval or support for such purely regional organizations as ASEAN. Except for the United Nations Economic Commission for Asia and the Far East (ECAFE), the USSR has chosen not to participate in regional organizations—not even such a relatively nonpolitical organization as the Asian Development Bank. Soviet policy reflects the small influence of the USSR in much of East Asia, relative to that of the United States or Japan, as well as the difficulty the Soviets would face in handling the question of Chinese participation in any projected regional organization.

Future U.S.-Soviet Relations

The Soviets will doubtless continue their efforts to improve their position in East Asia at the expense of the United States. But there is no sharp, unavoidable clash of interests in this region comparable to that in Europe or the Middle East. China is likely to continue to be the primary Soviet concern in the area.

Not only is East Asia a secondary area for rivalry between the United States and the USSR, their interests there overlap to some extent. Both have an overriding interest in preventing the kind of instability and unpredictability in Asia that would increase the danger of a military confrontation between them. They may disagree on what needs to be done to achieve that aim, but their common concern brings them closer to each other than either is to China. Both tend to be more conservative than China, find the status quo more tolerable, and are satisfied with a slower pace of change. Consequently, should Chinese policy prove to be disruptive, the United States and the Soviet Union might have a common interest in strengthening the status quo, although the Soviets would be loath to admit this common interest.

Besides their common opposition to Chinese-backed revolution in

East Asia, the United States and the Soviet Union will probably find their interests overlapping in certain other respects. As the world's two leading naval powers, with large trade and shipping interests, both were disturbed by the declarations by Indonesia and Malaysia in early 1972 that the Malacca Strait was not an international strait, but was subject to control by the riparian states. China, on the other hand, strongly supported the position taken by the two Southeast Asian governments. It is ironic that both the United States and the USSR sought to preserve freedom of passage through this international strait largely to assure that their navies would not be impeded in their efforts to counter each other.

The United States will not, however, always have more in common with the USSR than with China when the interests of the three powers are interwoven, as the episode of Bangladesh has already demonstrated. Should the Chinese continue to shift the emphasis of their policy toward state-to-state relations and away from the support of revolutionaries, other occasions may arise where U.S. interests are more closely aligned with Chinese than with Soviet interests. Indeed, one result of the dialogue begun with President Nixon's visit to China may be the identification of areas where U.S. and Chinese interests overlap and parallel policies can be followed.

Nevertheless, the four-power system in East Asia will probably serve Soviet purposes in this decade reasonably well. Although present alignments appear to favor the United States more than they do the USSR, working within the system probably appears less risky and more rewarding to the USSR than bold action to upset it. Even though the long-term Soviet aim is to press U.S. influence—and particularly the U.S. military presence—out of the region, the Soviets would probably prefer that this happen gradually, without extensive disorder and dangerous uncertainties that the Chinese might be better able to exploit than they.

If the USSR is to pursue a moderate and fairly modest policy in East Asia (except for possible renewed clashes and tension on the Sino-Soviet border), the United States will have to remain actively engaged in that region. For a combination of Soviet achievement of strategic parity, greater ability to project conventional force, U.S. military withdrawal from the region—particularly from Northeast Asia—and Soviet anxiety over possible Chinese gains might cause the Soviets to adopt a more aggressive policy in East Asia.

Despite the predominance of rivalry in U.S.-Soviet global relations, it may be easier to moderate this rivalry in East Asia, where Soviet interests are comparatively small, than elsewhere. Moreover, the Soviets are preoccupied militarily and politically by their conflict with China. And they are impelled by present conditions in Japan, and by the nature of U.S.-Japanese and Sino-Japanese relations, to rely more heavily on the carrot than the stick in seeking closer relations with Japan. Thus a U.S. policy that seeks to moderate clashes of interest within the four-power system, so as to reduce the danger of big-power war, has a good chance of success.

CHAPTER NINE

Lessening Tension in Korea

In Korea, more than in any other part of East Asia, important interests of all four big powers intersect. Hence, Korea is a possible flashpoint for a conflict that could draw in the big powers and destroy the hope for a peaceful and stable four-power system.

A conflict in Korea would have an immediate and potent effect on the Japanese, who have grown accustomed to peace in neighboring areas and therefore content with relatively weak armed forces. Acute political conflict would break out among the 600,000 Koreans in Japan, as well as between Japanese supporters of South Korea and those sympathetic to North Korea. If the reaction of the big powers to a Korean conflict should undercut Japanese confidence in the U.S. commitment to the defense of Japan, it would give strong impetus to Japanese rearmament. Although war in Korea appears unlikely, it would nevertheless be in the interest of the United States and the other big powers to find ways of diminishing the potential threat to peace posed by the uneasy confrontation between the two Koreas.

The Military Balance

Divided Korea is an unfortunate and unintended legacy of World War II. The longing of the Korean people for a unified state is frustrated by the confrontation at the 38th parallel that has turned North and South Korea into armed camps, imposing heavy burdens on the people of both sides, neither of which dares to fall behind in the arms race. The emphasis on armament grows out of the traumatic experience each government had of being nearly destroyed in war and saved only by the military intervention of a powerful ally. The incompatibility of the political and economic systems of the two Koreas and the personal stake of the leaders on each side in their own system make genuine overtures toward unification difficult. Rivalry between the big powers supporting each side tends to harden the division. The stalemate between the two could break down if provocative action and reaction should lead to expanding conflict and if one side or the other saw an opportunity to reunify Korea by force. An attempted reunification by force would draw in the big powers and endanger the general peace.

Until recently the hostility between the two Koreas was unrelieved. North Korea, with only 13.5 million people to South Korea's 32 million, has for years been preoccupied with preparations for war. Under the leadership of Kim Il-sung, the object of a personality cult surpassing that of Mao Tse-tung in China, the people of North Korea have been highly organized and disciplined. The public media have constantly reminded them of the hardships suffered during the Korean War and warned them that the "American imperialists" and their accomplices the "Japanese militarists" were plotting a new war. Devoting 20 percent of North Korea's gross national product to the defense budget, Kim has assiduously strengthened military preparedness, especially since 1966, building fortifications, placing important industrial plants underground, and training and equipping a nationwide militia to supplement the regular armed forces. Kim has also stressed self-reliance and, through large investments in heavy industry,[1] has greatly increased North Korea's ability to produce its own munitions and military equipment, although Pyongyang is still dependent on the Soviet Union for major items, such as aircraft and tanks.

Military preparedness has been a constant theme in South Korea also. Park Chung-hee, who has headed the government of the Republic of Korea since taking over in a military coup in 1961, has given high priority to strengthening the armed forces of the South against the threat of another invasion from the North. Pyongyang's strident propaganda attacks on the Park government and Kim's attempts to stir up a revolutionary movement in the South by subversion and the infiltration of armed agents have heightened anxiety among South Koreans. And the exposed position of Seoul, containing 20 percent of South Korea's population and only thirty miles from the demilitarized zone (DMZ)

1. Emphasis on heavy industry is continuing. The six-year plan ending in 1976 assigned 40.7 percent of government investment to heavy industry and 8.3 percent to light industry. See *Washington Post*, July 2, 1972.

separating the two parts of Korea, has caused South Korean leaders to fear a possible blitzkrieg by North Korean forces aimed at the capital city.

It is difficult to judge whether North Korea or South Korea holds the edge in the competition for military advantage. South Korea has the larger army—560,000 to North Korea's 360,000—but up to 1972 Pyongyang's military budget was twice that of Seoul.[2] Pyongyang also appears to have some advantage in the quantity of its military equipment. It probably has more tanks and artillery pieces than South Korea, but does not possess an overwhelming superiority in such weapons—even according to the estimates least favorable to the South. It does have a large quantitative superiority in aircraft, though even that is probably not large enough to be decisive in battle.[3] In a North Korean attack, it would be offset to some extent by advantages a defender would have over an attacker. Moreover, more important than quantity of equipment are such intangible factors as leadership, morale, quality of weapons and their deployment, and the effectiveness of the logistical system in backing them up. In air warfare, particularly, the quality of the aircraft and the skill of the air crews can be decisive, as demonstrated in the 1950–53 Korean War.

Of course, the military balance in Korea is not static. Pyongyang's quantitative superiority in certain items of military equipment gave Seoul a plausible case for demanding more U.S. military aid to redress

2. International Institute for Strategic Studies, *The Military Balance, 1971–72* (International Institute, 1971), pp. 47 and 48, and *The Military Balance, 1972–73* (1972), pp. 50 and 51; and *United States Security Agreements and Commitments Abroad,* Hearings before the Subcommittee on U.S. Security Agreements and Commitments Abroad of the Senate Committee on Foreign Relations, 91 Cong. 2 sess. (1970), pt. 6, pp. 17–29.

3. Estimates of numbers of major items of military equipment in the hands of North and South Korea vary considerably. In early 1972 William D. White of the Brookings Institution estimated that North Korea had 2,500–3,000 field artillery pieces (75 mm or larger), and South Korea 1,300–1,800; the North 800–1,100 tanks and assault guns (75 mm or larger), the South 650–850; the North 500–900 other armored vehicles, the South 500–650; the North 420–550 fighter-interceptor aircraft (MIG-15s, -17s, and -21s), the South 190–220 (F-86s and F-5s); the North 50–80 fighter-bombers (MIG-19s and SU-7s), the South 18 (F-4s); the North 50–80 bombers (IL-28s), the South none. These figures exaggerate the North's military strength. For example, the figures on North Korean tanks include about 150 armored assault guns, which are not comparable to South Korean tanks, although they cannot be classed with ordinary artillery pieces.

the balance when the United States in 1971 withdrew one of its two divisions stationed in Korea and talked of possible further withdrawals. The United States then agreed to a large-scale modernization program for the South Korean armed forces, projected at some $1 billion to $1.5 billion between 1971 and 1975, part of it in ammunition and equipment left behind by the U.S. division. An important objective of the program was to reduce the disparity in air power between North and South largely created by the Soviet provision of MIG-21s and IL-28s to the North Koreans in the mid-1960s. To this end the United States supplied the South Koreans with a squadron of F-4s and has begun to replace the obsolete F-86s with modern F-5s. The ability of the South Koreans to defend themselves depends not only on what the United States supplies them but also on whether the North Koreans prevail on the Soviet Union and China to provide them with more weapons. It appears now that the South Koreans could, with U.S. air and logistic support, defend their territory against an attack by North Korean forces, and perhaps do so without U.S. aid.[4]

Throughout the nearly twenty years since the Korean armistice, the most potent deterrent to North Korean attack has been the ability and willingness of the United States to intervene with its forces. As an earnest of its intentions, the United States has retained substantial forces in South Korea. A principal theme of Pyongyang's foreign policy, supported by the Soviet Union and China, has been the demand for the withdrawal of the U.S. forces, so that the Korean problem could be settled by the Koreans themselves "without outside interference." Seoul, with equal persistence, has insisted that U.S. forces remain in order to continue to deter an attack by North Korea—possibly strengthened by Chinese forces.

Recent improvements in relations between the United States and China and the beginning of political talks between North and South Korea, considered together with the strengthening of South Korea's armed forces under the modernization program, have raised questions in the United States as to the desirability of continuing to keep these U.S. forces in Korea.

4. Conclusion of William D. White, based on discussions with military analysts in Washington; it assumes no large influx of new weapons into North Korea. That the South Koreans could defend themselves without U.S. air and logistic support is a minority view.

The Political Confrontation

The arms race in Korea reflects the conflicting political objectives of the two governments. Each would like to see Korea unified under its own authority. The government of South Korea bases its claim on its recognition by the United Nations as the only legitimate government in Korea and on the existence of the United Nations Command as evidence of the continuing commitment of the UN. It has called on North Korea to solve the problem of divided Korea by means of UN-supervised elections throughout Korea.

North Korea has denied the competence of the United Nations to deal with Korea, and until 1973, its representatives were not permitted to attend the annual UN debate on the Korean question. Pyongyang has also demanded the abrogation of the UN resolution condemning North Korea and China as aggressors in the Korean War and has called for the UN Command to be dismantled. It has denounced the idea of UN-supervised elections for Korea, insisting instead on the reunification of the country through negotiations between the two governments, without outside interference.

Since the advent of the Park Chung-hee government in 1961, South Korea has adopted a long-term approach to reunification. Park has repudiated the use of military force to unify Korea, stressing the importance of strengthening the South economically and politically in order to offer a way of life superior to that in the North. He declared that the reunification of Korea should be deferred until the late 1970s when he expected South Korea to be far more developed economically than North Korea. Throughout the 1960s Pyongyang's various proposals for negotiations between the two Koreas were rejected by Seoul, which countered by demanding that Pyongyang first renounce the intent to overthrow the government of the Republic of Korea, stop armed infiltration of the South, and allow the UN to participate in a settlement.

North Korea has more actively and aggressively sought to establish conditions for reunification than has South Korea. Its various proposals have all aimed ultimately at creating a unified central government by elections in the North and South, conducted by Koreans without outside supervision. The intermediate steps it has proposed include economic and cultural exchange, the reduction of the armed forces on each side, and establishment of a confederation until the manner of creating a unified central government could be agreed on. South Korea has viewed these proposals as propaganda, for they were conditioned on the removal of U.S. forces from South Korea and the elimination of the government headed by Park Chung-hee.

Pyongyang's violent denunciations of the Park government, accompanied by the infiltration of large numbers of armed saboteurs and agents attempting to organize a revolutionary party in South Korea, gave the South Korean leaders ample reason to suspect Kim's offers to negotiate. North Korea's efforts to stimulate revolutionary activity in South Korea reached a high point in 1967–68. In December 1967 Kim Il-sung declared that "the northern half of the Republic is the revolutionary base for accomplishing the cause of national liberation on a nationwide scale"—a cause to be accomplished "at all costs."[5] The number of incidents of subversion and violence carried out by the North against the South soared from 50 in 1966 to 729 in 1967 and 761 in 1968. These included an audacious foray of January 21, 1968, by a specially trained team of 31 assassins against President Park's official Seoul residence and the landing of 120 commandos on the east coast of South Korea about fifty miles below the DMZ. Captured infiltrators said that hundreds of additional members of the North Korean army were receiving specialized training in espionage and terrorism.[6] In 1968, also, the North Koreans demonstrated their belligerence by the capture of the U.S.S. "Pueblo" and the shooting down of a U.S. EC-121 reconnaissance plane.

Kim Il-sung's intensive campaign of propaganda and armed infiltration of South Korea failed, however, to create a revolutionary movement. Infiltrators appear to have received little cooperation from the people of South Korea and the harsh methods used by some of them to force cooperation probably hurt their cause. North Koreans may have been misled by their own dogma and underestimated the strength of anticommunist sentiment in the South created by the brutality of northern troops during the Korean War and solidified by subsequent

5. Report of the United Nations Command to the United Nations, transmitted by U.S. Ambassador Arthur Goldberg's letter of Jan. 26, 1968 (UN Doc. S/8366, Jan. 27, 1968).

6. Report of the United Nations Command to the United Nations, transmitted by U.S. Ambassador Charles Yost's letter of May 8, 1969 (UN Doc. S/9198, May 8, 1969); and *American-Korean Relations*, Hearings before the Subcommittee on Asian and Pacific Affairs of the House Committee on Foreign Affairs, 92 Cong. 1 sess. (1971), p. 11.

indoctrination. A principal result of the infiltration campaign was South Korea's decision to organize and arm a homeland reserve of over two million men to detect and resist armed infiltrators.

Thus the North Korean campaign not only failed but probably was counterproductive, leaving South Korea better prepared to defeat infiltration than it had been before. By the end of 1968 Pyongyang appeared to have acknowledged the failure of these tactics. In 1969 the number of incidents fell to 134, in 1970 to 106, and in the first five months of 1971 only 15 occurred.[7] Further evidence of the failure of the campaign of violence—which cost the lives of 521 North Korean infiltrators in two years—was the replacement during 1968 and 1969 of all the key officials responsible for paramilitary actions against the South, including the minister of social security, the chief of the general liaison bureau of the Korean Workers party, and the chief of the reconnaissance bureau of the Ministry of National Defense.[8]

North-South Negotiations

The unsatisfactory result of the campaign to instigate revolution in South Korea was probably only one of the factors that caused Kim Il-sung to switch to a serious effort to engage the South in negotiations. Changes within Korea and in international relations affecting Korea helped to alter South Korean attitudes toward North Korea as well.

Kim's shift in tactics toward the South may have grown in part out of changes in the relative economic positions of the two Koreas. In the early years North Korea made impressively rapid progress in economic development, especially in industrialization, while South Korea lagged. But by the mid-1960s, under the double burden of minimizing dependence on outside economic help and diverting a large proportion of the national income to the defense budget, North Korean economic growth appears to have slowed sharply. The six-year plan extending to 1967 had to be stretched out three years. At precisely this time the South Korean economy, stimulated by a large influx of foreign capital and the expansion of foreign trade, began to grow rapidly. From 1966 to 1971 South Korea's gross national product increased in real terms by nearly 12 percent annually. Although South Korea emphasized light industry

7. *American-Korean Relations*, Hearings, p. 11.
8. *New York Times*, Sept. 22, 1969.

rather than heavy industry like North Korea, industrialization pro-
gressed substantially, with an average increase in real industrial production of 23 percent per year.

South Korea was making significant headway in its effort to outpace
North Korean economic growth and thus establish a more reliable base
from which to seek reunification. While Pyongyang continued to emphasize the slogan of "self-reliance," it showed increasing interest in expanding foreign trade, especially trade with Japan. Wider access to
Japanese technology could contribute significantly to North Korea's
economic growth. Moreover, North Korea's defense expenditures were
being "drastically reduced."[9] A period of economic competition with
South Korea was apparently under way.

One stimulant to South Korean growth was Japanese economic influence there. By 1970 public and private Japanese capital invested in
or pledged to South Korea amounted to at least $1.2 billion; in 1973 two-
way trade exceeded $3 billion—$1 billion more than Japan's trade
with mainland China. South Korea had become Japan's largest market
except for the United States. In the Nixon-Sato communiqué of November 1969, Sato described the security of South Korea as essential to the
security of Japan; since then North Korean propaganda has been filled
with harsh denunciations of Japanese economic ties with South Korea,
which are portrayed as evidence that Japanese militarists are again
scheming to take over Korea. Kim's switch to a softer policy toward
negotiations with South Korea may arise in part from fear of driving
the Park government into even closer cooperation with Japan.

The most important of the changes in the international situation
affecting North Korean policy toward South Korea, however, was probably the improvement in relations between the United States and China.
It must have dimmed the prospects of Chinese support for a policy of
seeking to take over South Korea by violence. Small but significant
modifications of the North Korean position began to appear in 1971,
after the announcement that President Nixon planned to visit Peking.
By the middle of 1972 Pyongyang was no longer insisting on prior withdrawal of U.S. forces from South Korea or the elimination of the Park
government as conditions for agreement on steps toward reunification.
Moreover, North Korea invited increasing numbers of influential visitors from Japan and pressed the Japanese government to open its doors

9. Kim's interview with Moto Goto, managing editor of *Asahi Shimbun,* published in *Asahi Evening News,* Sept. 28, 1971.

to travel by North Koreans. It also for the first time since the Korean War admitted a number of American correspondents and held out the prospect of expanding people-to-people exchanges with the United States. Kim's new strategy was a comprehensive "peace campaign," which placed Seoul on the political defensive.

Although South Korea's accomplishments in economic development and the failure of North Korea's infiltration campaign bolstered the confidence of South Korean leaders, they continued to feel at a disadvantage in countering the North Korean political offensive. South Korea had come a long way since the days of Syngman Rhee in developing a relatively stable political system, but many weaknesses remained that could be exploited by the North Koreans, such as the wide gap between rich and poor, extensive corruption, excessive reliance on foreign capital for investment, and the social dislocations resulting from rapid urbanization. South Korea was not as monolithic, tightly controlled, and sealed off from outside influence as North Korea, and its leaders feared that its relative freedom of expression and movement could make it vulnerable to Pyongyang's maneuvers, should negotiations begin between North and South.

Nevertheless, U.S. moves to improve relations with China and the USSR and the withdrawal of a U.S. division from South Korea radically changed the atmosphere. South Korea's foreign policy could no longer be conducted as it had been at the height of the cold war. President Nixon's policy of shifting emphasis from confronting major adversaries to negotiating with them had created a more complex international environment requiring greater flexibility in South Korean foreign policy. Hence, South Korea also began to make subtle changes in its posture both toward China and the USSR and toward North Korea.

The first fruit of the changing attitudes in North and South Korea was an agreement in August 1971 that the heads of their Red Cross societies would meet at Panmunjom to discuss arrangements for members of families separated by the division of Korea to communicate with and visit each other. This seemingly modest beginning was a radical step for two governments that had faced each other with unmitigated hostility for over twenty years and had totally prohibited contacts between people on either side of the DMZ. The talks moved at a slow pace and it was not until June 1972 after twenty meetings that the two sides were able to agree on an agenda for formal negotiations.

More important negotiations were proceeding behind the scenes, however. On July 4, 1972, even close observers of the Korean scene were taken by surprise by the announcement that senior officials of the two governments had agreed on a set of principles for the unification of Korea: that unification should be achieved by Koreans without outside interference; that it should be achieved by peaceful means, not by the use of force; that neither side would defame the other or engage in armed provocations, and that both would take measures to prevent inadvertent military incidents; that exchanges would be carried out in many fields; that both would cooperate positively in the Red Cross talks; that a direct telephone "hot line" would be installed between Seoul and Pyongyang; and that a North-South coordinating committee would be established to solve various problems between the two sides and settle the unification problem on the basis of the principles agreed on.

This development is unlikely to lead to early reunification of Korea, given the deep-seated mistrust between North and South, the differences in their political systems, and the conflicting views and objectives of leaders on the two sides. The principal purpose of each side in entering into the talks was probably to manipulate them so as to gain political advantages over the other. Nevertheless, the shift of emphasis from military confrontation to political maneuver represented by their willingness to talk to each other probably has further reduced the risk of war.

By the end of 1973 the coordinating committee established to pursue the dialogue had held four meetings, but had made no significant progress, either toward reunification or toward exchanges between North and South. In the meantime, President Park Chung-hee revised the constitution and took a number of other steps to strengthen his authority over South Korea and make it possible for him to remain in power indefinitely. He justified these actions primarily on the ground that the South Korean government would be at a disadvantage in negotiating with North Korea unless the South Korean body politic were more highly organized and disciplined and opposition to the government were repressed. He may be able to maintain his authoritarian rule for a long time by these means. But if he should rely increasingly on repression rather than on building a broad base of popular support for his government, economic growth probably would be slowed, internal opposition stimulated, and the danger increased that North Korea would resume large-scale efforts to infiltrate and subvert South Korea.

Thus, although tension between the two Koreas has been somewhat relaxed and both governments are placing greater emphasis on the political aspects of their confrontation, the danger of renewed conflict remains. Whether that danger increases will depend not only on the evolution of relations between the two Koreas, but on the attitudes of the big powers toward each other and toward Korea.

Attitudes of the Soviet Union

For twenty-five years, since the Soviet Union established the government in North Korea during its occupation by Soviet forces, the USSR has been North Korea's strongest protector and supporter. Kim Il-sung owes his early ascendancy over his rivals to Soviet support. The Chinese may have given more material aid than the Soviet Union, but it has consisted mainly of consumer goods and other items less important to North Korea than Soviet-supplied machinery and weapons. The North Korean military forces have relied heavily on the USSR for modern weapons: planes, tanks, artillery, and missiles.

North Korea is not, however, a mere puppet. Like North Vietnam, it has taken advantage of the Sino-Soviet dispute to maintain a degree of independence by maneuvering astutely between its two great protectors. Koreans are blunter than Vietnamese, however, and Pyongyang has been in less peril than Hanoi, so the North Koreans have not trod as narrow a path as the North Vietnamese. They have swung more widely from pro-Peking to pro-Moscow and back again. From their carefully balanced position between the two in 1961, when within a few days they signed similar defense treaties with both Moscow and Peking, the North Koreans swerved to pro-Peking, anti-Moscow in the early 1960s, to anti-Peking, pro-Moscow in the mid-1960s, and back to a roughly balanced position again in 1969–70.[10]

Throughout these gyrations Kim Il-sung's persistent theme has been self-reliance. In a remarkable speech to the Korean Workers party conference on October 5, 1966, he proclaimed the need for Korea to maintain an independent position and denounced "flunkeyism" toward the great powers.[11] He flailed at both "modern revisionism" and "left oppor-

10. For discussions of relations between North Korea, China, and the USSR, see Joungwon Alexander Kim, "Soviet Policy in North Korea," *World Politics*, vol. 22 (January 1970), pp. 237–51; Robert R. Simmons, "The Peking-Pyongyang-Moscow Triangle," *Current Scene*, Nov. 7, 1970, pp. 8–17; and Joseph C. Kun, "North Korea: Between Moscow and Peking," *China Quarterly*, No. 31 (July–September 1967), pp. 48–58.

11. U.S. Government, Foreign Broadcast Information Service (FBIS), *Daily Report: Far East (Supplement)*, Oct. 12, 1966.

tunism," condemning the "great power chauvinism" that caused the big communist powers to interfere in the internal affairs of the smaller communist parties. Over the years Kim has purged from the top ranks of his party the pro-Chinese Koreans and the pro-Soviet Koreans, surrounding himself mainly with loyal and long-time associates who fought with him against the Japanese in Manchuria in the 1930s.

Thus Moscow has found Kim a prickly and sometimes intractable partner. Anyone who took the Chinese side on Yugoslavia, the Indian border conflict, and the Cuban missile crisis, as Kim did, is obviously not trustworthy in Moscow's eyes. So it is, perhaps, not surprising that the Soviet Union has not supplied North Korea with the military equipment that would be needed to assure an overwhelming victory over the South, or that Moscow behaved cautiously in the "Pueblo" and EC-121 incidents, pointedly not endorsing Pyongyang's belligerence.

Soviet interest in Korea stems naturally from its location on the Soviet border and is reinforced by the need to compete with China for influence on a communist state. But there is little evidence that the Soviets have in recent years regarded the relatively small number of U.S. forces in South Korea as a threat to their security. Only after the Soviet dispute with China had become acute did the USSR substantially increase the military forces in its Far Eastern provinces. There is also little reason to believe that the Soviets consider the unification of Korea so important that they would be willing to assume large risks or burdens to accomplish it.

The USSR would appear to share with China, the United States, and Japan an interest in avoiding being drawn into war over Korea. Growing tension and risk of war in Korea would interfere with improving Soviet relations with the United States and Japan, both of which Moscow clearly regards as important objectives at the present time. It would in particular dash Soviet hopes for obtaining U.S. and Japanese assistance in developing the resources of Siberia.[12]

Attitudes of the Chinese

Although the North Koreans rely on the Soviets for vital military equipment and for deterrence of U.S. strategic nuclear power, ideologi-

12. Shigeo Hatada, director of the Japan Afro-Asian Solidarity Committee, reported that North Korean leaders had the impression that "the Soviet Union is only wishing for peace, making earnest efforts to maintain the status quo." *Yomiuri*, July 30, 1970.

cally and politically they have more in common with the Chinese. Like China, North Korea is a developing country and part of a divided state, claiming the right to territory under the control of a government allied to the United States. The North Koreans share with the Chinese a great suspicion of Japan and tend to see the trend of world affairs more through Chinese than through Russian eyes. Internally, they seem to have been influenced more by Peking than by Moscow, with their own versions of the Great Leap Forward and the cult of the leader.

The Chinese profess to be more dedicated than the Russians to promoting violent revolution, but there is little evidence that they would run serious risks to back an attempt by Kim Il-sung to unify Korea by force. On the contrary, the emphasis on "peaceful reunification" in Chinese statements of support for North Korea is striking.

The Chinese have strong reasons for desiring relatively peaceful and stable conditions in Korea during the next few years. Trouble in Korea could aggravate the strain of China's recovery from the shocks of the Cultural Revolution and of a possible severe succession struggle when Mao dies. It could also wreck Peking's progress toward improved relations with the United States and Japan, carefully planned to strengthen its position relative to the Soviet Union. Moreover, it could result in reinforcing the U.S.-Japanese alliance and accelerating Japanese rearmament. If the Chinese were drawn into military conflict in Korea, they could not count on the bountiful flow of Soviet military supplies they received before; instead, they would have to guard against the Soviets taking advantage of their involvement.

There is ample reason to believe that the Chinese see stability in the Korean peninsula as being in their interest. Competition with the Soviet Union for influence in North Korea will probably ensure firm Peking support for Kim Il-sung in political maneuvers to improve his position relative to that of the South Korean government, but the Chinese are unlikely deliberately to espouse policies that would provoke rising tension and danger of military conflict in Korea.

Attitudes of the Japanese

Japan's proximity to Korea and past wars with China and Russia, fought in large part over Korea, cause its leaders to see Korea as intimately related to Japan's own security. They would be alarmed if the entire peninsula were to come under the domination of a great power unfriendly to Japan. A truly neutral, unified Korea, not closely tied to any one of the big powers, would, of course, be no threat to Japan. But this is at best a distant goal, and until relations among the big powers and between the two Koreas change enough to make it possible, Japan's interests will be best served by a low-tension, stable balance between the two Koreas.

Because of Japan's security concerns, and its economic interests in South Korea, which have grown rapidly since the two established diplomatic relations in 1965, the outbreak of conflict in Korea would have a heavier impact on Japan than conflict anywhere else in Asia. Armed conflict in Korea would not only jeopardize important economic interests, it would call into question Japan's fundamental assumption that peace will prevail in Asia, allowing Japan to continue to prosper as a lightly armed big power pursuing its economic goals by peaceful means. War in Korea would cloud the prospects for expanded trade and improved relations with China and the Soviet Union. But even more damaging would be its precipitation of a bitter political struggle. The dominant political party—the Liberal Democratic party—and its supporters would tend to favor South Korea, while many among the opposition would sympathize with North Korea. Opposition to the use of bases in Japan by U.S. forces to carry out operations in Korea might provoke violent demonstrations. The Japanese government would be placed in a difficult position, as it strove to pacify its own people, while seeking to maintain good relations with the United States and to contribute to a favorable outcome of the conflict in Korea. U.S.-Japanese relations could become severely strained if the Japanese government were unable to share the burden of the conflict to the extent the U.S. government believed it should.

Thus the Japanese government has strong reasons for doing all it can to prevent conflict in Korea. It will give firm support to measures it believes will contribute to peace and stability in Korea and will try to avoid actions that might have the effect of heightening tension there. Its efforts will be hampered, however, by deep-seated animosity between Japanese and Koreans. Whenever serious incidents arise, as in the abduction of opposition leader Kim Tae-chung from Tokyo to Korea by South Korean agents in August 1973, tempers and suspicions flare on both sides The Japanese government will probably continue to favor a U.S. military presence in Korea or readily deployable to that area as a necessary deterrent to renewed conflict until negotiations between the Koreas and the improvement of relations among the big powers have further diminished the risk of war.

The Big Powers and Korean Unification

By the end of 1973 the portents for continued peace in Korea were favorable. Russia, China, and Japan, the neighboring great powers that had fought over Korea in the past, all seemed to have a greater stake in stability than in supporting a Korean leader in an effort to unify Korea by force. The United States had been able to reduce its forces in Korea without seriously undermining the confidence of the South Koreans or alarming the Japanese, a process that could be carried further if favorable trends continue in and around Korea. The United States and Japan had both made progress in reducing tension and expanding relations with the USSR and China. The continuing arms race between the two Koreas posed the potential danger of upsetting the military balance, but, for the time being at least, hostility between the two Koreas had been diminished by the agreement to seek unification not by force, but by peaceful means.

Despite these favorable portents, divided Korea remains a threat to peace. The tradition of a unified state is strong among Koreans. They are a homogeneous people with a distinct and ancient culture and a long history as a single independent nation. Resistance to Japanese colonization intensified their nationalistic sentiments. Thousands of members of Korean families separated from each other for years by the DMZ want to renew contacts. The concept of reunification therefore has an emotional appeal that can be exploited by Korean leaders. The danger is that as each Korean government maneuvers for a position from which to reunify the nation on its own terms, there will be temptations to resort to force should favorable opportunities arise.

The road to reunification is likely to be rocky, and the journey is unlikely to be completed within this decade. The vested interests that have grown up during the past twenty years in the differing political systems north and south of the DMZ will block their amalgamation. Even the opening of trade and travel between the two will be attended by many difficulties. The most important consideration, both for Koreans and for the big powers, as negotiations for expanding relations between the two Koreas proceed, is that neither side gain a sharply destabilizing advantage over the other.

To preserve stability, the military forces of the two Koreas must be in an approximate balance, the international relationships of each of the governments diversified, so that each develops relations with all four of the big powers, and the direct dependence of each Korea on big-power sponsors lessened.

If both Koreas had diplomatic, trade, and a variety of other relations with all four big powers, the intensity of the military confrontation that has dominated the peninsula since the Korean War would be diluted. Big powers would be less inclined to identify their own national interest closely and exclusively with one part of divided Korea. As a result it would be more difficult for a Korean leader to exert pressure on a big power to provide additional military equipment. The overriding emphasis on military power by the Korean governments would tend to decline, as economic power and diplomatic and political skills became increasingly important.

Changes in the relations of the big powers to the two Korean governments should occur gradually, however, and in a balanced way, so that neither Seoul nor Pyongyang feels it is being put at a serious disadvantage. The needed accommodations could be accomplished partly by actions of the two Korean governments, partly by shifts in policies toward Korea initiated by the big powers, and partly by international agreement among the big powers.

Diversification of the two Koreas' relations with the big powers has begun. Both Korean governments have recognized the need to open communications with nations whose governments have been regarded for years as implacable enemies. Park Chung-hee has declared that South Korea is prepared to "open its door" to all nations of the world and has urged countries with different ideologies and social systems to open their doors also to South Korea. It remains to be seen whether Peking and Moscow will respond. Kim Il-sung has been pressing for more trade and travel between Japan and North Korea and has admitted private Americans.

Diversification of relations could be advanced more rapidly if the relationship of the UN to the Korean problem were brought into line with current realities. Park Chung-hee, in a surprise move that gave him the political initiative over Kim Il-sung, declared on June 23, 1973, that his government would not object to the admission of both North

Korea and South Korea to the UN. He proposed a dual membership as an "interim measure" because he had concluded that unification could not be accomplished "within a short period of time."[13] The South Korean government has continued to insist, however, on the retention of the UN Command. The North Korean government, placed on the defensive, rejected the idea of separate memberships for North and South Korea, arguing that it would perpetuate division of the country. It proposed instead that a confederation be formed first, so that Korea could enter the UN as a single state, and it has continued to demand the dissolution of the UN Command.

For the UN debate on the Korean issue, the big powers have lined up, predictably, with the United States and Japan supporting the South Korean position and China and the USSR supporting that of North Korea. The stalemate may continue for some time, but it seems probable that both Koreas will ultimately enter the UN. Pyongyang might demand as its price for dual membership the dissolution of the UN Command, long one of its principal objectives. If so, the United States and South Korea could counter with a demand that a UN peace observation force, composed of units from nonaligned countries, be stationed in the DMZ. Dissolution of the UN Command would not, in itself, require the withdrawal of U.S. forces from South Korea, for they could be retained under the provisions of the U.S.-Republic of Korea security treaty. But a peace observation force in the DMZ would reduce the danger of incidents and help to create an atmosphere favorable to the gradual withdrawal of U.S. forces. Pyongyang would probably oppose outside interference in Korean affairs, but the North Koreans might, nevertheless, be persuaded to agree to an observation force in exchange for the elimination of the UN Command.

To maintain the balance of military force between the two Koreas while they negotiated, it would be highly desirable to limit the rapid buildup of weapons in both Koreas. Not only does the arms race place an unnecessarily heavy burden on the people of the two Koreas, it also increases anxiety on each side that the other may get ahead. Kim Il-sung has proposed that both sides reduce their armed forces to 100,000 and has even indicated he would not deprive the South of its numerical advantage. Despite uncertainties about how serious Kim is and how the difficult problem of verifying reductions of forces would

13. Park Chung-hee, *Special Statement Regarding Foreign Policy for Peace and Unification* (Seoul: Korea Information Service, June 23, 1973).

be resolved, force reductions or limitations are likely eventually to become a topic for discussion between Seoul and Pyongyang.

Since the big powers concerned with Korea appear to have a substantial interest in maintaining stability in the peninsula, it is not inconceivable that they could agree on actions to check the arms race. Even if formal agreement among the principal arms suppliers—the United States, the USSR, and China—were not practicable, tacit understandings might be reached among them that certain major items of military equipment that would create serious imbalance between North and South would be withheld. Placing a ceiling on the supply of offensive aircraft, the presence of which could be readily verified, would be especially desirable.

Another formula that might be seriously considered is a set of interlocking agreements in which the two Korean governments and the big powers would agree to renounce the use of force in Korea and to respect the peninsula as a nuclear-free zone. For example, the two Korean governments might in time convert their informal agreement not to use force against each other into a formal government-to-government agreement with the additional proviso that neither would manufacture nuclear weapons or permit them on its territory. The four big powers would then endorse the agreement, agree not to use force themselves in Korea, and pledge to respect the peninsula as a nuclear-free zone.

A set of agreements along these lines would provide assurance that all four big powers indeed perceived stability in Korea as in their interest and would thus improve the climate for further progress in the negotiations between the two Koreas. It would provide a framework for Japan to undertake a more active role in safeguarding peace in Northeast Asia.[14] By creating a nuclear-free zone it would diminish the risk that nuclear weapons might be used in a Korean conflict and would, for the first time, make China a participant in negotiating a limited arms control arrangement, thus increasing the prospect that the Chinese might come to see advantages in other forms of arms control agreements.

Agreement to a nuclear-free zone in Korea would not seriously handicap the United States in fulfilling its defense commitment to the Repub-

14. A self-denying agreement among the big powers would not imply an international guarantee of peace in Korea, and therefore would not obligate the guarantors to use force against a violator—an obligation the Japanese constitution prohibits.

lic of Korea, for the interlocking nature of the renunciation of force and nuclear-free zone agreements would provide for the parties to be released from the agreement if any one of them were to violate a part of it. Thus, the only military disadvantage to the United States would be the inability to position nuclear weapons in Korean territory.[15] Moreover, the high political costs and military risks attached to use of nuclear weapons in Korea make their use unlikely and diminish their deterrent effect.

A set of arms agreements among the big powers and the two Koreas would improve the atmosphere for continuing negotiations between Seoul and Pyongyang and would discourage temptations to seek reunification by force. Even though it is difficult today to see how reunification might be achieved, so long as some progress were being made in expanding peaceful relations between the two Koreas, neither Korea gained a destabilizing advantage over the other, and the big powers used their influence to help maintain these conditions, the danger of armed conflict in Korea would be kept low.

Implications for U.S. Policy

In pursuit of its long-term interests in East Asia, the United States should work to prevent armed conflict between the two Koreas, to strengthen the interest of all four big powers in peace in Korea, and to avoid actions toward Korea that would undermine Japanese confidence in the U.S. defense commitment to Japan.

The United States therefore should remain substantially involved in Korea and assure that its defense commitment to South Korea remains credible. Were the United States to abandon this commitment—or behave so as to convince Korean, Chinese, Soviet, and Japanese leaders that it intended to do so—the favorable trends in and around the peninsula could easily be reversed. But if the United States maintains its commitment and is successful in expanding and improving its relations with China and the USSR, the stake that all four big powers have in a stable peace in Korea will increase. As the danger of conflict recedes, the emphasis on military preparedness declines, and the Korean leaders pursue their goals increasingly through economic and political

15. A fuller exposition of the implications of a set of international agreements on Korea is contained in Ralph N. Clough and others, *The United States, China, and Arms Control* (Brookings Institution, forthcoming).

measures, the U.S. defense commitment to South Korea will fade in significance—just as the U.S. defense commitment to Taiwan will fade under the influence of improving relations between Washington and Peking. A gradual reduction in the U.S. military presence in South Korea would encourage this process, but an abrupt disengagement would endanger it.[16]

Whether some U.S. forces are withdrawn in the next several years or not, it would be advisable to continue the military aid to South Korean forces planned under the $1.5 billion modernization program. A continuing substantial flow of military aid would help to maintain the military balance on the peninsula essential to keep low the risk of large-scale conflict and would also bolster the political position of the South Korean government relative to North Korea. Sharp reduction or termination of military aid would endanger the military balance and raise questions as to the firmness of the U.S. commitment to the defense of South Korea.

Part of the military aid probably should go to expanding South Korea's military production facilities in order to diminish its dependence on a continuing high level of U.S. military aid and bring its military production capacity closer to that of North Korea. The degree of self-sufficiency attainable by South Korea in the next few years would not significantly increase the risk that its leaders would invade North Korea. They would still not be in a position to engage in large-scale conflict for more than a few weeks without U.S. logistic support.

The rapid growth of the South Korean economy has made possible a substantial reduction in U.S. economic aid to South Korea. Nevertheless, some economic aid, primarily in the form of agricultural products under Public Law 480, should continue to be supplied as needed to help maintain the momentum of economic growth and to evidence the continuing concern of the U.S. government with the health of the South Korean economy. It should no longer be necessary, however, to make official loans to South Korea on concessionary terms. Loans from the Japanese government and from international financial institutions should be ade-

16. See Hahm Pyong-choon, "Korea and the Emerging Asian Power Balance," *Foreign Affairs*, vol. 50 (January 1972), pp. 339–50, for a South Korean rationale for a continued "close special relationship" between South Korea and the United States. He believes that the United States, as a distant, detached power, can play an important role in preventing the revival of contention over Korea among Korea's big neighbors.

quate to meet those financial needs that cannot be supplied through foreign private loans and investment.

In order to further the balanced diversification of the international relationships of the two Koreas, the broadest possible support should be mobilized for the admission of both Koreas to the United Nations, as proposed by South Korea. In addition, the United States should make clear that it can enter into official relationships with North Korea only to the extent that the Soviet Union and China are willing to have relations with South Korea. Japan and other friendly states should be urged to adopt similar positions. Obviously, it is not possible for the United States, and still less for Japan, to control intercourse between their citizens and North Korea as Moscow and Peking control their peoples' contacts with South Korea. Substantial and growing trade and a small amount of travel back and forth already exist between North Korea and Japan, but virtually none between the communist states and South Korea. Even though private contacts with North Korea cannot be tightly regulated by the United States and Japan, the prospects for any softening of their official policies toward Pyongyang can be expressly linked to the expectation of comparable actions by Moscow and Peking.

The most difficult decisions for the United States will probably relate to the timing of further withdrawals of U.S. forces stationed in Korea. Paradoxically, present favorable trends in Korea probably owe their origin both to the withdrawal of 20,000 U.S. forces from South Korea and the fact that 40,000 remain. President Nixon's policy of reducing the U.S. military presence in the western Pacific created an essential condition for the improvement of relations with China, which, in turn, helped to persuade the Korean governments to enter into serious negotiations with each other. At the same time, the continued presence of a U.S. military force in South Korea may have been a factor in dissuading Kim Il-sung from relying on force to unify Korea; he may have concluded that in the changing international circumstances a relatively soft policy focused on negotiations with South Korea was more likely to secure the removal of U.S. forces from Korean territory than the threat of violence.

Over the next few years the presence of U.S. forces in South Korea is likely to be a major issue in the maneuvering between the two Koreas. North Korea will continue to demand their removal, which South Korea will continue to oppose. When Second Vice Premier Pak Song-chol on July 4, 1972, announced North Korea's agreement to the principles of reunification, he asserted that failure to achieve reunification earlier was entirely due to the "splitting policy of outside forces." He declared that the agreement showed that no threat of aggression from the north against South Korea existed. Therefore, Pak concluded, "the U.S. imperialists . . . must withdraw at once, taking with them all their forces of aggression."[17]

China and the Soviet Union will probably support the North Korean position, although they are unlikely to press the United States hard on this issue, for it is less important to them than a number of other issues. Moreover, the Chinese, in particular, may fear that a precipitate withdrawal of U.S. forces from South Korea would force the South Koreans into greater dependence on Japan, increasing the danger that Japan would add to its armaments to be better able to protect its interests in Korea. Chou En-lai, in discussing U.S. troop withdrawals from Korea, significantly noted that if things did not go well, the Japanese might use their treaty with South Korea "to get into South Korea immediately upon the withdrawal of U.S. forces." Though he referred to the withdrawal of U.S. forces from foreign territory as a "question of principle," he stated that when, where, and how the withdrawals would take place were concrete matters that would have to be discussed and agreed with the governments concerned.[18]

A year later, Chinese officials, including Chou, seemed considerably less concerned about the dangers posed by Japanese military forces. In fact, Chou reportedly told Tanaka that a "reasonable growth" of Japanese military strength would serve as a potential counterweight to the Soviet Union's "aggressive designs" in Asia.[19] This change in Chinese views may have been, at least in part, a tactical move related to the negotiations for the normalization of relations with Japan. But even if the Chinese are genuinely less concerned than before about the potential dangers in the strengthening of Japanese military forces, they remain deeply concerned about the potential Soviet threat and for this reason also may not be keen to see U.S. forces withdrawn soon from Korea. Hence, the Chinese, while wanting the United States to agree in principle to withdraw all its forces from Korea, probably would not be averse to a fairly lengthy period of withdrawal. Consequently, a gradual withdrawal of U.S. forces, timed so as not to upset the balance

17. FBIS, *Daily Report: People's Republic of China,* July 11, 1972, pp. A3–A5.
18. *New York Times,* Aug. 10, 1971.
19. Ibid., Dec. 14, 1972.

that now exists between the two Koreas, would be compatible with a U.S. policy of seeking improved relations with China.

Of course, an early total withdrawal of U.S. forces from South Korea would not necessarily result in renewed conflict in Korea, and it would have the great advantage, if conflict unexpectedly did occur there, of giving the United States the option of not becoming militarily involved —an option that would not be available if U.S. forces were present in South Korea when conflict broke out.

This course of action would, however, have serious disadvantages. It would heighten South Korean fears of an attack, especially the obsessive fear of a blitzkrieg against Seoul. It would also undermine the growing self-confidence that has made it possible for South Korean leaders to enter into negotiations with Pyongyang, despite their misgivings about the effect negotiations might have on domestic tranquility. Consequently, it would reduce chances of progress in North-South negotiations and probably cause both sides to place greater emphasis on military preparedness.

Moreover, a rapid withdrawal of all U.S. forces from South Korea would probably strengthen the hand of advocates of stronger armed forces in Japan, who would argue that a United States that no longer concerned itself about an area so closely related to Japan's security could not be relied on to defend Japan.

The most serious objection to early withdrawal of all U.S. forces from South Korea is the significant increase in the possibility of renewed conflict there, since it is uncertain how Kim Il-sung would react to the removal of U.S. forces from the military equation in Korea.

The risk of either renewed conflict or the reversal of recent favorable trends would be limited if future withdrawals of U.S. forces were contingent on further improvement of the relations among the big powers and between the two Koreas, and were arrived at after close consultation with the Japanese and South Korean governments. At present the Japanese and U.S. governments agree that U.S. forces in South Korea are important to the stability of the peninsula, both as a deterrent to renewed conflict and as a psychological support to the South Koreans as the delicate negotiations and political maneuvers between North and South proceed. The Japanese government did not object, however, to the withdrawal of the first U.S. division from South Korea and would probably not be disturbed by further withdrawals so long as, in its judgment, the stability of the peninsula were not threatened.

While an offer of greater military aid might overcome South Korean objections to the ultimate withdrawal of all U.S. forces from the peninsula, the probable result would be to intensify the arms race and perhaps to tempt a militarily strengthened South Korea to march north. The focus of attention in Korea would be shifted from diplomatic negotiations to the military balance.

Tensions would probably remain at a lower level if the United States kept some forces in South Korea until negotiations between the two Koreas had begun to develop cooperation between the governments. Judging from past experience, the presence of U.S. forces would continue to have a stabilizing effect on the peninsula.

It would probably be possible, however, to withdraw most U.S. ground forces within the next two or three years without destabilizing consequences. By keeping some U.S. air power in Korea, the United States would avoid leaving the South Koreans feeling exposed to the danger of an attack by a superior North Korean air force or having to supply them with additional expensive modern aircraft, which would speed up the arms race.

When the proper time arrives, total withdrawal of U.S. forces from Korea might be facilitated by agreement on the UN observer force in the DMZ or by agreements among the big powers concerning Korea.

The recommended U.S. actions to enhance prospects for peace in Korea assume a reasonably stable and effective government in South Korea. Whether that government will continue to be as stable and effective as in the recent past has been called into question by Park Chung-hee's actions to strengthen his authoritarian rule and suppress the opposition. Should South Korea be afflicted with a mounting cycle of disorder and repression, the United States would have to reconsider its policies.

CHAPTER TEN

Loosening Links with Thailand

By August 1973 all U.S. military forces had been withdrawn from Vietnam and bombing by U.S. aircraft throughout Indochina had ended. But President Nixon had warned in March that "the leaders of North Vietnam should have no doubt as to the consequences if they fail to comply with the [cease-fire] agreement," implying resumption of the massive U.S. air and sea attacks employed at critical junctures before the signing of the cease-fire agreement in January 1973.[1] Henry Kissinger reportedly made it clear to the North Vietnamese when the agreement was signed that the United States would not hesitate to use its air and sea power again if Hanoi should blatantly violate the cease-fire,[2] and the South Vietnamese stated that they had received similar assurances.[3] Moreover, U.S. officials indicated that the United States would keep some air power in the region for at least a few years to deter North Vietnam from mounting a major assault on South Vietnam.[4]

President Nixon clearly took the view that it was essential to keep alive the threat of U.S. air and sea power in order to buy time for the complicated play of diplomatic negotiations, internal political negotiations, military aid to friendly local forces, and economic aid programs to improve the prospects for the survival of a noncommunist South Vietnam. The threat of renewed U.S. bombing of battered and weary North Vietnam no doubt reduces the probability that Hanoi might launch an all-out offensive. But the potency of the threat has already been brought into question by congressional action forcing an end to bombing in Cambodia. Should Hanoi defy the United States and mount a large-

1. *New York Times*, March 30, 1973.
2. Article by William Beecher, *New York Times*, Jan. 23, 1973.
3. *New York Times*, Jan. 28, 1973.
4. Beecher, *New York Times*, Jan. 23, 1973.

scale attack, the cost to the U.S. government of overriding domestic and foreign opposition and resuming massive bombing would be high. It would be hard to convince most Americans and the principal U.S. allies that the U.S. interest in maintaining a containment line through Indochina at the present stage in the evolution of world politics was important enough to pay that price. Moreover, there is no assurance that massive U.S. bombing would suffice to preserve a noncommunist South Vietnam.

U.S. Alignments in Southeast Asia

The conclusion that U.S. interests in Southeast Asia are not critically important to the security of the United States argues for a long-term strategy of "loosening alignments" with governments of the region rather than continuing to keep U.S. forces poised to intervene if the containment line is threatened. Under such a strategy the survival of any particular Southeast Asian government would not be regarded as important enough to obligate U.S. forces to ensure its survival. Existing U.S. defense commitments in the region would be interpreted as providing for possible U.S. military intervention only against an attack by China (or the USSR—an eventuality even less probable than an overt large-scale attack by Chinese forces), not against lesser threats. Southeast Asian governments formerly dependent on the U.S. military capacity would have to compensate for the change in U.S. policy by improving their own ability to assure their security, by getting additional support from countries other than the United States, or by reaching compromise settlements with their enemies.

Although the United States would take the initiative to loosen alignments, the impetus would not come solely from the United States. Some local governments would want to loosen their ties with the United States in order to improve their diplomatic flexibility. Signs of such a tendency have already appeared in Thailand and the Philippines as a result of the withdrawal of U.S. forces from combat in Indochina.

As interest in the containment line waned, the line would gradually become blurred. It is not a natural line of demarcation rooted in long-standing differences between Southeast Asians. Some portions of the line, such as that dividing North and South Vietnam, have been politically significant in the past, and the fighting in recent years has created vested interests in other portions among those defending them. But the line as a whole, extending through Vietnam, Laos, and Cambodia, is a recent and artificial creation. Its location has been determined largely by decisions of the big powers as to whom they would support, and the high level of conflict has been made possible only by their provision of a large and continuing flow of equipment and supplies to each side. Where the fighting continues without U.S. forces, local forces and interests will assert themselves more, tending at places to reach across the containment line and blur it, rather than reinforce it.

The goal of a policy of loosening alignments would be to create an environment in which the states of Southeast Asia, acting singly or in cooperation with each other, would be less bound by the global rivalry between the big powers, and the big powers would be less affected by actions taken by those states. This would not mean a decline in trade, travel, aid programs, cultural exchange, and other types of intercourse. On the contrary, the inexorable trend toward greater interdependence among nations would cause these to increase. But the exclusiveness of the relationship with a particular big power demanded by close defense ties would be broken. Southeast Asian nations would increasingly develop relations of various sorts with all four big powers, as well as with other major industrial states in the world. The changed environment would give the Southeast Asian states more room for maneuver, particularly through the use of diplomacy rather than force in attempting to settle local conflicts.

The loosening of U.S. alignments alone would not necessarily lessen the impact of big-power rivalry on Southeast Asian states. But once the threat of U.S. intervention in local conflicts was removed, North Vietnam would probably seek a looser alignment with China. Even in wartime, the Sino-Soviet split has enabled Hanoi to preserve for itself considerable freedom of action. The attractiveness of Japan as a trading partner, which has made it one of the chief noncommunist traders with both the USSR and China, would also appeal to North Vietnam. Substantial Japanese trade with and economic aid to both North and South Vietnam would help to blur the containment line. An important step in this direction was taken in September 1973, when Japan and North Vietnam agreed to establish diplomatic relations.

Loosened alignment would also imply greater diversity in the political and economic systems of Southeast Asia. Because the line between "communist" and "anticommunist" would be drawn less sharply, mixed systems incorporating elements from both East and West could more easily develop. National leaders might feel freer to experiment with various ways of adapting aspects of the traditional culture to the demands of modernization. The United States, being less intimately attached to particular Southeast Asian governments, would not be preoccupied with the political complexion of those governments. Even North Vietnam, less dependent on China than when at war, might allow its internal policies to depart further from the Chinese model.

If the big powers relax their interests in Southeast Asia, the states of the region will draw closer to each other. Already the trend toward regional cooperation has been strengthened by the withdrawal of U.S. forces from South Vietnam. Eventually, the big powers may come to recognize Southeast Asia as a zone of peace and neutrality, as was proposed in 1971 by the foreign ministers of the states constituting the Association of Southeast Asian Nations.[5] A formal agreement may not be feasible for years, for conflicts of interest among the big powers are still sharp. But once the decision has been taken to keep U.S. forces out of local conflicts, and assuming that the Chinese do not change their policy of not intervening with their own forces, the principle of non-intervention by outside military force might come gradually to be accepted. A tacit understanding could develop that, although Big Four rivalry continued in Southeast Asia by a variety of nonmilitary means, none of the Big Four would see its interests in the region as important enough to risk a big war. Eventually, this tacit understanding might be converted into a formal pledge.

Loosening alignments would, of course, involve risks. The most immediate question would be its effect on South Vietnam and Cambodia, where embattled governments are struggling for survival. Their situation is too volatile to examine in detail. A U.S. decision not to use military force, even in the event of a large-scale offensive by North Vietnam, probably would reduce their chances. Yet the certainty that they had only their own military forces to rely on could result in improved performance. The South Vietnamese government responded well to the total withdrawal of U.S. forces from combat and the Cambodian government survived the termination of U.S. bombing support; it need not be assumed that a clear-cut U.S. decision not to intervene militarily again would cause either government to collapse.

5. *Washington Post*, Nov. 27, 1971.

A continuing flow of U.S. military and economic aid would be necessary if the South Vietnamese and Cambodian governments were to survive. But the logic of a policy of loosening alignments would require a declining level of such aid. The rate at which it was phased down would depend on circumstances in the countries and the level of aid to North Vietnam by China and the USSR.

A policy of loosening alignments in Southeast Asia would, then, increase the risk that Hanoi would gain control over South Vietnam and preponderant influence over Laos and Cambodia. Should that happen, would it bring a chain reaction that produced within a few years a Southeast Asia composed of communist states under Chinese domination?

Outside the Indochina states themselves, Thailand would provide the gravest test for the policy of loosening alignments, because the Thai government committed itself so deeply to the success of the U.S. policy of holding a containment line through Indochina. Thailand is a formal ally of the United States in the Southeast Asia Treaty Organization (SEATO), it provided bases for U.S. aircraft being used against North Vietnam, it sent a division of its own troops to fight in South Vietnam, it provided "volunteers" to aid the Royal Laotian government, and it helped to train the Cambodian armed forces. Moreover, because Thailand borders on Laos and Cambodia, it would feel more immediately threatened by North Vietnamese ascendancy in Indochina than would any other Southeast Asian state. And because it also borders on Burma and Malaysia and is closely associated with Indonesia, the Philippines, and Singapore in ASEAN, the shock waves of the impact on Thailand resulting from the proposed change in U.S. policy would be felt throughout Southeast Asia.

Thai-U.S. Relations

The Thais have been more concerned than any other Southeast Asian people about affairs in neighboring Indochina. Their intimate relationship with the United States has grown out of this concern. Thailand's military-dominated government, disturbed by the communist victory in China, cast its lot with the United States in deciding to contribute troops to the United Nations action in Korea. In the fall of

1950 the United States began programs of military, economic, and technical assistance to Thailand.

With the Vietminh victory at Dienbienphu and the subsequent agreement at Geneva in 1954 for French combat forces to withdraw from a partitioned Vietnam, the Thais saw Chinese Communist influence spreading further in their direction and pressed for formal defense arrangements with the United States. They were strong advocates of the Manila Treaty of 1954, which established SEATO.

Under the treaty "each Party recognizes that aggression by means of armed attack in the treaty area against any of the parties . . . would endanger its own peace and safety, and agrees that it will in that event act to meet the common danger in accordance with its constitutional processes." And if "the inviolability or the integrity of the territory or the sovereignty or political independence of any Party in the treaty area . . . is threatened in any way other than by armed attack or is affected or threatened by any fact or situation which might endanger the peace of the area, the Parties shall consult immediately in order to agree on the measures which would be taken for the common defense."[6]

The SEATO treaty has been particularly important for Thailand, because it is the only member of SEATO that is not also protected by some other defense treaty with the United States. Hence, when alarmed by the advance of North Vietnamese-supported Pathet Lao forces in Laos in 1962, it sought assurance that the United States would fulfill its treaty commitment. The United States, in the Rusk-Thanat communiqué, declared that it "regards the preservation of the independence and integrity of Thailand as vital to the national interest of the United States and to world peace," and that the obligation of the United States under SEATO "does not depend upon the prior agreement of all other parties to the Treaty, since this Treaty obligation is individual as well as collective."[7]

The belief that North Vietnam's effort, backed by both the Chinese and the Russians, to bring communist parties into power in South Vietnam, Laos, and Cambodia posed a serious threat to Thailand led the governments of Thailand and the United States to take a variety of actions to meet this perceived threat.

6. Royal Institute of International Affairs (London), *Collective Defense in Southeast Asia: The Manila Treaty and Its Implications* (Oxford University Press, 1956), p. 169.

7. *Department of State Bulletin*, March 26, 1962, p. 498.

To demonstrate its determination to fulfill its SEATO commitments, the United States sent 10,000 U.S. ground and air force personnel to Thailand after the flare-up in the fighting in Laos in 1961–62. A Military Assistance Command for Thailand (MACTHAI) was established to coordinate U.S. military activities. Although the U.S. ground forces were withdrawn after the Geneva Accords on Laos were signed in July 1962, the two governments agreed to improve facilities in Thailand to support future deployment of U.S. forces there should they be required. As the North Vietnamese pressed their attacks further in both Laos and South Vietnam during 1963–64, the United States began to improve Thai airfields and logistic facilities and to increase its air force units in Thailand. It also began joint military planning with the Thais to meet contingencies that might arise under the SEATO treaty.

From 1965, when the United States began bombing North Vietnam and sent ground forces in large numbers into South Vietnam, U.S. military activities in Thailand in support of the war in Vietnam and Laos increased sharply. The United States also supported the Thai government's efforts to contain the communist insurgency that broke out in northeast Thailand in 1965. Its military construction program reached a peak in 1966 and 1967, amounting to $336 million in those two years. By August 1969 the authorized strength of U.S. military personnel in Bangkok and eight major military bases totaled 48,000. Moreover, the United States paid for the dispatch of the Thai division that fought in South Vietnam and provided military and economic aid to the Thai government averaging over $100 million annually from 1966 to 1970. Total U.S. assistance to Thailand during the twenty years 1949–69, plus U.S. military expenditures in that country, exceeded $2 billion.[8]

The bare figures on the U.S. military presence and expenditures in Thailand and on U.S. aid to the Thai government fail to convey the closeness of the association between the United States and Thailand. The United States sent thousands of military advisers to help strengthen the Thais' ability to defend their country against a conventional attack and to cope with the spreading insurgency within Thailand. Large numbers of American civilians also advised the Thais on economic development, government administration, and counterinsurgency methods. Well over ten thousand Thai military personnel received training from

8. *United States Security Agreements and Commitments Abroad,* Hearings before the Subcommittee on U.S. Security Agreements and Commitments Abroad of the Senate Committee on Foreign Relations, 91 Cong. 1 sess. (1969), pt. 3, p. 748.

Americans, either in the United States or in Thailand, as well as smaller numbers of Thai civilians.

With the announcement of the Nixon Doctrine and the adoption of the Vietnamization program in South Vietnam, the United States began reducing its involvement in Thailand. By June 1971 its forces had been reduced by one-third to 32,000. The levels of military and economic aid had also declined and many U.S. advisers had been withdrawn. But in the spring of 1972 the number of U.S. forces rose again in order to counter with increased U.S. air power the large-scale offensive launched by Hanoi in South Vietnam. The forces declined again following the cease-fire in Vietnam and the termination of bombing in Cambodia, but in early 1974 they still constituted one of the largest groups of U.S. military personnel in any one country outside the United States.[9]

The critical choice in U.S. relations with Thailand now is whether to work to cement its close ties even more firmly, in order to keep facilities in Thailand available for U.S. forces, or to move to loosen the alignment, on the grounds that there is no longer a need for U.S. forces or bases there.

Should the United States decide it would no longer provide forces to assist in holding the containment line through Indochina, it could elect to commit its forces to the defense of the borders of Thailand, in effect establishing a new containment line. Such a course of action would have several disadvantages. Most important, this policy would keep the United States more deeply involved with the fortunes of a particular Southeast Asian government than its interests in that region would justify. And even if the United States were willing, Thai leaders might very well prefer not to maintain so close a relationship with the United States; they might decide that their interests would be better served by accommodating themselves to the enhanced influence of China and North Vietnam, following their past policy of conforming their diplomatic stance to changes in the relative influence projected into Southeast Asia by the big powers. Moreover, the long-term goal of big-power agreement on respecting Southeast Asia as a zone of peace and neutrality could not be attained so long as the United States was so deeply committed in Thailand.

The alternative policy of loosening alignments with Thailand would

9. *Thailand, Laos, Cambodia, and Vietnam: April 1973*, Staff Report prepared for the Subcommittee on U.S. Security Agreements and Commitments Abroad of the Senate Committee on Foreign Relations, 93 Cong. 1 sess. (1973), p. 5.

also pose risks. Communist dominance in Indochina would come as a severe shock to Thai leaders, who would be further unnerved by U.S. moves to diminish relations with Thailand. U.S. influence in Thailand would be sharply reduced, and a period of political uncertainty and possibly some disorder might result.

The fundamental question is whether these trends would result in Thailand's falling under Chinese control. This might conceivably happen in one of several ways: through an attack on Thailand by Chinese or North Vietnamese forces, through a successful revolution by the Chinese-dominated Thai Communist party, or by a decision of the Thai government to ally Thailand closely with China.

The Threat of Overt Attack on Thailand

A Chinese military attack on Thailand in the next few years is highly improbable, even if Indochina should come under communist dominance and the United States followed a policy of loosening alignment with Thailand. China, of course, has the power to overrun Thailand with its military forces, even without brandishing nuclear weapons. But there is little evidence either in their declared policy or their military doctrine and deployment that the Chinese intend to achieve their goals by military conquest. On the contrary, the doctrine of "people's liberation war" emphasizes self-reliance for local revolutionaries. It promises help, but not Chinese combat forces. And Chinese policies for the past twenty years toward Thailand's neighbor, Burma, which has had no defense alliance, suggest that in this respect the Chinese mean what they say.

The disinclination of the Chinese to send their own military forces into neighboring countries would probably be reinforced, not weakened, by a strengthened communist role in Indochina and a looser U.S. tie. Peking would probably see prospects improving both for revolution in Thailand and for increased Chinese influence on the Thai government. The more the Thais turned away from the United States and sought accommodation with Peking, the less reason the Chinese would have for invading Thailand. Even if the Chinese had some motivation for an attack on Thailand, it is difficult to imagine Peking not only casting aside its improved relations with the United States, but risking a military confrontation with the United States in the south at a time when it is obsessed with the Soviet threat to the north.

Of course, the Chinese might support the invasion of Thailand by a proxy: North Vietnam. If the North Vietnamese were able to consolidate their hold on Laos up to the Mekong River, they might go on into northeast Thailand, perhaps in the guise of Thai revolutionary forces, following the pattern of their intervention in Laos. But it is hardly credible that after twenty-five years of constant warfare the North Vietnamese would have the strength or inclination for a large-scale invasion of Thailand. Even if they achieved dominance in Indochina, they would be heavily involved in consolidating their position there and their people would need a respite from fighting. It would be hard to arouse much nationalist enthusiasm for fighting and dying in Thailand.

It is possible, of course, that military conflict between Thailand and North Vietnam might come about, not because of a deliberate decision by Hanoi to invade Thailand in support of Thai communist rebels, but because the two governments were backing different contenders for power in Laos or Cambodia. This could lead to clashes between the regular forces of the two nations and perhaps even result in large-scale conflict.

The danger that Thailand would fall under Chinese control, if the United States limited its support to military and economic aid, is not great. The situation would be different from that in Vietnam in many ways. It would be harder to justify the presence of North Vietnamese troops in Thailand than in South Vietnam, and it is especially doubtful that either the Soviet Union or China would be willing to provide large-scale support for such an enterprise if U.S. forces were not involved. China, particularly, would be unlikely to see an intervention by North Vietnamese forces as being in Chinese interest. China has always been the principal backer of the Thai Communist party and would hardly wish to see its influence in Thailand eclipsed by Hanoi's.

Moreover, as appears to have occurred in the Vietnam negotiations, China's and Russia's developing relations with the United States would probably dispose them against supporting an adventurous policy by Hanoi in Thailand. Thus the alignment of big-power interests would favor efforts to bring the conflict to an early negotiated settlement— or at least to avoid actions tending to prolong it. The nonparticipation of U.S. forces in the fighting would tend to enhance, rather than reduce, prospects for big-power cooperation to this end.

Insurrection by Chinese-directed Communists

A greater threat to Thai freedom than invasion is the seizure of power by the Chinese-backed Thai Communist party. But even this contingency is not very likely. The communist movement has never developed the strength in Thailand that it has had at various times in other Southeast Asian countries. As an independent state, Thailand offered a less hospitable climate than did the Southeast Asian colonies to exponents of Lenin's anti-imperialist theories. Moreover, since 1933 the Thai government has outlawed and suppressed the Thai Communist party, except for the six years from 1946 to 1952 when it was permitted to function legally. From its beginning the Thai Communist party has maintained close associations with the Chinese Communist party, causing the Thai government and many Thais to regard it as primarily an instrument by which China could exercise influence on Thailand through the overseas Chinese community.

Armed communist insurrection against the government, which began in most Southeast Asian countries between 1945 and 1950, did not begin in Thailand until 1965. Four sizable groups of insurgents are now operating in border areas far from Bangkok. In the forested mountains of the northeast, not far from the Mekong River, armed rebellion began in 1965. The northeast was a logical place to start a revolt, for the people of the region were poor and neglected by the central government and the region was not far from communist-held parts of Laos. For a while the rebels were able to increase their numbers and expand their area of operations, but by 1967 government countermeasures began to take effect and forced them to change their tactics. The armed rebels may number as many as 2,000. They continue to recruit and organize, but have had to reduce overt violence to avoid Thai security forces.

The insurgents in the north, unlike those in the northeast, are not ethnic Thais, but mainly Meo tribespeople, with a cadre of Thais, some of whom had experience as guerrillas in the northeast. Their rugged and remote mountain homeland is well suited to guerrilla warfare, and long-standing Meo grievances against Thai authorities provide a basis for communist recruiting. The Meos, who began their insurgency in 1967, get direction, training, and some supplies from camps across the border in Laos. Their numbers have gradually increased, reaching perhaps 2,900 by late 1972.

In the midsouth, some 600 Thai communists have been active, attacking village defense forces and capturing weapons. They may have contacts with a fourth group that operates in the south. The southern group began in the late 1950s with several hundred members of the Malayan Communist party who fled across the border into Thailand. This group, which may number as many as 2,000, is composed mainly of ethnic Chinese, with some Thai Muslims. It is unlike the other communist guerrilla groups in Thailand, because it is directed by the Malayan Communist party and its attacks are aimed at the Malaysian government.[10]

The Thai Communist party, which directs the insurgents in the northeast, north, and midsouth, makes no secret of its close relationship with Peking. It is the leading element in the two principal front organizations for Thailand, the Thailand Independence Movement and the Thailand Patriotic Front, whose chief officers have resided for many years in Peking.[11] The party's activities are made known primarily through broadcasts by the Voice of the People of Thailand, a clandestine radio station located in China, and by the New China News Agency. Peking gives the insurgents strong propaganda support and provides funds and training. In return, the Thai Communist party has adopted a firmly Maoist stance and has denounced the "Soviet revisionist clique."[12] Its central committee has declared that "under the guidance of the great thought of Mao Tse-tung we are full of confidence that we will be able to drive the U.S. imperialists out of Thailand, overthrow the traitorous Thanom clique, and set up a people's revolutionary political power on the soil of Thailand."[13]

10. Data on communist insurgents in Thailand are estimates by U.S. Embassy, Bangkok, quoted in ibid., p. 7.

11. See Donald E. Weatherbee, *The United Front in Thailand* (University of South Carolina Press, 1970).

12. Voice of the People of Thailand on March 1, 1968, declared that "the Communist Party of Thailand has held high the great red banner of Mao Tse-tung's thoughts, which are the present greatest ideas of Marxism-Leninism, and has determinedly insisted on resisting modern revisionism led by the Soviet revisionist clique in order to defend the purity of Marxism-Leninism." Ibid., p. 67.

13. U.S. Government, Foreign Broadcast Information Service (FBIS), *Daily Report: Communist China*, April 9, 1969, p. A3.

When the party in 1969 created a supreme command to direct the insurgent activities of the Thai People's Liberation Armed Forces, the first task outlined for these forces was to "study and firmly grasp the thoughts of Mao Tse-tung."[14] Guerrillas returned from training in China reportedly wore Mao Tse-tung badges.

References to Mao's thought became less frequent and less glowing among the Thais as the high-flown rhetoric of the Cultural Revolution faded in China. But as recently as August 1972, on the occasion of the forty-fifth anniversary of the Chinese People's Liberation Army, the Voice of the People of Thailand declared that the Thai Communist party was integrating "the theory of Marxism-Leninism-Mao Tse-tung thought" with revolutionary practice in Thailand and pledged "to learn from the great example set by the People's Liberation Army."[15]

The Thai government has watched with growing concern the construction by Chinese army engineers of two roads from the Chinese border across the northwest corner of Laos toward the Thai frontier. Work on one road has been intermittent since 1962; by April 1973 it stretched over one hundred miles from Mengla in Yunnan Province to Pak Beng, only twenty miles from the Thai border. The second road, on which work had only begun in 1973, lies to the west of the first road. The purpose of these roads may be primarily to strengthen Chinese influence in this part of Laos. If it is, however, to open supply routes to Thailand, the roads would improve considerably the ability of the Chinese to step up supplies to the insurgents.

The Thai government, aided by U.S. funds, equipment, advice, and training, has substantially improved the ability of its security forces, including regular armed forces, border patrol police, ordinary police, and the village-based volunteer defense corps, to control the insurgency. It has also undertaken a variety of social and economic measures intended to improve the lot of the people, especially in the northeast, and to make them less susceptible to communist influence. Programs for building roads, digging wells, establishing farm cooperatives, building schools, providing medical service, training local officials, improving crops, aiding village projects, and disseminating information are aimed at strengthening ties between the government and the people and demonstrating that the government can help meet the people's needs. Despite the increased resources being used to increase popular support

14. Weatherbee, *The United Front in Thailand*, pp. 70–71.
15. FBIS, *Daily Report: People's Republic of China*, Aug. 7, 1972, p. J4.

for the government and to repress the rebellion, the number of armed insurgents has slowly increased.[16]

The government, however, has been able to contain the insurgents in their remote mountain strongholds, and the communists have found little popular support in the populous parts of Thailand. The few thousand communist rebels have depended on outside support for both training and weapons. And because they have identified themselves with China, the government has been able to mobilize nationalist sentiment against them.

Thai Strengths and Weaknesses

The chances that the rather weak Chinese-oriented Thai Communist party may gain control over Thailand are much slimmer than those of the insurgents in South Vietnam. The Thais are more homogeneous than the people of South Vietnam. Close to 90 percent of Thailand's 40 million people speak the same language, adhere to the Buddhist religion, and follow similar customs. The 2.5 million Chinese in Thailand are the most important minority, because of the large number concentrated in Bangkok and their key role in industry and commerce. But they are better assimilated than the Chinese in other Southeast Asian countries because of the similarity of their religion and customs to those of the Thais and because Thai government policy has promoted assimilation. Other non-Thai peoples in Thailand, such as Malays, Cambodians, Vietnamese, and miscellaneous tribespeople, total only a little over a million, scattered around the margins of the country.

A more important difference between Thailand and South Vietnam than the makeup of their populations, however, is the fact that Thailand has never been a colony. Consequently, there was no anticolonial war to raise up thousands of armed and experienced guerrillas like those who became fervent nationalists fighting the French in Vietnam and formed the backbone of communist forces there. Moreover, the Thai communist insurgents have no charismatic nationalist leader like Ho Chi-minh, whereas the Thai government can rally the population around the traditional symbol of authority—the king. Finally, Thailand is not a divided country.

16. *U.S. Security Agreements,* Hearings, pp. 629–32; *Thailand, Laos,* Staff Report, pp. 7–8.

Besides lacking important advantages that the Vietnamese communists possessed, the Thai communists face many obstacles in mounting a revolution in the countryside. Even though Thailand is the most rural of all Southeast Asian states except Cambodia, with only 13 percent of its people living in towns and cities, the countryside is rather stable. Banditry has been eliminated in all but the most remote areas. Traditional values, respect for authority, and traditional social organizations still have a strong hold. Thailand's gross national product grew at 7–8 percent annually in the 1960s, so that even with a population growth of 3.3 percent the standard of living has improved. Thailand has ample resources and its concentration of land ownership is relatively low. Despite inevitable economic setbacks when the prices of its export commodities fall, as happened in 1970–71, the prospects for maintaining a rate of economic growth substantially higher than that of most developing countries are reasonably good.[17] The Thai bureaucracy, army, and police force are experienced and relatively effective, by Asian standards. Thailand does not have the characteristics of a country in which large numbers of the populace are ripe for revolt.

Of course, Thailand possesses weaknesses common to most developing countries. There is considerable corruption and inefficiency. Modernization is increasing the gaps between the rich and poor, the city and the countryside, the wealthier regions and the poorer ones, and the old and the young. There is danger of a widening gulf between the aspirations of the people and the ability of the government to satisfy them. Landlords are expanding their holdings and more smallholders are being forced to become tenant farmers, especially in drought years, when farmers are compelled to borrow money at very high rates of interest. Rapidly industrializing Bangkok has seen for the first time strikes by dissatisfied workers.

Most significant of all, in October 1973 tens of thousands of rioting university students brought down the government, forced the three principal military leaders to flee the country, and caused the king to call on the rector of a Bangkok university to form the first Thai civilian government in sixteen years. Given the tradition of military rule in Thailand and the country's lack of experience in constitutional government and democratic procedures, it will be difficult for a civilian government to govern effectively. The military will retain substantial

17. See United Nations, *Economic Survey of Asia and the Far East, 1969*, pp. 204–11, and *1971*, pp. 6 and 151–53.

power behind the scenes. Thailand might go the way of South Korea, where the civilian government brought to power by the student-instigated ouster of Syngman Rhee was overthrown within less than two years by a military coup. Whatever may happen, Thai politics will never be the same as before the October riots. The formerly docile Thai students have demonstrated a capacity for exerting political pressure that no future Thai government can ignore.

Should the student riots of 1973 prove to be the beginning of a period of political disorder, with frequent changes of government, opportunities would increase for the Thai Communist party to gain in strength. But customary public order in Thailand has not been seriously undermined. Respect for the monarchy provides an element of stability that does not exist in most Southeast Asian countries. The bulk of politically active Thai students appear interested in reform, not in revolution. Consequently, their pressure could strengthen the Thai government's ability to counter communist insurgency in Thailand, by inhibiting government leaders from indulging in some of the worst excesses of the past. The odds against a successful communist revolution soon in Thailand do not appear to have been significantly altered by recent events. Suppose, however, communist dominance in Indochina and a U.S. policy of loosening alignments. How would the ability of Thailand to avoid Chinese domination be affected?

The chief immediate change would be in the ability of the Chinese or North Vietnamese to establish infiltration routes, supply depots, and sanctuaries; the whole length of Thailand's border with Laos and Cambodia would be open to them. It would become more difficult for Thai security forces to restrict the movement of supplies and persons across the border. Operating out of sanctuaries in Laos or Cambodia, the rebels would have access to a wide belt on the Thai side of the border in which they could work at building a communist organization by the usual combination of threat and promise.

But the limited gains the rebels have made over the past seven years in Thailand, even though the Chinese and North Vietnamese already had access through parts of Laos to large sections of the porous Thai border, suggest that other factors determine the effectiveness of the insurgents. The failure of the Burmese Communist party to duplicate the success of the North Vietnamese communists reflects differences in internal conditions in the two countries, rather than differences in the accessibility of outside help, for both countries have long borders with

China and both parties have received Chinese assistance. In Thailand, as in Burma, better access to cross-border sanctuaries would not give the rebels a decisive advantage.

More important would be the psychological boost to the rebels and the corresponding shock to government supporters. Knowing that they had an invulnerable rear area extending all the way to China and the support of the largest nation in the world, the rebels would be encouraged to persevere against unfavorable odds. The Thai government, on the other hand, worried by the advance of hostile forces to the Thai border, would be forced to spread its forces out thinly over a broad area and would be frustrated by inability to reach the rebels' supply bases. More of the already strained Thai budget would have to be diverted to countering the insurgency. Moreover, there would be a tendency for the fence-sitters in Thailand to assume that China would replace the United States as the nation with the greatest influence on Thailand, and many would withhold their support from the government, if not shift to active support for the rebels, as a hedge against the future.

Still, the Thai Communist party would have to recruit and train cadres, expand party and front organizations, and work for the cooperation of the people necessary to create secure base areas. Lacking the nationalist advantages that the Chinese Communists had in mobilizing resistance to a Japanese invasion and that Vietnam's communists had in fighting against a colonial ruler, the Thai Communist party would probably face a long, uphill struggle, even with the advantages conferred on it by communist dominance in Indochina and U.S. withdrawal from a close relationship with the Thai government.

Judging from the experience of communist parties in Asia during the past twenty-five years, the Thai Communist party is unlikely to be able to seize power unless it can convince a sizable group of disaffected citizens that it, and not the Thai government, is the authentic champion of nationalist sentiment in Thailand. The Thai Communist party would have to shake off the image of Chinese control that severely limits its appeal. The party's heavy dependence on Chinese support makes this difficult to do and any substantial increase in Chinese support would compound the problem. And if, over a period of years, the Thai Communist party were able to create extensive local support to replace its dependence on China, when it finally came to power it probably would not be a pliant tool of Peking.

Thai Foreign Relations

The Thais demonstrated impressive diplomatic skills in maintaining their national independence throughout the colonial period, an experience that they can draw on in the period ahead in order to avoid falling under the exclusive domination of China or any other major power. A U.S. policy of loosening the alignment with Thailand would cause the Thais to increase emphasis on their efforts, already under way, to balance their relations among the big powers.

China

Thailand would be more likely to fall under Chinese domination through Chinese diplomatic pressures on the Thai government, augmented by domestic political unrest, covert Chinese aid to the Thai Communist party, and Thai fear of Chinese power than through military conquest or an early seizure of power by the Thai Communist party. If Indochina came under communist dominance and the United States decided not to use its forces to support the Thai government except in the event of Chinese attack, many Thais would be convinced that the United States was "abandoning" Thailand. Chinese efforts to exploit this situation could combine pressure and inducement, ranging from the cultivation of influential Thai leaders to increased support of the Thai Communist party and other opposition groups. Some influential Thais would become leaders of pro-China groups, while a larger number would at least hedge their bets on the future by giving support to such groups. Thailand probably would become less stable politically, as a realignment of political forces occurred, and a military coup might bring to power new leaders to replace those associated with the discredited pro-American policies.

China would probably place primary emphasis on interstate relationships, unless an improbably rapid upsurge in the insurgency should place the Thai government in jeopardy. The cultivation of a broad range of diplomatic, trade, and people-to-people relations—the current emphasis in Chinese foreign policy—would place China in a better position from which to compete with other big powers for influence on the Thai government. As even the most fervent supporters of world revolution within the Chinese leadership would probably recognize, it would also strengthen the base for Chinese encouragement of revolutionary forces in Thailand over the long run.

By early 1971, the Thai government, already scenting the changes in big-power relations in East Asia, had informed the Chinese through third countries that it was interested in developing contacts with Peking and had begun a trade study in anticipation of the legalization of trade with China.[18] In mid-1972 an influential Thai official accompanied a Thai ping-pong team to Peking for important informal conversations with Chinese officials. By the autumn of 1973 the Thai government had approved in principle relaxing the embargo on trade with China and was proceeding methodically to amend trade regulations and to establish a state trading company through which trade with China would be conducted.[19] At the same time Thailand was moving cautiously to diminish its ties with Taiwan and to lay the groundwork for diplomatic relations with Peking. A new Thai government might move more quickly in this direction, if for no other reason than to show how its policies differed from those of the old regime. Communist dominance in Indochina and a U.S. decision to loosen alignments with Thailand would hasten this process. Thus, Chinese influence on Thailand would be certain to increase.

But the same deep-seated, historic fear of Chinese domination that governs Burmese reactions would militate against any Thai government's turning Thailand into a satellite of China. Even if new leaders of Thailand should repudiate the close association with the United States, they could not become Chinese puppets without losing their sources of support within the country. Any Thai leaders would strive to limit Chinese influence. Thailand might follow the Burmese example, seeking to placate China by severely restricting Thailand's international relationships. But the Thais are aware that Burma's policy of keeping all big powers at arm's length has had adverse effects on the country's economic growth and has not succeeded in dissuading Peking from continuing to support the Burmese Communist party's rebellion against the government. Hence, instead of following an isolationist policy, the Thais would be more likely to want to expand relations with other

18. Foreign Minister Thanat's news conference, Bangkok, Jan. 28, 1971, and his interview with *Washington Post* correspondent, in London, *Washington Post*, April 29, 1971.

19. FBIS, *Daily Report: East Asia and Pacific*, Aug. 15, 1973, p. J-1, and Sept. 12, 1973, p. J-1.

nations in order to compensate for the unwillingness of the United States to provide the kind of support that it had offered in the past.

The precise mix of international relationships that the Thais might work toward would be affected by their perception of the changing balance of power within Southeast Asia and in East Asia as a whole. It would also be affected by the balance of political power in Thailand, which in turn would be influenced by international trends. But Thai leaders could be expected to judge these trends shrewdly and to adjust Thailand's international relations slowly. In addition to accommodating to China's enhanced position, they would probably attempt to appear as the initiators of a loosened alignment with the United States and seek closer relations with Japan, the USSR, and Eastern Europe, a new modus vivendi with North Vietnam, and a closer association with their regional partners.

The United States

Generally speaking, the broader the communist influence in Indochina, the greater would be the Thais' loss of confidence in the United States and their leaders' tendency to diminish Thailand's identification with the United States and create alternative relationships. This would be true whether the present or new leaders were in power. Thus, instead of resisting or protesting a U.S. move to loosen the U.S.-Thai alignment, the Thais probably would take the initiative themselves, quite likely by requesting the withdrawal of U.S. military forces from Thailand. Once this highly visible symbol of the two countries' closeness had been removed, however, the Thai government would probably wish to retain substantial economic and cultural relations with the United States. The Thais would probably even wish to continue to receive military aid from the United States, although insisting that U.S. military advisers be as few and inconspicuous as possible. In general, the Thai government would want to play down its past close connection with the United States and emphasize its self-reliance and its ability to have good relations with all the big powers.

Japan

Japan has already surpassed the United States in trade with Thailand and in private investment there,[20] and is Thailand's principal trading

20. In 1972 Japan supplied 40 percent of Thailand's imports and took 24 percent of its exports, while the United States supplied 13 percent and took 12 percent.

partner. It exported almost as much to Thailand in 1972 as to mainland China.[21] So long as Thailand remains politically stable, Japan's economic relations with Thailand are likely to expand steadily and Thailand can expect to receive a significant share of the $4 billion flow of resources to less developed countries that Japan projects for 1975. The two countries are associated in the Ministerial Conference on Southeast Asian Economic Development and the Asian Development Bank. Moreover, the Mekong River development scheme planned by the Mekong Committee, of which Thailand is one of four members, has benefited substantially from Japanese government grants and contract work by Japanese companies.

There are limits, however, on the extent to which the Thais could draw on Japan to counter Chinese influence. Concern is mounting that Japan is gaining dominant influence in Thailand and using its superior economic strength to exploit the Thai economy. Strong antagonism caused Thai students in December 1972 to launch a movement to boycott Japanese goods and in January 1974 to demonstrate against Premier Tanaka during his brief visit to Thailand. Thus the Thai government will be wary of too close a Japanese embrace. Moreover, for the next several years at least, the Japanese government will probably hesitate to take political actions that the Chinese could construe as aimed at helping the Thai government limit the growth of Chinese influence. If Thailand should become less stable as the result of communist dominance in Indochina and the loosening of the Thai alignment with the United States, both the Japanese government and Japanese investors would be inclined to draw back, rather than incur significant risks in order to strengthen the position of the Thai government. The Japanese government will probably become less cautious on this score as a consensus develops among Japanese on their nation's role in Asia, but this will take time.

The USSR and Eastern Europe

The Thais would regard closer relations with the USSR and Eastern Europe as another means of striking an international balance that would

International Monetary Fund/International Bank for Reconstruction and Development (IMF/IBRD), *Direction of Trade Annual, 1968–72*. The *Far Eastern Economic Review*, Nov. 18, 1972, p. 39, estimated Japanese investment in Thailand at 852 million *baht* as compared to a U.S. investment of 478 million *baht*.

21. IMF/IBRD, *Direction of Trade, December 1973*, pp. 30–31.

ward off excessive Chinese influence. Thailand has trade agreements with Rumania, Bulgaria, and the Soviet Union. Trade with Russia is unlikely to become very significant (from 1958 to 1965 Thai exports to the USSR never exceeded 1.5 percent of total exports, and imports never exceeded 0.4 percent)[22] but Soviet economic aid to Thailand is not inconceivable. The Thais might also hope to derive some advantage from the fact that the Soviets are hostile to the Chinese-dominated Thai Communist party.

The Thais would be cautious, however, in developing relations with the USSR, for they have been suspicious of past Soviet activities in Thailand. In 1952 Soviet publications were banned, and many Thais suspected of being associated with the Russians were arrested. General Phao Siyanon, the commander of the national police, accused the Russians of being behind a plot for revolt. A Soviet official was expelled from Bangkok in 1959 and another in 1966. Suspicion of Soviet intentions may diminish but is unlikely to disappear under a new Thai government.

Because the Soviet Union regards Southeast Asia as a low-priority area, it is unlikely to make any significant commitment of its prestige or resources to Thailand. For this reason, and because of continuing Thai suspicions of Soviet purposes, the relationship between Bangkok and Moscow would probably remain much less important as a counter to Chinese influence than Bangkok's relations with Washington and Tokyo.

North Vietnam

While Thai leaders consider China the chief long-term threat to their country, they see North Vietnam as the more immediate danger. The Thai government has long given various forms of support to anticommunist Lao in order to help preserve a buffer zone against North Vietnamese forces, and it provided the bases for the U.S. aircraft that backed the Lao defenders.

If the fragile cease-fire in Laos collapsed and Hanoi gained a predominant position throughout Laos, the Thais' buffer zone would disappear. Without U.S. air support the Thais would be more likely to seek a negotiated settlement than commit large amounts of resources to prolonged warfare beyond their borders.

22. Paul R. Shirk, "Thai-Soviet Relations," *Asian Survey*, vol. 9 (September 1969), pp. 682–93.

The makings of a modus vivendi between Bangkok and Hanoi appear to exist. Both Thailand and North Vietnam have an interest in remaining independent and not being controlled by China, and their chances of doing so would improve if they could damp down the conflict between themselves. Thailand has withdrawn its forces from South Vietnam, thus eliminating one aspect of the conflict. The withdrawal of U.S. bombers from bases in Thailand would eliminate another. North Vietnam's principal objective has always been to gain control over South Vietnam; its operations in Laos and Cambodia are incidental to this purpose. Even though Hanoi gained predominant influence over Laos and Cambodia, it could find it in its own interest not to use this influence to the detriment of Thailand. Talks between Thai and North Vietnamese officials, in which the presence of U.S. bombers in Thailand was reportedly a major issue, took place in Vientiane in the spring of 1973, after the cease-fire agreement had been reached in Laos.

Southeast Asian Neighbors

The limitations of regional cooperation as a means of strengthening nations such as Thailand against Chinese pressure are severe. Nevertheless, the Southeast Asian nations have taken small steps toward breaking down the rigid barriers between them, creating a sense of common interest, reducing the feeling of isolation in the face of Chinese power, and inspiring greater confidence in the future. Thailand has been a leader in this effort and could be expected to pursue it more vigorously as a means of helping to offset a decline in U.S. support. Feeling that it had been left in an exposed position, the Thai government would probably increase its efforts to make regional cooperation more effective. Other ASEAN nations might, in a spirit of *sauve qui peut*, recoil from closer association with Thailand, but it seems more likely that the sense of common peril would increase the willingness of all of these governments to work together.

U.S. Policy toward Thailand

The odds seem clearly against Thailand's falling soon under the control of China and becoming a subservient base from which Peking could extend its sphere of influence outward to the rest of Southeast Asia. Not only are U.S. interests in Southeast Asia insufficient to justify the high costs and risks of continuing to defend a containment line with U.S. forces, but the probability is relatively low that even communist dominance in Indochina would cause this first Southeast Asian "domino" to topple. Chinese influence might conceivably become predominant in Thailand at some future time, but it is unlikely to sweep over that country with such speed and force as the result of a U.S. policy of loosened alignments that it would seriously damage the primary U.S. interest in East Asia—the relationship with Japan. The loosening of the U.S. alignment with Thailand might even enhance, rather than prejudice, Thailand's ability to remain free of Chinese control by strengthening the nationalistic posture and self-reliance of the Thai leaders.

The motivation and power to resist Chinese domination are substantial, not only in Thailand, but also in the states of Southeast Asia beyond Indochina and Thailand. Chinese influence will grow and communist parties might come to power in one or more states—but there is little risk that an irresistible tide would sweep through Southeast Asia, giving China hegemony over the whole region.

A policy of loosened alignments implies the withdrawal of all U.S. forces from Thailand. So long as any forces remained, all of the governments the United States had supported would be encouraged in the belief that U.S. forces would be sent into battle again in Indochina as a last resort. A lingering assumption of this kind would undermine the determination of these governments to do whatever may be necessary to enhance their own military strength. Furthermore, if one of these governments should be gravely threatened, the presence of U.S. bombers in Thai airfields could encourage efforts within the U.S. bureaucracy to reverse the decision not to use them again in Indochina.

A policy of loosened alignments would not preclude a commitment to help defend Thailand against possible attack by China, if the Thais wished that commitment maintained. But the probability of such an attack is so low that there would be no need to keep U.S. air forces on Thai bases either to deter or to defend against a possible Chinese attack. Facilities could be maintained at Thai airfields for possible future use by the United States, if desired by the Thai government, and small units of U.S. personnel could remain to keep the facilities usable.

So long as the probability of Chinese attack on Thailand remained low, there would be no need for the United States to maintain general purpose forces to meet a full-scale Chinese attack. Any increased Chinese military aggressiveness toward Southeast Asia would grow out of long-term trends that would provide the early warning needed to build up U.S. forces, trends such as the working out of a far-reaching détente between the Soviet Union and China, the rise of a more expansionist leadership in China, the failure of the U.S. policy of détente with China, or a basic change in Chinese foreign policy doctrine to justify use of Chinese forces outside of China and production of the military hardware needed to carry out such a policy.

The removal of U.S. aircraft from Thai bases would be the most dramatic manifestation of a U.S. policy of loosening alignments in Southeast Asia. It would symbolize a radical change in the U.S. view of Thailand as a critically important base for U.S. military forces engaged in maintaining a containment line in Southeast Asia.

Additional steps could be taken to lessen the heavy dependence of the Thai government on the United States and the paternalistic tendency of the U.S. government to assume a heavy responsibility for its success or failure. The U.S. objective should be not total disengagement, but a scaling down of official activity in Thailand. This would imply a considerably more relaxed attitude toward trends in that country and a recognition that U.S. policies can have only a marginal effect on their direction. Such an attitude would make for a healthier long-term relationship between the United States and Thailand and would tend to strengthen the nationalist appeal of the Thai leadership in the period ahead, when Chinese-backed communist insurgency is likely to be the main threat.

The United States might continue its military aid, but in declining amounts, except in the unlikely event that China or the Soviet Union should support an overt attack on Thailand by North Vietnam. An effective and strongly nationalist Thai leadership relying almost entirely on its own resources should be able to control Chinese-supported insurgency at least as successfully as the Burmese government has controlled the multiple insurgencies in Burma over the past twenty-five years. Added U.S. military aid would not compensate for ineffective leadership.

Thailand will continue to need economic aid in order to maintain an adequate rate of economic growth, but the bulk of it could be channeled through international lending institutions or through such multilateral programs as the Mekong project or economic projects developed by ASEAN. The shift away from bilateral economic aid would further loosen the close U.S. alignment with Thailand. A U.S. policy of loosening alignments would help to speed the trend toward closer regional cooperation among the states of Southeast Asia. Regional cooperation is likely to be more effective and lasting if the impetus comes from local initiative, and the loosening of the U.S. alignment with Thailand should help remove the taint of U.S. instigation that has made Thai overtures toward regional cooperation suspect in some quarters.

If individual Southeast Asian states can throw off their heavy dependence on particular big powers, and increasingly have relations of various kinds with all members of the four-power system, the big powers might ultimately agree to respect Southeast Asia as a zone of peace and neutrality in which none would intervene with its own forces.

CHAPTER ELEVEN

Avoiding Use of Force in Southeast Asia

The shock waves from a U.S. decision to loosen its alignment with its close allies in Southeast Asia—especially if it resulted in communist dominance in Indochina—would spread beyond Thailand, although with diminishing force to the rest of the region. For a time China's influence would increase, as Southeast Asians revised their judgments of future political trends in the region. Communist parties would gain confidence and adherents, and subversive and insurgent activities would probably be stepped up. Those Southeast Asian governments that had not yet established trade, diplomatic, and other relations with China would probably do so. The prospects of these states remaining free from control by China, or any other big power, rest primarily on the strength of nationalism and the ability of their leaders to draw on nationalistic feelings to mobilize resistance to foreign domination.

Nationalism, of course, has various manifestations. One form is that invoked by an ethnic minority within a state seeking autonomy or independence. But the dominant form of nationalism in Southeast Asia today is the sentiment that ruling groups invoke to maintain the sovereignty and territorial integrity of the new nation-states within the boundaries inherited from the colonial past. It has no specific content[1] and can thus be utilized for radically different purposes by communist revolutionaries, by military dictators, or by nonrevolutionary modernizers. It can be linked to historic anti-Chinese sentiments and used to mobilize resistance against communist-led insurrections assisted by Peking. It can also be used to rouse opposition to the economic policies of Japan or the United States. Since it is most intense when directed

1. Rupert Emerson, "Post-Independence Nationalism in South and Southeast Asia," *Pacific Affairs*, vol. 44 (Summer 1971), pp. 173–92.

against an external threat, it is a crucial determinant of Southeast Asian nations' prospects for avoiding Chinese control.

Burma

Burma maintains the strictest nonalignment policy in Southeast Asia. Its first three postwar governments struck a cautious balance in their relations with the big powers, East and West. Ne Win, the nation's ruler since 1962, has sharply reduced relations of all kinds with the outside world,[2] though Burma does have diplomatic relations with all four big powers.

The main long-term threat to Burmese nonalignment is the Burmese Communist party (the White Flag Communists), which has been conducting a rebellion since 1948. Containment of the rebellion has been made more difficult by simultaneous uprisings of the Karens, Shans, and Kachins—the latest phase of a centuries-old conflict between these minority peoples and the Burmans. One group of Kachins headed by a Kachin communist has, like the Burmese Communist party (BCP), received support from China. Up to the mid-1960s, Peking's operation was largely covert and its material aid to the BCP was small. In 1963, after Ne Win had come to power, a group of Burmese communists from Peking went to Rangoon to try to negotiate an end to the rebellion and legal status for the BCP. The negotiations failed.

With the Cultural Revolution in China, Peking's friendly relations with the Burmese government changed dramatically. Anti-Chinese riots in Rangoon, provoked by the aggressive peddling of Mao's thought by Chinese officials in Burma, strained relations between the two countries and the Chinese took the wraps off their covert backing of the BCP. Peking radio began vitriolic attacks on Ne Win[3] and provided an outlet

2. See John H. Badgley, "Burma and China," in A. M. Halpern, ed., *Policies Toward China: Views from Six Continents* (McGraw-Hill, 1965), pp. 303–28, for a perceptive account of Burma's foreign policy, especially its relationship to China up to 1964.

3. A typical New China News Agency (NCNA) broadcast on March 28, 1969, extolled the alleged military victories of the Burmese communists and asserted that "the reactionary Ne Win clique is trying to save itself from destruction by further hiring itself to U.S. imperialism and Soviet revisionism and by carrying out frantic counterattacks on and sanguinary suppression of the Communist Party of Burma and the revolutionary Burmese people." U.S. Government, Foreign Broadcast Information Service (FBIS), *Daily Report: Communist China*, April 2, 1969, p. A3.

for a vice chairman of the BCP and other important Burmese communists living in Peking to air their views to the world. Guerrilla attacks within Burma increased, especially in areas near the Chinese border, where groups trained and supplied by the Chinese could operate most easily.

Despite open and increased Chinese support and the widespread dissatisfaction produced by the economic stagnation[4] under Premier Ne Win's "Burmese way to socialism," the communists did badly. They were plagued by bloody factional infighting and were infiltrated by Burmese government agents. Under attack by government forces,[5] they abandoned their long-held main base area in central Burma for a strip of mountainous territory with ready access to Chinese sanctuary and support.

By 1971 Chinese policy toward Burma had begun to shift. Attacks on Ne Win by Peking radio ceased and the ambassadors of the two countries returned to their posts. Ne Win himself made an official visit to Peking in August 1971 during which he was given a conducted tour by Chou En-lai and was received by Mao. The two governments opened negotiations on the resumption of Chinese economic aid to Burma.

The Chinese did not, however, abandon support of the BCP. A clandestine radio in China continued to broadcast BCP propaganda. Two leading Burmese communists appeared on the rostrum in Peking on Army Day, August 1, 1971. Clashes between Chinese-supplied insurgents and the Burmese army in the remote border region continued; during the 1972 dry season the rebels succeeded in expanding their area of control; and during 1973 they threatened Keng Tung city. Peking clearly desired to keep the insurgency going, as an instrument for applying pressure on the Burmese government and also for ready use should "objective conditions" for revolution in Burma improve.

An important reason for the communists' failure to make progress in

4. From 1960 to 1971 Burma's per capita agricultural production index fell from 101 to 86 and exports dropped from $226 million to $123 million. U.S. Agency for International Development (AID), *East Asia: Economic Growth Trends* (August 1973), pp. 16, 24. Badgley argues that because of Burma's system of values, which puts political and cultural integrity ahead of economic development, Ne Win may be in a good deal stronger position than the economic deterioration would suggest. John Badgley, "The Union of Burma: Age Twenty-two," *Asian Survey*, vol. 11 (February 1971), pp. 149–57.

5. Documents captured in the fighting showed that the BCP had been controlled by Peking for years. Badgley, "The Union of Burma," p. 151.

Burma over the past decade is the strongly nationalistic character of the Ne Win regime. It has emphasized preserving Burmese culture and has taken commerce out of the hands of the alien Chinese and Indians. And it has carefully avoided close ties with any great power. In sharp contrast with Ne Win's nationalistic stance, the Burmese communists have advertised their close association with Peking and their reliance on Mao's thought to carry through the communist revolution in Burma. Consequently, Peking's attempts to stigmatize Ne Win as a running dog of the Americans and Russians and to hail the leaders of the BCP as true nationalists have probably convinced few Burmese.

The stigma of its image as a creature of Peking is difficult for the BCP to overcome. With its chief operations located close to the Chinese border, it seems more than ever dependent on Chinese support. So long as the Burmese government remains self-reliant and not heavily dependent on any big power, the prospects for a BCP victory seem remote.

A U.S. policy of loosening alignments would have relatively little effect on conditions in Burma. The increase in Chinese prestige that would result from communist dominance in Indochina would make the Burmese leaders more fearful of their great neighbor and even more careful to hew to strict nonalignment, but it would seem unlikely to have any dramatic impact on the complicated balance of forces within Burma. It is hard to produce convincing reasons why communist victory in Indochina and its subsequent effect on Thailand should rapidly and gravely weaken the politico-military grip of the nationalistic Ne Win regime over most of Burma or cause Burmans or ethnic minorities to flock in large numbers to the BCP banner.

Whatever turns civil conflict in Burma might take, the United States should avoid action that would add plausibility to Chinese charges that particular Burmese leaders depend on U.S. support. The best hope for any Burmese government to remain free of Chinese domination lies in the ability of Burmese leaders to maintain a convincing nationalist image. Burma's firmly established policy of nonalignment would fit well with a U.S. policy of loosened alignment in Southeast Asia and a long-term goal of neutralizing the whole region.

Malaysia

Although Malaysia has a loose defense arrangement with the United Kingdom, Australia, New Zealand, and Singapore, it regards itself as nonaligned and participates in the meetings of the nonaligned nations. Malaysia has diplomatic relations with Japan and with both the United States and the Soviet Union, the two principal buyers of its main export, rubber, and in May 1974 it established diplomatic relations with Peking.

The Malayan Communist party poses the chief long-term threat to Malaysia's nonalignment. About two thousand communist guerrillas harass Malaysian security forces along the Thai border. And a few hundred others, styling themselves the "North Kalimantan people's armed forces," operate across the Indonesia-Sarawak border. Both groups are strongly backed in broadcasts from China. They are said to follow the guidance of Mao's thought in seeking to overthrow "the puppet Rahman-Razak clique." Most of them are Malaysian Chinese.[6]

Border raids by the communist guerrillas impose a heavy burden on the Malaysian government. But the greatest danger to the government arises from communal tension between the 45 percent of the population who are Malays and the 35 percent who are Chinese (the other 20 percent of the population consists of Indians and a great variety of tribal peoples). The Malays predominate in government, the military, and the police, while the Chinese predominate in business. Because the Chinese minority is both large and powerful, the cultural gulf between the two communities is deep, and communal loyalties are strong, the problem of balancing the interests of the two groups and creating an overarching commitment to the multiracial Malaysian nation is delicate. The precariousness of the balance showed up in the bloody communal rioting of May 1969 that forced the suspension of parliamentary government for more than a year. In Malaysia nationalism is not as strong a barrier to foreign pressure as in most Southeast Asian countries. It is a new idea that must overcome the parochialism of the ethnic communities.

The explosion of racial hostility in 1969 shook the moderate leaders of both communities. The Malay leaders, under heavy pressure from militant Malays, are determined to keep power in Malay hands and to work vigorously to improve the lot of their mainly rural constituents, who have not shared equally with the largely urban Chinese in the

6. Peking rejected the union of Sabah and Sarawak with the Malay Peninsula to form Malaysia. Until 1971, when Peking began to give increasing attention to state-to-state relations, it refused to use the term *Malaysia*. The Malayan Communist party continues to use *Malaya*, and the communist rebellions going on in the two parts of Malaysia continue to be treated by Peking as two separate "liberation movements," presumably aiming at creating two separate states.

benefits of Malaysia's economic progress. Moderate Chinese leaders, fearful lest Malay extremists should gain power, are disposed to accept Malay dominance, to cooperate with the moderate Malay leaders, and to discourage Chinese militancy.

The government's ambitious goal is to make Malays within one generation full partners in the commercial and industrial life of the nation and wipe out the identification of race with economic function. Prime Minister Abdul Razak and his associates must move quickly to contain the pressures of Malay extremists without placing burdens on the Chinese community that would discredit moderate Chinese leaders. The government recognizes that the program is dependent on sufficiently rapid economic growth to ensure that the standard of living of the Chinese continues to improve, and that of the Malays improves even faster.[7]

The Malaysian government has some advantages in coping with its dangerous racial problem. Its economic prospects are good. The per capita gross national product in Malaysia in 1970 was $355, one of the highest in Asia, and GNP grew at the rate of 5.7 percent annually in 1970–71.[8] Malaysia has a favorable balance of trade and ample foreign exchange and is a large and efficient producer of its basic export products: rubber, tin, and palm oil. There is no shortage of domestic and foreign investment capital. Labor is plentiful and wages relatively low, providing an attractive incentive for investment in labor-intensive industry. Moreover, Malaysia enjoys the services of a well-trained and efficient civil service and has a tradition of moderation in politics. The key factor in the creation of an integrated national society is the political skill and sophistication of the moderate leaders of the two communities.

Both sides recognize the need for tolerance and concessions, but both races include angry young men who advocate strong, occasionally violent, measures. A disquieting portent for the future is the tendency of those coming out of the universities to take more extreme racial views than their elders. If the races should move further apart and the government be forced into more repressive measures against Chinese, many young Chinese might be drawn into the Malayan Communist party.

Malaysia's communal tension, combined with the fact that Peking

functions, in speech delivered to Parliament, March 5, 1971 (processed).

7. Tan Sri Ghazali bin Shafie, minister of information and minister with special

8. AID, *East Asia: Economic Growth Trends*, p. 13.

has supported a Malayan Communist party that is largely Chinese, creates a special diplomatic problem for Kuala Lumpur. The establishment of diplomatic relations with China creates a risk that a Chinese embassy in Kuala Lumpur, developing relations of all kinds with Malaysian Chinese, might intensify Malaysians' consciousness of being Chinese and thus work against government efforts to create an integrated society. In fact, Peking might see the prospects for revolution in Malaysia advanced by outbreaks of racial violence and increased repression by the Malay authorities that would drive more Chinese into the Malayan Communist party, despite assurances by Mao Tse-tung and Chou En-lai to Malaysian Premier Tun Abdul Razak that they regarded the communist rebels in Malaysia as an internal problem for the Malaysian government to deal with as it thought best.[9]

But it seems doubtful that Peking would deliberately use diplomatic relations to promote racial division in Malaysia. The Maoist theory of revolution calls for the broadest possible united front against the governing classes and for creating an armed force in the countryside largely composed of peasants and heavily dependent on the cooperation of the rural population. The Malaysian peasants are Malays, and a communist party composed of Chinese could not possibly function according to the classical Maoist model. Efforts by the Malayan Communist party to recruit Malays—not very successful so far—indicate its awareness of the problem. Perhaps a stronger deterrent to Chinese encouragement of a largely Chinese revolutionary movement is the grave risk that the Indonesians would offer strong support to crush it. Creating a multiracial revolutionary movement would seem as indispensable to communist success in Malaysia as the creation of loyalty to a multiracial state is to the present Malaysian government.[10]

Since the United States has no defense commitment to Malaysia, the

9. FBIS, *Daily Report: East Asia and the Pacific*, June 3, 1974, p. O1.

10. Peking's policy since 1957–58 of urging overseas Chinese to become citizens of the states where they reside and merge with the local people is further evidence that Peking would be unlikely to support a policy designed to set Chinese against Malays. See Stephen Fitzgerald, "China and the Overseas Chinese: Perceptions and Policies," *China Quarterly*, no. 44 (October–December 1970), pp. 1–37. In the communiqué announcing the establishment of diplomatic relations the Chinese government declared that it considered anyone of Chinese origin who had of his own will acquired Malaysian nationality as having automatically forfeited Chinese nationality and urged those who retained Chinese nationality to abide by the laws and respect the customs and habits of Malaysia. FBIS, *Daily Report: East Asia and the Pacific*, May 31, 1974, p. A29.

policy of loosened alignments would have no direct effect. Communist dominance in Indochina could reduce or eliminate Thailand's cooperation against the Malaysian communists on its border. Thailand and Malaysia might, however, be drawn into closer cooperation. More important is the possible effect on the communal problem within Malaysia. Increased fear of China among Malays might lead to measures against Chinese and greater polarization of the society. In short, communist dominance in Vietnam would increase uncertainties and make the task of the Malaysian government more difficult.

The existence of the five-power defense arrangement between Malaysia, Singapore, the United Kingdom, Australia, and New Zealand would somewhat cushion the psychological impact on Malaysia of communist dominance in Vietnam. It would not, however, provide any direct help to the Malaysian government if the insurgency in that country should become more active or if domestic political tension increased. Neither the outside powers nor the Malaysian government would want foreign forces used to maintain order within the country. The presence of token forces from stronger countries affords some sense of reassurance to a small nation in a dangerous world, but the principal assistance that its defense associates could give would be in the form of military and economic aid and training programs. The United States could provide long-term assistance by adopting trade and economic aid policies that would favor the rapid economic development essential to the success of the Malaysian government's program to create an integrated society. But outsiders could not do much to help the Malaysian government cope with an increase in communal tension or communist rebellion.

Although Malaysian leaders would be disturbed by communist dominance in Vietnam, they favor in principle the withdrawal of U.S. combat forces from Southeast Asia. As the leading advocates of a neutralized Southeast Asia, recognized by the United States, China, and the USSR, they would find congenial a U.S. policy of loosening alignments. They acknowledge that the neutralized Southeast Asia they propose cannot be achieved until the concept is accepted in principle by the other Southeast Asian states and by the United States, China, and the Soviet Union. They think it is more likely to be accepted if the Southeast Asian states can exhibit greater self-reliance and closer cooperation with each other. Hence, they are strong supporters of the Association of Southeast Asian Nations (ASEAN).

Singapore

Like Malaysia, Singapore pursues a policy of nonalignment while participating in the five-power defense arrangement with Malaysia, the United Kingdom, Australia, and New Zealand. It has diplomatic relations with the United States, the USSR, and Japan, but not with China, which until recently took a hostile attitude toward the Singapore government, referring to it as "the Lee Kuan-yew puppet clique." It is a member of ASEAN and a strong backer of regional cooperation.

Although subversion in Singapore by a communist party closely linked to China has been a continuing problem, security forces have kept it from becoming a serious threat. Effective government, prosperity, and rapid economic growth have inhibited the rise of dissidence. Communal friction is less serious than in Malaysia, for 75 percent of the population are Chinese and only 14 percent Malays. The government's principal worry is that severe communal trouble in Malaysia might send a flood of Chinese refugees into Singapore and thus strain relations between the two countries. Repression of Chinese in either Malaysia or Indonesia might incline Singapore Chinese to look to China as champion of the rights of the oppressed minority.

Even Chinese long resident abroad tend to look to China as their homeland. That is one of the problems Singapore's leaders face in trying to create loyalty to a tiny state, only a few years old, with no culture of its own or past history of independent existence. But nationalism will grow, stimulated by Singaporeans' pride in their governmental skills and economic growth that outdistance their neighbors' achievements. The task of inculcating nationalism will become easier as the rapidly widening gap between the ways of life in modernizing Singapore and in mainland China diminish the political importance of ethnic and cultural links. But nationalism will thrive only if economic prosperity continues and troubles in neighboring states do not severely threaten Singapore's security.

Fortunately, Singapore's economic prospects are bright. Efficient government and political stability have attracted substantial amounts of foreign and domestic capital into a successful program for rapid industrialization. The economy has grown at an annual rate of 12–13 percent the past several years and the per capita gross national product exceeded $1,100 in 1971, the highest in Asia, except for Japan. Singapore's population of 2 million carried on a foreign trade of nearly $6 billion in 1972, about the same as the total foreign trade of mainland China's 750 million. Singapore's rapid economic growth has created a labor shortage causing the government to modify its inducements to foreign investors so as to attract high-technology industries rather than those that are merely labor-intensive. Education and technical training programs are being revamped to facilitate this transition to a higher plane of industrialization.

Its rapidly growing economic bonds with the United States have helped to allay concern in Singapore about the withdrawal of British forces from Malaysia and Singapore and of U.S. forces from Indochina. The United States has been the largest investor in Singapore in recent years. Over three hundred American firms are established there, and U.S. investment is growing steadily. The oil drilling boom off Indonesia and Malaysia has not only brought a major expansion in Singapore's refining capacity, but an influx of firms to service oil exploration.

Singapore's economic ties are overwhelmingly with the noncommunist world. Japan is second only to Malaysia as a trading partner. Trade with mainland China in 1970 was $151 million, somewhat less than Singapore's trade with Australia and far less than its trade with Japan, the United States, or the United Kingdom. Trade with the USSR was an even less impressive $58 million.[11]

Of all the Southeast Asian states, Singapore is probably the least disposed to accept diplomatic relations with Peking. A Chinese diplomatic mission could interfere with government efforts to create an enduring loyalty to the new state. Moreover, the acceptance in Singapore of diplomats from Peking would nourish the suspicion, widely held among Indonesians, that Singapore serves as a center for Chinese subversion in the region. Nevertheless, the trend set by Peking's seating in the United Nation's, China's improvement in relations with the United States, and its softening policy toward noncommunist governments in Southeast Asia will probably lead to the establishment of diplomatic relations. Already Singapore trade delegations have attended the Canton

11. Economic data taken from Singapore, Department of Statistics, *Singapore External Trade Statistics—December 1970;* U.S. Embassy, Singapore, "American Investment in Singapore," Airgram A-333, Jan. 11, 1971, and "Semi-Annual Economic Review," Nov. 1, 1970.

fair and a Chinese ping-pong team has visited Singapore. But to protect its relations with Indonesia, Singapore may defer diplomatic relations with Peking until Jakarta has them.

Although Singapore would not be affected directly by a U.S. policy of loosening alignments, it is concerned about the possible repercussions, as evidenced by Lee Kuan-yew's appeal for U.S. forces to remain in Thailand. Communist dominance in Indochina would encourage procommunists in Singapore and could bring on serious political clashes in Malaysia, jeopardizing Singapore's self-confidence and threatening its security.

Singapore would probably wish to remain unaligned, and in order to temper China's increased influence in Southeast Asia would work to strengthen relations with the three other big powers, particularly the United States. It would want a continued flow of American capital and growing trade, as well as visits by ships of the Seventh Fleet and use of commercial ship and aircraft repair facilities by the U.S. military forces. It would also welcome increased trade and investment from Japan, despite lingering memories of the killing and mistreatment of Singapore Chinese by Japanese troops in World War II.

Singapore would probably also encourage some increase in Soviet commercial and diplomatic activity and accept Soviet naval visits, more to strengthen its nonaligned image than in the hope of countering Chinese influence. These varied associations, together with the five-power Commonwealth military arrangement, would help the Singapore government adjust to a U.S. policy of loosened alignments. The effects of such a U.S. policy would be substantial but would not critically threaten Singapore's independence.

Although Singapore is more skeptical of the feasibility of a big-power guarantee of a neutralized Southeast Asia than is Malaysia, it would not be averse in principle to such an arrangement, given adequate progress in regional cooperation and sufficient decline in tension among the big powers to offer promise that neutralization would work.

Indonesia

Indonesia, with a population of 120 million and a wealth of undeveloped resources, is strategically located between mainland Southeast Asia and the Philippines to the north and Australia to the south. Whether it follows a policy of confrontation, as under President Sukarno, or of regional cooperation, as under President Suharto, its policies inevitably have a strong influence on the whole region. Indonesia is nonaligned—less rigorously so than Burma, but more so than Malaysia. It maintains diplomatic relations with the United States, the USSR, and Japan, but relations with China have been suspended since 1966.

Indonesia's nonaligned posture could be threatened if the Indonesian Communist party (PKI) should revive with Chinese support. The PKI, closely linked to Peking and working intimately with Sukarno, had come close to achieving a dominant position in the country when it lost out as a result of its abortive coup in 1965. Now, having lost most of its leaders, it is an underground organization constantly harassed by the Indonesian security forces. Nevertheless, it could become a serious threat again if the Indonesian government should become ineffective and unpopular.

President Suharto and his colleagues have the great advantage, however, that the communists in Indonesia have always been overshadowed by noncommunist nationalists. The Indonesian army is the only non-communist army in Southeast Asia that fought for independence. The four-year war against the Dutch was led by noncommunists, who also crushed an attempted coup by the PKI in the course of the struggle. The war of independence instilled in the armed forces a strong sense of nationalism and gave them experience in mobilizing the population with nationalistic appeals, which they used to great effect against the PKI after the failure of its coup in 1965.

The PKI's close identification with China in recent years and the widespread belief among Indonesians that Peking was behind the PKI coup in 1965 severely handicap revival of the party. Many Indonesians fear that China's long-term goal is to dominate Indonesia. They also envy the relatively affluent overseas Chinese, and can easily be instigated to riot against them. The continued attacks on the Suharto government by Peking radio and by PKI leaders who have taken refuge in Peking reinforce the attitudes. Indonesian leaders can thus readily arouse the people to oppose the revival of a PKI identified with China.

The Suharto regime, although dogged by corruption and inefficiency, has made good progress toward economic stabilization. It has persuaded foreign creditors to stretch out the term for repayment of debts and has attracted a substantial flow of outside resources, both public and private. The multilateral framework for coordinating debt repayment and aid plans through the World Bank, the International Monetary Fund, and the Intergovernmental Group for Indonesia[12] has prevented Indonesia from becoming too closely identified with any single donor country. Prospects for economic progress in the next few years are favorable. The vigor, intelligence, and growing experience in governing of Suharto and his principal aides, combined with the influx of foreign firms to develop Indonesia's rich resources of oil, timber, and minerals and to help build a manufacturing industry, provide grounds for optimism.

Longer-range prospects are more uncertain. Indonesia is one of East Asia's poorest states, with a gross national product that probably does not exceed $100 per capita. The rate of population growth, estimated to be around 2.5 percent, will accelerate as health conditions improve, making difficult a sustained improvement of living standards. Already, the increase in population may be outrunning increases in production. The government's family planning program faces many obstacles.[13] Consequently, maintaining political order and achieving economic progress over the longer term throughout this sprawling chain of islands will be a herculean task.

The present relationship between the United States and Indonesia is a model that the United States should work toward in its relations with other Southeast Asian countries. The United States has no security treaty with Indonesia, but has given a general warning to other nuclear powers that it might intervene if they threaten military attack on non-nuclear states. A variety of donors supplies economic aid to Indonesia through a multilateral arrangement, and the U.S. share is less than half the total. Less than one-third of private investment from outside comes from the United States.[14] And the U.S. military aid program is relatively small.

Communist dominance in Indochina would have less impact on Indonesia than on other Southeast Asian states. Indonesia is big; it is

12. A group of nations that meets annually to consider Indonesia's economic plans and coordinates with them external aid to Indonesia and debt repayment schedules.

13. See Willard A. Hannah, *Population Review 1970: Indonesia*, American Universities Field Staff Report, Southeast Asia Series, vol. 19 (December 1970).

14. According to the U.S. Embassy, Jakarta, of $1.3 billion in investments approved by the Indonesian government from January 1967 to January 1971, U.S. investments amounted to $374 million. By the end of 1973 total approved investments had risen to $2.7 billion and the U.S. share to $843 million. *Far Eastern Economic Review*, March 4, 1974, p. 50.

some distance from Vietnam and Thailand; and its leaders are confident of their ability to maintain internal security. Moreover, they maintain diplomatic relations with the North Vietnamese and tend to regard them as national communists rather than as puppets of the Chinese.[15] The Indonesians would be seriously disturbed only if the U.S. policy of loosening alignments caused a rapid increase in insurgency in Thailand and Malaysia and a substantial deterioration in the positions of the governments of those ASEAN partners of Indonesia. In other ASEAN states, communist gains would affect Indonesian politics indirectly and only marginally improve prospects for the revival of the PKI. The PKI's prospects depend almost entirely on political developments within Indonesia, particularly on the pace of economic development and the extent to which influential political groups share the fruits of development. Thus, the possibility of China's gaining influence on Indonesia through the PKI would be only remotely related to a U.S. decision not to use U.S. forces to hold a containment line in Southeast Asia.

Most Indonesians would approve such a policy if it were not clearly damaging to other ASEAN governments. Their own policy of nonalignment contemplates a careful balancing of relationships among the four big powers. They look forward to the day when Indonesia can play the leading role in the region to which they believe it is entitled by size, population, and history. Consequently, they wish to avoid a close association with any one of the big powers that would dim the luster of such a role. They look on Indonesia as the central pillar of ASEAN and want to expand that association to include other Southeast Asian states such as Burma or Cambodia.

The desire for balance in the relationships with the four big powers reflects a deep commitment among the Indonesian elite to the principle of nonalignment, as well as certain reservations toward each of the Big Four. From the United States the Indonesians want a market for their goods, a substantial flow of capital and technical aid, some military aid, and a promise of enough military power—located "over the horizon"—to deter possible Chinese military aggression. They do not want to be tied to the United States by a security treaty. From Japan they also want trade and aid, but they are concerned that Japan might come to dominate their economy and eventually be ready to use mili-

15. Note Adam Malik's proposal, seconded by Abdul Razak, that North Vietnam be invited to attend the ASEAN meeting in Manila in March 1971.

tary force to protect its economic stake in Southeast Asia. From the Soviets they would accept economic aid, but they would not wish to become heavily dependent on the USSR again for military equipment and they fear that Soviet sympathy for the PKI might lead to active assistance to that party. As for China, the Indonesians recognize that their policy of nonalignment will require resumption of diplomatic relations with Peking, but suspect that the Chinese would use their mission in Jakarta to help the PKI or carry on undesirable activities among the overseas Chinese.

In principle, Indonesian leaders would favor as a long-term goal the neutralization of Southeast Asia to exclude the forces of the big powers from the region. This view is reflected in the declaration of August 8, 1967, when ASEAN was established, that "all foreign bases are temporary" and the foreign ministers' 1971 resolve to take steps to secure the recognition of Southeast Asia as a zone of peace, freedom, and neutrality. The Indonesians, however, would first have the Southeast Asian states demonstrate to the big powers strength of their own, growing out of increased cooperation. Having ten times the population of Malaysia, the Indonesians tend to put more stress on their own strength than the Malaysians and less reliance on guarantees by outsiders. Thus they would accommodate to a U.S. policy of loosened alignments more readily than most Southeast Asian nations.

The Philippines

The Republic of the Philippines is unique among the states of Southeast Asia because of its long association with the United States, first as a colony, then as an ally. Not only is it allied to the United States by the mutual defense treaty of 1951, it also has on its territory two of the principal U.S. bases in the western Pacific—Clark Air Force Base and Subic Bay Naval Base. It has diplomatic relations with the United States and Japan, but not with China or the USSR. Its economic ties are mainly with the United States and Japan, which together took 76 percent of Philippine exports and supplied 54 percent of its imports in 1971.[16] It has only token trade with China and none with the Soviet Union. The Philippines belongs to ASEAN.

16. AID, *East Asia: Economic Growth Trends*, pp. 28, 29.

The Philippine communists, the Hukbalahap, tried to use participation in guerrilla resistance to Japan as a springboard to power immediately after the war. They were outmaneuvered by other nationalist leaders and, like the communists in most countries of Southeast Asia, failed to seize control of the nationalist movement. The grant of independence by the United States eliminated the possibility of anticolonial war, such as occurred in Indochina and Indonesia. The Huks have made little headway during the past twenty-five years, but a small number are still active, as well as two newer rebel organizations. One of the latter, known as the New People's Army, is avowedly Maoist and its exploits are cited approvingly by Peking radio. Except for small areas in Luzon, where communist guerrillas operate, and a Muslim rebellion in the island of Mindanao, the Philippine countryside has been quite stable. Most of the disorder and violence has occurred in greater Manila.

Despite governmental inefficiency, the economy has been expanding. The growth rate has varied widely from year to year, but has averaged a respectable 6 percent in recent years. Most important of all, the Philippines—until recently—was one of the few Asian states in which the electoral method of changing heads of government was generally accepted as a way of life. Election campaigns and the lively, if biased, press offered a way of working off steam and forcing on the politicians a degree of responsibility to their constituents that did not exist in most of Asia.

Nonetheless, economic growth has been erratic and has tended to increase the gap between rich and poor. Moreover, the population, of 41 million in 1972, was growing at a rate of 3.3 percent annually—one of the highest growth rates in East Asia—and could be expected to double in twenty years if not checked. But until 1969 the government had no population policy and it did not permit the import and sale of contraceptive devices. And it had an abundance of disturbing short-term problems—the prevalence of crime and corruption, the failure to carry out land reform, the flooding of Manila with the poor and unemployed from the countryside, the overproduction of educated youth by Manila's colleges and universities, and the irresponsible behavior of venal Manila journalists—all capable of creating explosive conditions for revolutionaries to exploit.[17]

17. For a reassuring view of political conditions in the Philippines, see the study prepared for the U.S. Agency for International Development by H. A. Averch, F. H. Denton, and J. E. Koehler, "A Crisis of Ambiguity: Political and Economic Develop-

These problems help to explain why the political system that had existed in the Philippines since independence in 1946 came to an abrupt end with the imposition of martial law by President Ferdinand Marcos in September 1972. In January 1973 Marcos proclaimed a new constitution for the Philippines which gave him sweeping authoritarian powers and allowed him to continue in office indefinitely. He suspended an interim assembly that was to have served as a legislature under the new constitution and he continued martial law.

His avowed purpose was to bring about a "revolution" in Philippine society through land reform, cleaning out corruption, and imposing law and order. To this end he quickly had over six thousand people arrested, including some leading political opponents and newspapermen, and collected nearly half a million weapons that were in the hands of private individuals. He moved vigorously against the communist guerrillas and the Muslim rebels. The popular reaction to Marcos' unprecedented changes in the Philippine political system has been relief that public order has markedly improved, but the politically sophisticated have been concerned that Marcos' main objective may be to perpetuate his own power rather than to benefit the nation. If their view should prove to be correct, the result would be widespread disillusionment and a greater threat of armed rebellion than has ever existed.

Should a sizable revolutionary movement develop in the Philippines, the communist leaders might be in a stronger position than in most other Southeast Asian states to utilize nationalism to help them gain control of the movement. Chinese influence in the Philippines has been small, while that of the United States has been enormous. Consequently, demands for reform and manifestations of nationalism have often taken on an anti-American coloration. The colonial history, the pervasive American cultural influence, the U.S. military bases, the important American economic stake, and the large number of American residents present many targets for attack. A communist party that veiled its ties with Peking and had no apparent connection with the distrusted overseas Chinese could exploit latent anti-American sentiment.

But the Filipinos are ambivalent toward the United States. There

---

ment in the Philippines" (Rand Corp., August 1969; processed), which concludes that the Philippines is not a nation in crisis and that it is not particularly susceptible to revolution. Benedict J. Kerkvliet argues that the country is much less stable than the Rand study concludes; see *Journal of Asian Studies*, vol. 32 (May 1973), pp. 489–500.

is not only latent anti-American sentiment among them, there is also a large reservoir of goodwill. Moreover, they rely for security on the United States. As a Korean diplomat shrewdly put it: "Every nation needs friends and enemies. For the Philippines, the United States is both." Thus, although the communists can exploit Philippine nationalism, they would meet resistance from large numbers of Filipinos who see no necessary conflict between nationalism and friendly relations with the United States and who would fear domination by Communist China (or by a remilitarized Japan) if ties with the United States were severed. A Chinese-oriented communist party in the Philippines could become the chief vehicle of Philippine nationalism only if confidence in the political system should deteriorate radically and the United States were closely identified with an increasingly unpopular oligarchy striving to maintain its rule by force. Because of the Philippines' island location, it would under any circumstances be difficult for Peking to maintain control of a communist party that it had helped to power.

Both the United States and the Philippines have indicated that their patron-protégé relationship must change. As early as July 1969 President Nixon called for a new relationship between the two countries.[18] Since then, Sangley Point Naval Station has been returned to the Philippines and the United States has agreed to renegotiate the treaties governing the other military bases. Pursuant to the Nixon Doctrine, which calls for a lower U.S. military profile in the western Pacific, the authorized strength of U.S. forces in the Philippines was reduced from 28,000 to 18,900 by mid-1971.[19] The privileges granted to citizens of each country doing business in the other are unlikely to be continued after the Laurel-Langley Trade and Investment Agreement expires in 1974.

In adjusting future U.S. relations with the Philippines, a central problem will be Subic Bay Naval Base and Clark Air Force Base, which have been key links in the chain of U.S. military bases in the western Pacific. They could increase in relative importance as political pressures in Japan compelled the consolidation and reduction of U.S. military facilities in Okinawa and elsewhere in Japan.

Yet, continued U.S. reliance on Subic Bay and Clark Field would entail serious costs and risks. Unless there should be an overt military

18. U.S. Department of State, *United States Foreign Policy: 1969–70*, p. 62.
19. Ibid., p. 37, and U.S. Department of State, *United States Foreign Policy: 1971*, p. 50.

threat to the Philippines, which seems highly unlikely, nationalist pressures to restrict the U.S. use of bases in the Philippines will grow. In order to retain them, the United States might be compelled to give increasing support to an increasingly unpopular government, thus providing an easy target for revolutionaries to focus nationalistic resentment on. Moreover, the prospect that U.S. bases would remain in the Philippines indefinitely not only would limit Philippine interest in increasing the importance and effectiveness of ASEAN, but would also stand in the way of big-power understanding on the neutralization of Southeast Asia.

 It would be wiser for the United States to take the position that its bases in the Philippines would be turned over to the Filipinos, leaving the timing of the transfer and the possibility of subsequent use by U.S. forces open. Once the decision had been taken to withdraw U.S. forces from the rest of Southeast Asia and not to intervene there again except in the improbable event of military aggression by another nuclear power, the rationale for the maintenance of Subic Bay and Clark Field as U.S. bases would be much weakened. A U.S. statement of intent to turn these bases over to the Philippines would improve the prospects for a big-power understanding on the neutralization of Southeast Asia and would give Philippine leaders reason to cooperate more closely with their ASEAN partners. Finally, the less committed the United States felt to maintain permanent military bases in the Philippines, the easier it would be to adjust U.S. policies to unpredictable changes in the balance of domestic forces in that country.

A U.S. policy of loosening its alignment with the Philippines, and other Southeast Asian countries—even if it were associated with communist dominance in Indochina—would have relatively little effect on the prospects for revolution in the Philippines. There would be some damage to U.S. prestige, some increase in Chinese influence, and greater uncertainty among Filipinos about their own future. The international relationships of the Philippines would be more affected than would the balance of domestic political forces. The trend toward expanding trade and other relations with the Soviet Union, Eastern Europe, and China would be accelerated.[20] Negotiations for the estab-

20. In March 1972 the Philippines established diplomatic relations with Rumania and Yugoslavia; in 1972 Imelda Marcos, wife of the president, visited Moscow, and Ben Romualdez, special envoy of the president, visited Peking, as did various other individuals and groups, including Senator Salvador Laurel; in August 1972 a gift

plomatic relations with China would probably be speeded
ncern over Chinese backing for communist rebels in the

ʒ nationalist currents in the Philippines and their tendency
ti-American direction suggest that in that country, perhaps
ian elsewhere in Southeast Asia, the United States would in
stand to gain rather than lose from a policy of loosening
t. To be successful Philippine leaders increasingly will have
ɔ demonstrate that they are following a truly independent
poncy responsive to Philippine national interests. And if the forces of
revolution should grow stronger in the Philippines, the less the United
States were involved in supporting a government seeking to suppress
revolution, the more difficult it would be for agents of China to exploit
anti-U.S. feeling to gain control of the revolutionary movement.

Nationalism and Big-Power Rivalry

Nationalism can be an important bulwark against the domination of
individual Southeast Asian nations by China. But it does not work
exclusively against China. All the big powers, each desiring a Southeast
Asia compatible with its interests, will have to heed the demands of
nationalism in formulating their policies.

It will be difficult for any of the big powers to maintain good relations with strong leaders who rely on their appeal to nationalism to
retain and strengthen their authority over small states. Big powers are
natural targets for ultranationalists, and no leader in power can afford
to allow himself to be outflanked by appearing too complaisant toward
a big power. He must appear unequivocal in his defense of his nation's
rights and independence of action.

Thus, all the big powers will have problems in coping with Southeast
Asian nationalism in the 1970s. The Chinese have an advantage as Asians
and as the most energetic backers of revolution in Southeast Asia to
dispose of the vestiges of Western imperialism or "neo-imperialism."

---

of a shipload of relief supplies for flood victims from the People's Republic of China
arrived in Manila and the Philippines officially opened trade relations with China;
in May 1973 President Marcos announced that diplomatic relations with the USSR
and China were under active consideration and in November a Chinese trade mission visited the Philippines.

Their appeal has declined, but it may grow again if China continues to show stability and progress at home and increased prestige and influence abroad. But the Chinese also suffer from serious handicaps in working with nationalist leaders in Southeast Asia. In most of the states of that region China is feared and overseas Chinese are unpopular. Moreover, the Chinese communist system is so authoritarian, and doctrinal disputes within the communist world so fierce, that constraints on the freedom of speech or flexibility of action of Southeast Asian communists beholden to Peking for support are severe. Other leaders in the states of the region have greater freedom to appeal for support on nationalist grounds than do pro-Chinese leaders of communist parties. For example, they can demonstrate their independence by publicly criticizing both communist and noncommunist powers, but the pro-Chinese can rarely, if ever, utter public criticism of China. Perhaps the greatest handicap, in the long run, is Peking's tendency, on ideological grounds, to insist on uniform political and economic systems as the only acceptable final outcome in all Southeast Asian states.

These facts confront the Chinese with a dilemma: The firmer the control over a Southeast Asian communist party, the less chance it will have of succeeding; the greater the chances of success of a Southeast Asian communist party, the less responsive it is likely to be to Chinese influence. Bad local government, serious policy errors by the United States or Japan, and clever management of Peking's relations with Southeast Asian states and communist parties would ease the Chinese dilemma, but would not resolve it.

Local nationalists will probably cause the United States and Japan their greatest problems in economic relations with Southeast Asian states. It will be hard to avoid appearing to take advantage of the relative weakness of the economies of Southeast Asian states, and American and Japanese trade and investment will create increasingly visible and tempting targets to nationalist groups. Yet it will be difficult to accede to all economic demands that these groups put forward.

The Japanese are likely to have more trouble than the United States. They are already widely criticized in Southeast Asia for their aggressiveness, their clannishness, their single-minded preoccupation with selling more Japanese goods, and their preference for investing in the production of raw materials for Japan, rather than in manufacturing industries that would contribute more to the economic growth of the country concerned. Resentment against Japan exploded in the angry student demonstrations against Premier Tanaka during his visit to several Southeast Asian countries in January 1974. Local antagonism toward the Japanese is likely to increase in intensity as Japanese economic influence continues to expand, despite efforts by the Japanese government to mitigate it.

Peking's shift of emphasis in Southeast Asia from supporting communist rebels to cultivating Southeast Asian governments will make China in some respects a more formidable contender for influence in Southeast Asia—and would not bar it from shifting back to supporting communist rebels if conditions for insurrection improved. It is a welcome tactical shift from the U.S. viewpoint, for it signifies China's admission that successful communist revolutions in Southeast Asian states are unlikely in the near future. It requires China to compete in Southeast Asia with the other big powers by use of nonviolent means of influence, and the longer this policy emphasis continues, the more it will draw China into a network of relationships that in time will make it harder to turn to heavy reliance on support of revolutionary violence.

Regional Cooperation

One likely consequence of a U.S. policy of loosening alignments would be an acceleration of the trend toward regional cooperation. The past five years have seen growth in various forms of international cooperation among nations of Southeast Asia, mainly in the economic and cultural fields, and the trend appears to have accelerated in response to U.S. moves to reduce force levels in the western Pacific, improve relations with China, and encourage U.S. allies to assume greater responsibility for their own security. Were the United States to go further and loosen its alignments with its allies, the impulse among Southeast Asian countries to band closer together to strengthen their position in relation to the big powers would probably be further strengthened.

The principal regional organization created by the Southeast Asians themselves is the Association of Southeast Asian Nations. Founded in 1967 for the purpose of strengthening economic and cultural relations, ASEAN has no explicit security purposes, although some leaders in member countries have indicated their hope that these will evolve gradually. The organization has already provided a framework of common interest and concern within which bilateral security arrangements, such as those that Malaysia has with Indonesia and Thailand for coping with insurgents in border areas, can more easily develop. ASEAN has also demonstrated its value as a means of preventing conflict among its five members. It is doubtful if either Thailand or Indonesia would have made such strenuous efforts to mediate the serious dispute over Sabah between Malaysia and the Philippines had they not wanted to prevent the dispute from destroying their regional organization.

ASEAN leaders have announced long-term goals that are congruent with a U.S. policy of loosening alignments with Southeast Asian nations. When the five countries' foreign ministers asserted their nations' determination "to exert initially necessary efforts to secure the recognition of, and respect for, Southeast Asia as a zone of peace, freedom, and neutrality, free from any form or manner of interference by outside powers," they called on Southeast Asian countries to "make concerted efforts to broaden the areas of cooperation which would contribute to their strength, solidarity, and closer relationships."[21]

They recognize that persuading the big powers to respect Southeast Asia as a neutral zone may take a long time—hence their description of their immediate task as exerting "initially necessary efforts." Moreover, the foreign minister of the largest ASEAN country, Adam Malik of Indonesia, believes that it is not enough to secure pledges from the big powers to respect the neutrality of the area. "It is only through developing among ourselves an area of internal cohesion and stability, based on indigenous socio-political and economic strength, that we can ever hope to assist in the early stabilization of a new equilibrium in the region that would not be the exclusive diktat of the major powers."[22]

Former Thai Foreign Minister Thanat Khoman was one of the most forceful proponents of regional cooperation in Southeast Asia. In his view of regional cooperation in Southeast Asia, reliance on outside manpower to help in resisting the revolutionary wars that Peking was trying to impose on these nations had no place.[23] Friendly big powers might supply material aid, but threatened governments should not rely on it. They had "no better course to follow than to rely largely on themselves, on their own human and material resources."

And states facing the same threat should cooperate with each other

21. FBIS, Daily Report: Asia and Pacific, Nov. 29, 1971, p. O-2.
22. Far Eastern Economic Review, Sept. 26, 1971, p. 32.
23. Permanent Mission of Thailand to the United Nations, "Alternatives for Southeast Asian Security," press release 11, Feb. 24, 1970.

on a practical basis on many specific matters, rather than through formal treaties. "The old concept of security based on military power and alliance, even if it may still be valid as far as nuclear and world powers are concerned, is likely to yield its place to a new concept of political security, or more exactly, a security founded on concerted and coordinated political actions, particularly in regard to smaller non-nuclear states." This new concept would require "novel methods of consultation, cooperation, and coordination" among the states of the region and with those outside powers that "show an interest in the task of peace-building." It would call for "frequent and regular meetings at high and intermediate levels," as well as "joint implementation" of economic, social, cultural, and technical undertakings. In relations with great powers, political and military matters would be deemphasized in favor of intensified cooperation in the economic field in areas such as the Mekong project.

"The nations on the spot, by joining together and combining their moral, political and diplomatic resources and ingenuity may present a worthwhile persuasive opportunity to Peking to alter its militant intentions and follow a more peaceable course of coexistence with fellow Asian and Pacific nations." It was a problem for the Asian peoples themselves, Thanat concluded, to find ways of convincing China that its aspirations for the status of a great power could be better achieved in the framework of regional cooperation than by "aggressive and truculent actions against smaller nations of the area."

Achieving both the internal national strength and the regional cohesion that Malik and Thanat regard as necessary to gain the respect of the big powers for the neutralization of Southeast Asia will be difficult and, at best, a lengthy process. Each nation has serious internal weaknesses which cannot be readily overcome. Furthermore, the nationalism that is these nations' most effective weapon against external pressure can also stand in the way of regional cooperation. The confrontation between Indonesia and Malaysia and the quarrel over Sabah between Malaysia and the Philippines showed how emotional appeals to patriotism can upset regional harmony. The need to use nationalism as a unifying and modernizing force in the new nations makes it hard for their leaders to accept the restrictions on sovereign freedom of action demanded by close regional ties.

In addition to the obstacles posed by nationalism, the paucity of intercourse among Southeast Asian states and the many differences in culture, language, and customs are likely to make extensive regional cooperation slow in coming. Thus, even though regional cooperation is likely to be accelerated by a U.S. policy of loosening alignments, it would be unrealistic to expect it to develop rapidly enough to offset the short-term destabilizing effects of such a U.S. policy.

In the long run, however, assuming that local conflicts can be contained and big-power military intervention in the region prevented for a number of years, regional organization could become one of the principal means by which Southeast Asian states protect their collective interests.

Summing Up

The former Indonesian ambassador to Washington, Soedjatmoko, outlined the prospects for a Southeast Asia no longer divided by a containment line backed by U.S. military force:

The dynamics of the multipolar constellation of forces in the East Asian-Pacific region therefore may well open the door to a new period in Southeast Asian history—a period in which finally, for the first time after so many centuries, Southeast Asia will be free to deal with its problems in terms of its own history and its own aspirations for the future, and capable of dealing with the major powers with increasing autonomy. It will mean the real end of the colonial period and the beginning of a Southeast Asia that is finally coming into its own and dealing with its problems in its own terms rather than in the distorting terms of the old external power bipolarity, with its built-in exploitation of ideological Pavlovian reflexes.

Of course it would be an illusion to think that all pieces in this picture will automatically fall into place. There will most likely be a period in which some of the major powers—but possibly also some Southeast Asian states—will want to do some probing, in various degrees of risk-taking, in order to test the strength and the will of others, and in this way to determine at which point cost and risk outrun benefit, and accommodation may be called for.

In the face of such a possibility, a great deal of toughness, dexterity, perseverance, and, above all, coolheadedness will be required on the part of the nations so tested. Still, it may be an inevitable learning period in which, at times through rational discussion and negotiations, but at times also through the bitter experience of conflict, the "rules of the game" inherent in the new dynamic balance will become explicit and acceptable. The period of adjustment that is in the offing therefore may be a dangerous one, full of uncertainties and tensions. The danger may be especially acute if out of desperation with seemingly insoluble internal problems, some Southeast Asian countries experience a revival of virulent Communism of local vintage or of extreme xenophobic nationalism, both reflecting deepseated primitive yearnings for immediate salvation and requiring aggressive actions to sustain them. Still, with some understanding of the nature of the problems and stakes involved, this period of adjustment should not be an entirely unmanageable one.[24]

The United States should encourage such local resolve by withdrawing its forces permanently from defense of a containment line in Southeast Asia, despite the substantially increased prospect that all of Indochina might fall under control of Hanoi and that Chinese influence would increase throughout the region. It should first act to remove U.S. forces from Thailand. If these forces are no longer to be used in Indochina, they serve no useful purpose in Thailand. On the contrary, their presence provides a target for opponents of the Thai government, they become more of a burden than a benefit in U.S.-Thai relations, and the Thai government itself will probably wish them withdrawn.

The United States should endorse the ASEAN proposal to make Southeast Asia a zone of peace and neutrality. It should seek the advice of the ASEAN nations as to ways in which it might most effectively support this initiative. Its objective should be to get tacit or explicit understandings with the USSR, China, and Japan on means of limiting conflict in Southeast Asia and of keeping big power forces out of this region.

The United States should announce its decision in principle to turn Clark Air Force Base and Subic Bay Naval Base over to the Philippines. Given the possibility that armed rebellion in the Philippines may become much more serious in the future, the United States could only be sure of retaining these bases if it were prepared to go to great lengths to support an increasingly beleaguered government. That would be unwise. The United States should allow the bases to become Philippine bases but defer the turning over of the bases until after the effects of the withdrawal of U.S. forces from Thailand had been absorbed. Two such jolts in rapid succession would be unnecessarily disturbing to other states in East Asia and, more important, would lend greater plausibility to the view held by some Japanese that the United States intends to withdraw all forces from East Asia. Moreover, U.S. bases in the Philip-

24. Soedjatmoko, "The Role of the Major Powers in the East Asian Pacific Region," in Harald B. Malmgren, ed., *Pacific Basin Development: The American Interests* (Heath, 1972), p. 133.

pines could be a useful element in the negotiations with the Soviets and Chinese on concrete measures to convert Southeast Asia into a zone of peace and neutrality. The United States should gradually reduce its bilateral military and economic aid programs. Its interests in Southeast Asia, while not important enough to justify the use of U.S. forces there— except to deter or defend against an attack by a nuclear power— are important enough to deserve continued, although diminishing aid to governments that are following sensible policies to preserve their independence. Eventually, all military assistance should be placed on a reimbursable basis, so that countries can make their own decisions about how to use fungible external resources. Supporting assistance should be provided as needed. Multilateral economic aid should be expanded, as bilateral economic aid declines, with a view to increasing the total scale of development aid.

The speed with which U.S. military aid is reduced should be related in part to the degree to which the heavy reliance of the North Vietnamese on Chinese and Soviet military aid is modified. The United States should make a strong effort, if possible with Japanese cooperation, to convince the Soviet Union and China that it would be in the interests of all big powers to establish some kind of ceiling or limitation on the supply of weapons to Southeast Asia, in order to hold down the intensity and scope of conflict in the region and thus reduce the danger that big-power forces might be drawn in.

Southeast Asia will nevertheless remain a troubled region in this decade and perhaps for much longer, as nations struggle to modernize and big powers contend with each other for influence. A U.S. decision to remove its forces from the defense of the containment line will not, at least in the short term, reduce the chances of turmoil. But perhaps, as Soedjatmoko hopes, the period of adjustment ahead for Southeast Asia "will not be an entirely unmanageable one."

Whatever troubles may be ahead for individual Southeast Asian nations, they will not so seriously affect vital U.S. interests that U.S. military forces should be used in that region, and it is doubtful that U.S. efforts to determine the course of history in Southeast Asia through use of U.S. military forces would succeed. Consequently, the United States should focus its efforts in East Asia in this decade on protecting its primary interest there—the relationship with Japan—and in Southeast Asia should aim at more modest goals than in the past.

CHAPTER TWELVE

New Directions

The probability of persisting friction between the Soviet Union and China, without war, and Japan's strong inclination to remain lightly armed and forgo nuclear weapons present an exceptional opportunity to consolidate the present relatively stable four-power equilibrium in East Asia, provided the United States remains active in that region. The prospect is favorable for carrying further the Nixon administration's shift from military containment of China to the improvement of relations with China and the USSR.

In adjusting the deployment of its armed forces pursuant to this policy, the United States should draw a sharp distinction between Southeast Asia, where U.S. interests are minor, and Northeast Asia, where they are very important. Therefore, while U.S. forces should no longer be maintained in Thailand poised to intervene in Indochina, substantial forces should be maintained in Northeast Asia as long as needed to protect the important U.S. interests there.

Crucial to the success of a strategy aimed at consolidating the four-power equilibrium is a lightly armed, nonnuclear Japan. The historical precedent that great economic powers inevitably become great military powers may not hold true for a nation as vulnerable to nuclear attack as Japan, which has the option of relying on the U.S. nuclear umbrella. Therefore, the United States should not fatalistically assume that Japan will eventually acquire nuclear weapons. But it would be unwise for the United States to complacently assume that Japan will not do so. The working of Japan's domestic politics, friction with nuclear-armed neighbors, and declining confidence in the U.S. defense commitment to

Japan could combine to produce the unexpected. By treating Japan as a respected partner and keeping a sufficient military presence in Northeast Asia, the United States can reduce that risk.

The remarkable success of the U.S. and Japanese governments over the past twenty years in maintaining their connection has produced a complacency, a sense that the advantages of the alliance to both sides are so obvious that no unusual effort is required to keep it healthy. But in the uncertainties of a multipolar world, severely shaken by the energy crisis, the cement that has held that connection together may loosen. Some differences are inevitable, as Japan's role and views change; indeed, the question is not whether the two countries will drift apart, but whether the drift can be held within tolerable limits. Only greater consciousness of the importance of the connection, sensitivity to the interaction between domestic and international trends that threatens it, and energetic action to limit the drift will assure its preservation.

The firmer the connection between the United States and Japan, the more effectively can both take advantage of the disposition of Moscow and Peking to seek improved relations with them. Both favor in principle expanding relations with the USSR and China, but the tactics employed may give rise to misunderstanding and recrimination, as produced by the "Nixon shock" of July 1971, if there is not close consultation and effective coordination of policies. According the connection the importance it deserves should prevent such damaging surprises.

If rivalry between Japan and China increases, as seems likely, the United States will find it both more important and more difficult to maintain Japanese confidence in the U.S. connection. Pressure on the United States to take a stand on Sino-Japanese differences may well pose the greatest test of the U.S.-Japanese relationship. There will be no easy or risk-free response to that test—which underlines the importance of trying to reduce its risks by reinforcing trends toward declining emphasis on military force in big-power rivalries in East Asia.

By pressing ahead vigorously with coordinated policies to create more extensive relations with China, the United States and Japan may be able to achieve a momentum that would make reversal of the trend difficult for the successors of Mao and Chou. Pursuit of the détente with China and the USSR should be kept in reasonable balance, however. Actions that might increase the risk of war between China and the USSR should be sedulously avoided. Pressure on Japan to achieve an even balance in its parallel policies will be greater than on the United States and the United States should be sensitive to this problem.

Recurrence of conflict in Korea would jeopardize the four-power equilibrium and could severely strain U.S. relations with Japan. Therefore, U.S. military strength in South Korea, which is a significant deterrent to conflict, should be reduced only gradually. Recent trends indicate that most U.S. ground forces probably could be withdrawn from South Korea within the next several years without disturbing repercussions. If relations among the big powers should continue to improve, productive interchange should develop between the two Koreas, and Seoul and Pyongyang should come to have important relations with each of the four powers, the U.S. defense commitment to South Korea would gradually fade in significance.

Conflict over Taiwan would also be a severe blow to big-power equilibrium. The risk of conflict can be kept low, however, if the United States, China, and Japan adhere to the spirit of the Shanghai communiqué of 1972, abjuring any step to establish Taiwan as an independent state, keeping the door open for reassociation of Taiwan with the China mainland, and insisting that any resolution of the Taiwan issue must be peaceful. The significance of the U.S. defense commitment to Taiwan will decline as relations between the United States and China expand and Taiwan recedes in importance as an issue between them.

Conflict in parts of Southeast Asia is probable during the remainder of the 1970s. North Vietnam may gain dominance over Indochina and local communist parties may expand their influence elsewhere. But the possibility that China might achieve hegemony over the region, either by invasion or by support of local communist insurgents, is remote. The United States should decline to intervene militarily against any force indigenous to Southeast Asia, for direct U.S. interests there are minor and the chance is small that turmoil there might seriously damage the vital U.S. interest in Japan.

Conflict confined to Southeast Asia need not upset the four-power equilibrium in East Asia. The United States should utilize its own decision to refrain from military intervention in Southeast Asia as a means of securing similar pledges from the other big powers. Thus the withdrawal of U.S. forces from Thailand and the decision in principle to convert U.S. bases in the Philippines to Philippine bases can provide leverage for obtaining from the USSR, China, and Japan agreement to respect Southeast Asia as a zone of peace and neutrality, as desired by the ASEAN nations. The preoccupation of the Soviet Union and China with their own confrontation, the disposition of Japan to avoid massive rearmament, and the disinclination of the American people to fight again in Southeast Asia offer the prospect of securing a big-power concord on that region.

Henry Kissinger, in his first appearance as secretary, called on his colleagues in the Department of State to seize the "unparalleled opportunity to help bring about a peaceful international structure, a world which the major participants feel that they have had a share in creating and which, therefore, they have an interest in maintaining. It is an opportunity that comes not often in a century, and then through a combination of historical events that, inevitably, cannot be repeated."[1]

A fragile beginning has been made in East Asia in the long-term process of building a peaceful international structure. The exceptional opportunity for involving the four big powers more deeply in that process offers the possibility of replacing military confrontation with an expanding network of constructive relations. Success in this enterprise depends largely on overcoming the problems that could drain the U.S.-Japanese connection of its vitality. How the United States and Japan manage their relationship will determine whether in the nuclear age a great power can abjure great military strength and still satisfy the aspirations of its people. It will also test whether two peoples of different race and dissimilar culture, and not long ago enemies in battle, can cooperate effectively for peace and stability.

The U.S.-Japanese relationship is already threatened. Should the drift apart gather so much momentum that neither government could check it, Japan could eventually become a heavily armed, free-wheeling power, no longer closely cooperating with the United States. Fortunately, U.S. policymakers can exert more control over the condition of relations between the United States and Japan than over most factors in East Asia affecting U.S. security. Of course, the health of the alliance depends as much on Japanese policymakers as on American, and both must be willing to make sacrifices and compromises to maintain it.

Ultimately, the success of U.S. policies in East Asia depends on the relationship between the United States and Japan and their relations with the USSR and China. The political orientation of the smaller states

1. Department of State Press Release No. 354, Sept. 28, 1973, p. 3.

of the region is not vital to U.S. security, and their relations with the United States therefore will not seriously affect the broad purposes and continuity of U.S. policy. If the 1970s should end without a major war in East Asia, with the Japanese satisfied with their nonnuclear role, and with substantial progress toward turning the four-power system away from an emphasis on military confrontation toward an increasing interest on the part of each power in finding ways of forestalling or containing international conflict, the American people would be more secure.

Members of the Brookings Study Group on U.S. Policy in East Asia

Organizations are those with which members were affiliated in the period during which the study group met (August 1969–April 1970).

A. Doak Barnett *Brookings Institution*
Seyom Brown *Brookings Institution*
William P. Bundy *Massachusetts Institute of Technology*
Ralph N. Clough (study director) *Brookings Institution*
John C. Culver *U.S. House of Representatives*
Hiram L. Fong *U.S. Senate*
Max Frankel *The New York Times*
Peter H. B. Frelinghuysen *U.S. House of Representatives*
Leslie H. Gelb *Brookings Institution*
Bernard Gordon *Research Analysis Corporation*
Kermit Gordon *Brookings Institution*
Marshall Green *U.S. Department of State*
Morton H. Halperin *Brookings Institution*
Lee H. Hamilton *U.S. House of Representatives*
Samuel P. Huntington (chairman) *Harvard University*
Amos J. Jordan, Colonel USA *U.S. Military Academy*
George McT. Kahin *Cornell University*
Edward M. Kennedy *U.S. Senate*
Gale W. McGee *U.S. Senate*
F. Bradford Morse *U.S. House of Representatives*
David Mozingo *Cornell University*
Henry Owen *Brookings Institution*
Lucian W. Pye *Massachusetts Institute of Technology*
Edwin O. Reischauer *Harvard University*
James Thomson *Harvard University*
Paul C. Warnke (vice chairman) *Clifford, Warnke, Glass, McIlwain & Finney*
Kenneth T. Young *Council on Foreign Relations*

Index

Acheson, Dean, 6n, 7, 10, 21
Aichi, Kiichi, 63, 68
Akimov, V., 75n
Andreev, M., 154n
ANZUS treaty, 154
Aron, Raymond, 52n
Arms control, 32, 53, 120, 143–44
ASEAN. *See* Association of Southeast
 Asian Nations
Asian and Pacific Council, 154
Asian Development Bank, 25, 202
Association of Southeast Asian Nations
 (ASEAN), 25, 154, 155, 185, 186,
 204, 206, 215, 221, 222, 226, 229–30,
 238
Australia, 10, 24, 30, 33, 123, 211, 215
Averch, H. A., 223n

Badgley, John H., 209n, 210n
Balance of power, 44–45. *See also*
 Four-power system
Bandung conference, second (*1965*),
 128
Batsavage, R. E., 121n
Beecher, William, 182n
Bell, Coral, 45n
Bieda, K., 105n
Biryukov, A., 72n
Brezhnev, Lenoid I., 132n, 153, 154
Brown, Seyom, 8n
Brzezinski, Zbigniew, 95n
Burma, 23, 24, 221; and China, 209–11;
 communist rebellions in, 19, 126,
 197, 198, 200, 206, 209; effect of
 U.S. loosening alignments policy on,
 211
Butterfield, Herbert, 44n

Cambodia, 10, 11, 27, 185–86, 187,
 197, 204, 221

Canada, 24, 123
Ceylon, 123
Chen Pao Tao. *See* Damansky Island
Ch'en Yi, 128
Chiang Kai-shek, 7
China, People's Republic of, 16, 18, 19,
 23, 83; attempt to influence Southeast Asia, 87–88, 228, 229; Communist party, 124, 192; defensive
 military strategy, 119–20; foreign
 policy, 119, 126, 127, 129–30; increasing emphasis on diplomacy, 127–
 28; and Indonesia, 219, 221–22; and
 Japan, 55, 62, 70, 76–80, 85–88, 90,
 99, 142, 236; and Malaysia, 123, 127,
 149, 212–14; military policy, 16,
 130–31, 133, 134; Nixon *1972* visit
 to, 1, 49, 61, 73, 80, 85, 129, 156;
 and North Korea, 169–70; and North
 Vietnam, 150, 151, 152, 153; nuclear
 power, 3, 31, 47, 60, 76, 120, 121,
 128, 143, 144; past humiliation, 117,
 122; revolutionary doctrine, 118, 126;
 role in four-power system, 45–46;
 and Singapore, 216, 217–18; and
 Soviet Union, 130–34; subversion in
 Southeast Asia by, 14, 86, 127; succession problems, 124–25, 137; and
 Taiwan, 16, 36–37, 138–43; and
 Thailand, 190, 191, 192–94; trade,
 20, 78–79, 80, 121–24; and United
 Nations, 85, 127, 128; and U.S., 31,
 127–28, 135–37. *See also* Sino-Soviet
 differences
China, Republic of. *See* Taiwan
Chou En-lai, 80, 84, 86n, 102n, 119,
 124, 125, 140, 146, 179, 210, 214,
 236
Chrysler Corporation, 33n, 100n
Clifford, Clark, 13n